INSTANT QUOTATION DICTIONARY

Compiled by

Donald O. Bolander, B.S., M.A.

Director of Education, Career Institute

Dolores D. Varner

Gary B. Wright, B.A.

Stephanie H. Greene

4800 Quotations

on

More Than 600 Subjects

Complete Author Index

Published by

CAREER PUBLISHING, INC.

1500 Cardinal Drive   Little Falls, New Jersey 07424

Instant Quotation Dictionary

a quick, handy reference guide
especially prepared for the use of

Authors	Speechwriters
Students	Lecturers
Businessmen	Copywriters
Teachers	Reporters
Clergymen	Editors
Executives	Parents
Secretaries	Librarians

and for those in any occupation or activity where concise
and meaningful quotations can greatly increase the
effectiveness of written or verbal communication.

1981 Edition
Copyright © 1969, 1972 by
CAREER PUBLISHING, INC.
Library of Congress Catalog Card No. 74-104786
Printed in the United States of America
All rights reserved

ISBN   0-911744-05-3

QB 81-1

Purpose of This Book

The main purpose of the *Instant Quotation Dictionary* is to provide a quick and easy way to find just the right quotation, just the right thought, on a wide variety of subjects. It is a book for everyone—perfect for browsing or finding your own personal thought for the day.

Whether you are preparing a speech, writing a report or term paper, preparing a story or delivering a sermon, a famous quotation is always an effective foundation for building your theme. Even a not-so-famous quotation can be effective if it contains the thought and the punch you want to develop.

In this *Instant Quotation Dictionary* you will find the thoughtful words of the wise and the witty on many interesting and timely subjects. The quotations were selected to include the widest possible range of thought, from the provocative or controversial, the sentimental and inspirational, to the satirical, the witty and the humorous. Varying points of view are presented under controversial subjects. There are quotations from the Bible, the Talmud, the early philosphers, and from the literary masters of several centuries ago. Also included are quotations from the speeches of statesmen and political leaders, educators, scientists, clergymen and church leaders, and from the moralists and humorists of modern times.

This self-indexing dictionary is alphabetically arranged by subject headings, making it easy to find the quotation you need. Cross-referencing of the subjects will lead you to additional pertinent quotations that are listed under other headings.

When you want to locate the words of your favorite writer or speaker, regardless of subject, there is a complete author index at the end of the book.

A

ABILITY *Also see:* ACTION, CHARACTER, DISCRETION, FORCE, GEN-
IUS, PERSEVERANCE, POWER, STRENGTH, SUCCESS.

There is something that is much more scarce, something finer far, something
rarer than ability. It is the ability to recognize ability. *Elbert Hubbard*

Consider the postage stamp: its usefulness consists in the ability to stick to
one thing till it gets there. *Josh Billings*

The question "Who ought to be boss?" is like asking "Who ought to be
the tenor in the quartet?" Obviously, the man who can sing tenor.
Henry Ford

Executive ability is deciding quickly and getting somebody else to do the
work. *John G. Pollard*

Men are often capable of greater things than they perform. They are sent
into the world with bills of credit, and seldom draw to their full extent.
Horace Walpole

They are able because they think they are able. *Vergil*

Ability is of little account without opportunity. *Napoleon Bonaparte*

Natural abilities are like natural plants; they need pruning by study.
Francis Bacon

The wind and the waves are always on the side of the ablest navigators.
Edward Gibbon

Ability hits the mark where presumption overshoots and diffidence falls
short. *John Henry Newman*

ABSENCE *Also see:* LONELINESS, MEMORY, WANT.

. . . that common cure of love. *Miguel de Cervantes*

Is not absence death to those who love? *Alexander Pope*

Absence diminishes little passions and increases great ones, as wind extin-
guishes candles and fans a fire. *François de La Rochefoucauld*

The absent are never without fault. Nor the present without excuse.
Benjamin Franklin

When a man is out of sight, it is not too long before he is out of mind.
Thomas à Kempis

The absent are like children, helpless to defend themselves. *Charles Reade*

The absent are always in the wrong. *English Proverb*

Absence and death are the same—only that in death there is no suffering.
Walter S. Landor

ABSTINENCE   *Also see:* DRUNKENNESS, MODERATION, SACRIFICE.

Complete abstinence is easier than perfect moderation.   *St. Augustine*

Always rise from the table with an appetite, and you will never sit down without one.   *William Penn*

All philosophy lies in two words, sustain and abstain.   *Epictetus*

The only way for a rich man to be healthy is by exercise and abstinence, to live as if he were poor.   *William Temple*

Abstaining is favorable both to the head and the pocket.   *Horace Greeley*

Once during Prohibition I was forced to live for days on nothing but food and water.   *W. C. Fields*

ABSURDITY   *Also see:* RIDICULE, SARCASM.

The privilege of absurdity; to which no living creature is subject but man only.   *Thomas Hobbes*

In politics, an absurdity is not a handicap.   *Napoleon Bonaparte*

There is nothing so absurd or ridiculous that has not at some time been said by some philosopher.   *Oliver Goldsmith*

It is the height of absurdity to sow little but weeds in the first half of one's lifetime and expect to harvest a valuable crop in the second half.   *Percy Johnston*

The intelligent man finds almost everything ridiculous, the sensible man almost nothing.   *Johann Wolfgang von Goethe*

Almost all absurdity of conduct arises from the imitation of those whom we cannot resemble.   *Samuel Johnson*

ABUSE   *Also see:* CRUELTY, INJURY, POLLUTION, SLANDER.

Abuse is the weapon of the vulgar.   *Samuel Griswold Goodrich*

The best security against revolution is in constant correction of abuses and the introduction of needed improvements. It is the neglect of timely repair that makes rebuilding necessary.   *Richard Whately*

I never yet heard man or woman much abused that I was not inclined to think the better of them, and to transfer the suspicion or dislike to the one who found pleasure in pointing out the defects of another.   *Jane Porter*

There are none more abusive to others than they that lie most open to it themselves; but the humor goes round, and he that laughs at me today will have somebody to laugh at him tomorrow.   *Seneca*

Anyone entrusted with power will abuse it if not also animated with the love of truth and virtue, no matter whether he be a prince, or one of the people.   *Jean de la Fontaine*

ACCURACY   *Also see:* FACTS, FIDELITY, PUNCTUALITY, SCIENCE.

Accuracy is the twin brother of honesty; inaccuracy, of dishonesty.
Charles Simmons

Accuracy is to a newspaper what virtue is to a lady, but a newspaper can always print a retraction.
Adlai E. Stevenson

Accuracy of statement is one of the first elements of truth; inaccuracy is a near kin to falsehood.
Tryon Edwards

Insanity is often the logic of an accurate mind overtaxed.
Oliver Wendell Holmes

Even a stopped clock is right twice a day.
Anonymous

Facts are God's arguments; we should be careful never to misunderstand or pervert them.
Tryon Edwards

From principles is derived probability, but truth or certainty is obtained only from facts.
Nathaniel Hawthorne

ACHIEVEMENT   *Also see:* ACTION, AIM, AMBITION, DECISION, LABOR, PURPOSE, SUCCESS, WORK.

Let us, then, be up and doing,
With a heart for any fate;
Still achieving, still pursuing,
Learn to labor and to wait.
Henry Wadsworth Longfellow

I feel that the greatest reward for doing is the opportunity to do more.
Jonas Salk

Mere longevity is a good thing for those who watch Life from the side lines. For those who play the game, an hour may be a year, a single day's work an achievement for eternity.
Gabriel Heatter

Do not attempt to do a thing unless you are sure of yourself; but do not relinquish it simply because someone else is not sure of you.
Stewart E. White

Death comes to all
But great achievements build a monument
Which shall endure until the sun grows cold.
Georg Fabricius

The mode by which the inevitable comes to pass is effort.
Oliver Wendell Holmes

Every man who is high up loves to think that he has done it all himself; and the wife smiles, and lets it go at that.
James Matthew Barrie

Life affords no higher pleasure than that of surmounting difficulties, passing from one step of success to another, forming new wishes and seeing them gratified.
Samuel Johnson

7

ACTION

Also see: ACHIEVEMENT, DESIRE, LABOR, PROGRESS, WORK.

Thought is the blossom; language the bud; action the fruit behind it.
Ralph Waldo Emerson

Mark this well, you proud men of action! you are, after all, nothing but unconscious instruments of the men of thought.
Heinrich Heine

Positive anything is better than negative nothing.
Elbert Hubbard

Our grand business is not to see what lies dimly at a distance, but to do what lies clearly at hand.
Thomas Carlyle

Every action of our lives touches on some chord that will vibrate in eternity.
Edwin Hubbel Chapin

The actions of men are the best interpreters of their thoughts.
John Locke

Think like a man of action and act like a man of thought.
Henri Bergson

The best way out is always through.
Robert Frost

What you do speaks so loud that I cannot hear what you say.
Ralph Waldo Emerson

Action may not always bring happiness; but there is no happiness without action.
Benjamin Disraeli

It is by acts and not by ideas that people live.
Anatole France

Thought and theory must precede all salutary action; yet action is nobler in itself than either thought or theory.
William Wordsworth

Good actions ennoble us, and we are the sons of our own deeds.
Miguel de Cervantes

Action to be effective must be directed to clearly conceived ends.
Jawaharlal Nehru

Indolence is a delightful but distressing state; we must be doing something to be happy. Action is no less necessary than thought to the instinctive tendencies of the human frame.
Mahatma Gandhi

Periods of tranquility are seldom prolific of creative achievement. Mankind has to be stirred up.
Alfred North Whitehead

Give me the ready hand rather than the ready tongue.
Giuseppe Garibaldi

ADAPTABILITY *Also see:* CONFORMITY.

The weather-cock on the church spire, though made of iron, would soon be broken by the storm-wind if it . . . did not understand the noble art of turning to every wind.   *Heinrich Heine*

Make yourself necessary to somebody.   *Ralph Waldo Emerson*

Complete adaptation to environment means death. The essential point in all response is the desire to control environment.   *John Dewey*

One learns to itch where one can scratch.   *Ernest Bramah*

Adaptability is not imitation. It means power of resistance and assimilation.
                                                        Mahatma Gandhi

We must make the best of those ills which cannot be avoided.
                                                        Alexander Hamilton

---

ADMIRATION *Also see:* FAME, FOOL, LOVE, PRAISE, RESPECT.

Admiration is the daughter of ignorance.   *Benjamin Franklin*

We always love those who admire us; we do not always love those whom we admire.   *François de La Rochefoucauld*

The only things one can admire at length are those one admires without knowing why.   *Jean Rostand*

Fools admire, but men of sense approve.   *Alexander Pope*

A fool always finds a greater fool to admire him. *Nicolas Boileau-Despréaux*

Admiration is a very short-lived passion, that immediately decays upon growing familiar with its object.   *Joseph Addison*

Distance is a great promoter of admiration!   *Denis Diderot*

ADVANCEMENT . . . See PROGRESS

ADVENTURE *Also see:* DANGER, DISCOVERY, INVENTION, SPACE, TRAVEL.

Without adventure civilization is in full decay.   *Alfred North Whitehead*

Adventure is not outside a man; it is within.   *David Grayson*

Who dares nothing, need hope for nothing.   *Johann von Schiller*

You can't cross the sea merely by standing and staring at the water. Don't let yourself indulge in vain wishes.   *Rabindranath Tagore*

We live in a wonderful world that is full of beauty, charm and adventure. There is no end to the adventures that we can have if only we seek them with our eyes open.   *Jawaharlal Nehru*

ADVERSITY *Also see:* AFFLICTION, CALAMITY, MISERY, PROSPERITY.

By trying we can easily learn to endure adversity—another man's I mean.
Mark Twain

No man is more unhappy than the one who is never in adversity; the greatest affliction of life is never to be afflicted.
Anonymous

Adversity makes men, and prosperity makes monsters.
Victor Hugo

Little minds are tamed and subdued by misfortune; but great minds rise above them.
Washington Irving

Prosperity is not without many fears and distastes; adversity not without many comforts and hopes.
Francis Bacon

Friendship, of itself a holy tie,
Is made more sacred by adversity.
Charles Caleb Colton

Adversity is the first path to truth.
Lord Byron

The good things of prosperity are to be wished; but the good things that belong to adversity are to be admired.
Seneca

Prosperity is a great teacher; adversity is a greater. Possession pampers the mind; privation trains and strengthens it.
William Hazlitt

Constant success shows us but one side of the world; adversity brings out the reverse of the picture.
Charles Caleb Colton

―――――

ADVERTISING *Also see:* ART, BUSINESS, PUBLICITY.

Advertising is 85% confusion and 15% commission.
Fred Allen

Advertising may be described as the science of arresting the human intelligence long enough to get money from it.
Stephen Butler Leacock

The business that considers itself immune to the necessity for advertising sooner or later finds itself immune to business.
Derby Brown

Advertising is the foot on the accelerator, the hand on the throttle, the spur on the flank that keeps our economy surging forward.
Robert W. Sarnoff

Doing business without advertising is like winking at a girl in the dark. You know what you are doing, but nobody else does.
Steuart H. Britt

Advertising is the life of trade.
Calvin Coolidge

The product that will not sell without advertising will not sell profitably with advertising.
Albert Lasker

Sanely applied advertising could remake the world.
Stuart Chase

Advertising promotes that divine discontent which makes people strive to improve their economic status.
Ralph S. Butler

ADVICE *Also see:* CAUTION, EXPERIENCE, HELP, WISDOM.

Advice is like snow; the softer it falls the longer it dwells upon, and the deeper it sinks into the mind.
Samuel Taylor Coleridge

Advice is seldom welcome, and those who need it the most, like it the least.
Lord Chesterfield

We give advice by the bucket, but take it by the grain.
William Rounseville Alger

Advice: the smallest current coin.
Ambrose Bierce

It is easy when we are in prosperity to give advice to the afflicted.
Aeschylus

In those days he was wiser than he is now—he used frequently to take my advice.
Winston Churchill

Men give away nothing so liberally as their advice.
François de La Rochefoucauld

He that gives good advice, builds with one hand; he that gives good counsel and example, builds with both; but he that gives good admonition and bad example, builds with one hand and pulls down with the other.
Francis Bacon

No man is so foolish but he may sometimes give another good counsel, and no man so wise that he may not easily err if he takes no other counsel than his own. He that is taught only by himself has a fool for a master.
Ben Jonson

Advice is like castor oil, easy enough to give but dreadful uneasy to take.
Josh Billings

It is only too easy to make suggestions and later try to escape the consequences of what we say.
Jawaharlal Nehru

The only thing to do with good advice is to pass it on. It is never of any use to oneself.
Oscar Wilde

He that won't be counselled can't be helped.
Benjamin Franklin

Write down the advice of him who loves you, though you like it not at present.
Proverb

It takes nearly as much ability to know how to profit by good advice as to know how to act for one's self.
François de La Rochefoucauld

There is as much difference between the counsel that a friend giveth, and that a man giveth himself, as there is between the counsel of a friend and a flatterer.
Francis Bacon

Consult your friend on all things, especially on those which respect yourself. His counsel may then be useful where your own self-love might impair your judgment.
Seneca

AFFECTION *Also see:* ADMIRATION, FRIENDSHIP, KISS, LOVE.

Affection, like melancholy, magnifies trifles; but the magnifying of the one is like looking through a telescope at heavenly objects; that of the other, like enlarging monsters with a microscope. *Leigh Hunt*

A slight touch of friendly malice and amusement towards those we love keeps our affections for them from turning flat. *Logan P. Smith*

Talk not of wasted affection; affection never was wasted.
Henry Wadsworth Longfellow

Caresses, expressions of one sort or another, are necessary to the life of the affections as leaves are to the life of a tree. If they are wholly restrained, love will die at the roots. *Nathaniel Hawthorne*

The affections are like lightning: you cannot tell where they will strike till they have fallen. *Jean Baptiste Lacordaire*

A woman's life is a history of the affections. *Washington Irving*

I never met a man I didn't like. *Will Rogers*

The moment we indulge our affections, the earth is metamorphosed; there is no winter and no night; all tragedies, all ennuis, vanish, —all duties even.
Ralph Waldo Emerson

AFFLICTION *Also see:* ADVERSITY, CALAMITY, DISEASE, PAIN, SORROW, SUFFERING.

The gem cannot be polished without friction, nor man perfected without trials. *Chinese Proverb*

Strength is born in the deep silence of long-suffering hearts; not amid joy.
Felicia Hemans

Affliction, like the iron-smith, shapes as it smites. *Christian Nestell Bovee*

I thank God for my handicaps, for through them, I have found myself, my work and my God. *Helen Keller*

To bear other people's afflictions, everyone has courage and enough to spare. *Benjamin Franklin*

As threshing separates the wheat from the chaff, so does affliction purify virtue. *Richard E. Burton*

Humanity either makes, or breeds, or tolerates all its afflictions. *H. G. Wells*

Affliction comes to us, not to make us sad but sober; not to make us sorry but wise. *Henry Ward Beecher*

Though all afflictions are evils in themselves, yet they are good for us, because they discover to us our disease and tend to our cure. *John Tillotson*

By afflictions God is spoiling us of what otherwise might have spoiled us. When he makes the world too hot for us to hold, we let it go. *John Powell*

AGE *Also see:* AVARICE, YOUTH.

I refuse to admit I'm more than fifty-two, even if that does make my sons illegitimate.   *Lady Astor*

At 20 years of age the will reigns; at 30 the wit; at 40 the judgment.
Benjamin Franklin

If wrinkles must be written upon our brows, let them not be written upon the heart. The spirit should never grow old.   *James A. Garfield*

Age—that period of life in which we compound for the vices that we still cherish by reviling those that we no longer have the enterprise to commit.
Ambrose Bierce

Age . . . is a matter of feeling, not of years.   *George William Curtis*

Age does not depend upon years, but upon temperament and health. Some men are born old, and some never grow so.   *Tryon Edwards*

Only the young die good.   *Cynic's Calendar*

A man is not old as long as he is seeking something.   *Jean Rostand*

The woman who tells her age is either too young to have anything to lose or too old to have anything to gain.   *Chinese Proverb*

The older I grow the more I distrust the familiar doctrine that age brings wisdom.   *H. L. Mencken*

AGGRESSION *Also see:* ANGER, ENEMY, WAR.

The truth is often a terrible weapon of aggression. It is possible to lie, and even to murder, with the truth.   *Alfred Adler*

It is the habit of every aggressor nation to claim that it is acting on the defensive.   *Jawaharlal Nehru*

Aggression which is flagitious when committed by one, is not sanctioned when committed by a host.   *Herbert Spencer*

Civilized society is perpetually menaced with disintegration through this primary hostility of men towards one another . . .   *Sigmund Freud*

AGITATION *Also see:* ARGUMENT, DISSENT.

Agitation is that part of our intellectual life where vitality results; there ideas are born, breed and bring forth.   *George Edward Woodberry*

Those who profess to favor freedom, and yet depreciate agitation, are men who want rain without thunder and lightning. They want the ocean without the roar of its many waters.   *Frederick Douglass*

Agitation is the marshalling of the conscience of a nation to mold its laws.
Robert Peel

AGNOSTICISM   *Also see:* ATHEISM, GOD, SKEPTICISM.

Agnosticism simply means that a man shall not say he knows or believes that for which he has no grounds for professing to believe.   *Thomas Huxley*

Agnosticism is the philosophical, ethical and religious dry-rot of the modern world.   *F. E. Abbot*

There is only one folly greater than that of the fool who says in his heart there is no God, and that is the folly of the people that says with its head that it does not know whether there is a God or not.   *Otto von Bismark*

I am an agnostic; I do not pretend to know what many ignorant men are sure of.   *Clarence Darrow*

Don't be an agnostic—be something.   *Robert Frost*

AGREEMENT   *Also see:* COMPROMISE, CONFORMITY, UNDERSTAND-
ING, UNITY.

We hardly find any persons of good sense save those who agree with us.
   François de La Rochefoucauld

He that complies against his will is of his own opinion still.   *Samuel Butler*

When two men in business always agree, one of them is unnecessary.
   William Wrigley, Jr.

There is no conversation more boring than the one where everybody agrees.
   Michel de Montaigne

I have never in my life learned anything from any man who agreed with me.
   Dudley Field Malone

If you wish to appear agreeable in society, you must consent to be taught many things which you know already.   *Johann Kaspar Lavater*

The fellow that agrees with everything you say is either a fool or he is getting ready to skin you.   *Kin Hubbard*

You may easily play a joke on a man who likes to argue—agree with him.
   Ed Howe

AIM   *Also see:* AMBITION, DESIRE, END, IDEAL, PURPOSE, PURSUIT.

Perhaps the reward of the spirit who tries is not the goal but the exercise.
   E. V. Cooke

Aim at the sun, and you may not reach it; but your arrow will fly far higher than if aimed at an object on a level with yourself.   *Joel Hawes*

In great attempts it is glorious even to fail.   *Cassius*

Not failure, but low aim, is crime.   *James Russell Lowell*

High aims form high characters, and great objects bring out great minds.
   Tryon Edwards

AMBIGUITY *Also see:* DOUBT.

Those who write clearly have readers, those who write obscurely have commentators. *Albert Camus*

I fear explanations explanatory of things explained. *Abraham Lincoln*

Clearly spoken, Mr. Fogg; you explain English by Greek. *Benjamin Franklin*

That must be wonderful; I have no idea of what it means. *Molière*

AMBITION *Also see:* AIM, CONSCIENCE, DESIRE, EFFORT, GLORY, IDEAL, PURPOSE, SUCCESS, WORTH, ZEAL.

You can't hold a man down without staying down with him. *Booker T. Washington*

Ambition is the last refuge of failure. *Oscar Wilde*

The tallest trees are most in the power of the winds, and ambitious men of the blasts of fortune. *William Penn*

Ambition has one heel nailed in well, though she stretch her fingers to touch the heavens. *William Lilly*

We grow small trying to be great. *E. Stanley Jones*

Too low they build who build below the skies. *Edward Young*

Hitch your wagon to a star. *Ralph Waldo Emerson*

Most people would succeed in small things if they were not troubled with great ambitions. *Henry Wadsworth Longfellow*

The noblest spirit is most strongly attracted by the love of glory. *Cicero*

He who surpasses or subdues mankind, must look down on the hate of those below. *Lord Byron*

Ambition should be made of sterner stuff. *William Shakespeare*

Ambition is so powerful a passion in the human breast, that however high we reach we are never satisfied. *Niccolò Machiavelli*

All ambitions are lawful except those which climb upward on the miseries or credulities of mankind. *Joseph Conrad*

Nothing is too high for the daring of mortals: we storm heaven itself in our folly. *Horace*

Ambition is not a vice of little people. *Michel de Montaigne*

15

To be ambitious of true honor and of the real glory and perfection of our nature is the very principle and incentive of virtue; but to be ambitious of titles, place, ceremonial respects, and civil pageantry, is as vain and little as the things are which we court.
Philip Sidney

It is the constant fault and inseparable evil quality of ambition, that it never looks behind it.
Seneca

If you wish to reach the highest, begin at the lowest.
Publilius Syrus

When you are aspiring to the highest place, it is honorable to reach the second or even the third rank.
Cicero

Ambition often puts men upon doing the meanest offices: so climbing is performed in the same posture with creeping.
Jonathan Swift

A noble man compares and estimates himself by an idea which is higher than himself; and a mean man, by one lower than himself. The one produces aspiration; the other ambition, which is the way in which a vulgar man aspires.
Henry Ward Beecher

Ambition is the germ from which all growth of nobleness proceeds.
Thomas Dunn English

Some folks can look so busy doing nothin' that they seem indispensable.
Kin Hubbard

Ambition is a lust that is never quenched, but grows more inflamed and madder by enjoyment.
Thomas Otway

A life spent in constant labor is a life wasted, save a man be such a fool as to regard a fulsome obituary notice as ample reward.
George Jean Nathan

The men who succeed are the efficient few. They are the few who have the ambition and will power to develop themselves.
Herbert N. Casson

Where ambition can cover its enterprises, even to the person himself, under the appearance of principle, it is the most incurable and inflexible of passions.
David Hume

No bird soars too high if he soars with his own wings.
William Blake

There are glimpses of heaven to us in every act, or thought, or word, that raises us above ourselves.
Arthur P. Stanley

It seems to me we can never give up longing and wishing while we are thoroughly alive. There are certain things we feel to be beautiful and good, and we must hunger after them.
George Eliot

The very substance of the ambitious is merely the shadow of a dream.
William Shakespeare

AMERICA *Also see:* DEMOCRACY, NATION, PARTY, PATRIOTISM, PRESIDENT.

America has believed that in differentiation, not in uniformity, lies the path of progress. It acted on this belief; it has advanced human happiness, and it has prospered. *Louis D. Brandeis*

America is the only nation in history which miraculously has gone directly from barbarism to degeneration without the usual interval of civilization. *Georges Clemenceau*

Ideals are the "incentive payment" of practical men. The opportunity to strive for them is the currency that has enriched America through the centuries. *Robert E. Hannegan*

America is the country where you buy a lifetime supply of aspirin for one dollar and use it up in two weeks. *John Barrymore*

America is not a mere body of traders; it is a body of free men. Our greatness is built upon our freedom—is moral, not material. We have a great ardor for gain; but we have a deep passion for the rights of man. *Woodrow Wilson*

A citizen of America will cross the ocean to fight for democracy, but won't cross the street to vote in a national election. *Bill Vaughan*

If there is one word that describes our form of society in America, it may be the word—voluntary. *Lyndon Baines Johnson*

Intellectually I know that America is no better than any other country; emotionally I know she is better than every country. *Sinclair Lewis*

America is a country of young men. *Ralph Waldo Emerson*

I am certain that, however great the hardships and the trials which loom ahead, our America will endure and the cause of human freedom will triumph. *Cordell Hull*

I would rather see the United States respected than loved by other nations. *Henry Cabot Lodge*

Wake up, America. *Augustus P. Gardner*

America lives in the heart of every man everywhere who wishes to find a region where he will be free to work out his destiny as he chooses. *Woodrow Wilson*

I was born an American; I live an American; I shall die an American. *Daniel Webster*

Our country is still young and its potential is still enormous. We should remember, as we look toward the future, that the more fully we believe in and achieve freedom and equal opportunity—not simply for ourselves but for others—the greater our accomplishments as a nation will be. *Henry Ford II*

The interesting and inspiring thing about America is that she asks nothing for herself except what she has a right to ask for humanity itself.
Woodrow Wilson

America is a large, friendly dog in a very small room. Every time it wags its tail, it knocks over a chair. *Arnold Joseph Toynbee*

If the American dream is for Americans only, it will remain our dream and never be our destiny. *René de Visme Williamson*

Our country, right or wrong. When right, to be kept right; when wrong, to be put right. *Carl Schurz*

If there is a country in the world where concord, according to common calculation, would be least expected, it is America. *Thomas Paine*

America, thou half-brother of the world;
With something good and bad of every land. *Philip James Bailey*

The country's honor must be upheld at home and abroad.
Theodore Roosevelt

In the field of world policy, I would dedicate this nation to the policy of the good neighbor. *Franklin Delano Roosevelt*

Let our object be our country, our whole country, and nothing but our country. *Daniel Webster*

America has meant to the world a land in which the common man who means well and is willing to do his part has access to all the necessary means of a good life. *Alvin Saunders Johnson*

America . . . a great social and economic experiment, noble in motive and far-reaching in purpose. *Herbert Hoover*

There is a New America every morning when we wake up. It is upon us whether we will it or not. *Adlai E. Stevenson*

Why is it, whenever a group of internationalists get together, they always decide that Uncle Sam must be the goat? *Bertrand H. Snell*

America is not merely a nation but a nation of nations.
Lyndon Baines Johnson

Every time Europe looks across the Atlantic to see the American Eagle, it observes only the rear end of an ostrich. *H. G. Wells*

The less America looks abroad, the grander its promise.
Ralph Waldo Emerson

For this is what America is all about. It is the uncrossed desert and the unclimbed ridge. It is the star that is not reached and the harvest that's sleeping in the unplowed ground. *Lyndon Baines Johnson*

AMIABILITY *Also see:* AGREEMENT, CHEERFULNESS, COURTESY, HAPPINESS.

Natural amiableness is too often seen in company with sloth, with uselessness, with the vanity of fashionable life. *William Ellery Channing*

When the righteous man turneth away from his righteousness that he hath committed and doeth that which is neither quite lawful nor quite right, he will generally be found to have gained in amiability what he has lost in holiness. *Samuel Butler*

How easy to be amiable in the midst of happiness and success. *Anne Sophie Swetchine*

An inexhaustible good nature is one of the most precious gifts of heaven, spreading itself like oil over the troubled sea of thought, and keeping the mind smooth and equable in the roughest weather. *Washington Irving*

AMUSEMENT *Also see:* ENJOYMENT, JOY, PLEASURE, REVERIE.

. . . the happiness of those who cannot think. *Alexander Pope*

Life would be tolerable but for its amusements. *George Bernard Shaw*

The only way to amuse some people is to slip and fall on an icy pavement. *Ed Howe*

True enjoyment comes from activity of the mind and exercise of the body; the two are ever united. *Humboldt*

You can't live on amusement. It is the froth on water—an inch deep and then the mud. *George MacDonald*

Amusement to an observing mind is study. *Benjamin Disraeli*

I am a great friend to public amusements, for they keep people from vice. *Samuel Johnson*

If those who are the enemies of innocent amusements had the direction of the world, they would take away the spring, and youth, the former from the year, the latter from human life. *Honoré de Balzac*

The real character of a man is found out by his amusements. *Joshua Reynolds*

Life is worth living, but only if we avoid the amusements of grown-up people. *Robert Lynd*

The mind ought sometimes to be diverted, that it may return the better to thinking. *Phaedrus*

> Cards were at first for benefits designed,
> Sent to amuse, not to enslave the mind. *David Garrick*

When I play with my cat, who knows whether she is not amusing herself with me more than I with her. *Michel de Montaigne*

ANCESTRY *Also see:* ARISTOCRACY.

Everyone has ancestors and it is only a question of going back far enough to find a good one.
Howard Kenneth Nixon

The happiest lot for a man, as far as birth is concerned, is that it should be such as to give him but little occasion to think much about it.
Richard Whately

Whoever serves his country well has no need of ancestors.
Voltaire

Every man is his own ancestor, and every man his own heir. He devises his own future, and he inherits his own past.
H. F. Hedge

My father was a Creole, his father a Negro, and his father a monkey; my family, it seems, begins where yours left off.
Alexandre Dumas

Everyone has something ancestral, even if it is nothing more than a disease.
Ed Howe

Birth is nothing where virtue is not.
Molière

Some decent, regulated pre-eminence, some preference given to birth, is neither unnatural nor unjust nor impolite.
Edmund Burke

Some men by ancestry are only the shadow of a mighty name.
Lucan

The man who has nothing to boast of but his illustrious ancestry, is like the potato—the best part under ground.
Thomas Overbury

It is of no consequence of what parents a man is born, so he be man of merit.
Horace

We inherit nothing truly, but what our actions make us worthy of.
George Chapman

I would like to be like my father and all the rest of my ancestors who never married.
Molière

It is indeed a desirable thing to be well descended, but the glory belongs to our ancestors.
Plutarch

Our ancestors are very good kind of folks; but they are the last people I should choose to have a visiting acquaintance with.
Richard Brinsley Sheridan

We are all omnibuses in which our ancestors ride, and every now and then one of them sticks his head out and embarrasses us.
Oliver Wendell Holmes

The fathers have eaten sour grapes, and the children's teeth are set on edge.
Ezekiel. 17:2

Breed is stronger than pasture.
George Eliot

ANGER *Also see:* AGGRESSION, QUARREL, TEMPER.

When angry count four; when very angry, swear. *Mark Twain*

Men often make up in wrath what they want in reason.
William Rounseville Alger

Anger blows out the lamp of the mind. *Robert Green Ingersoll*

To rule one's anger is well; to prevent it is still better. *Tryon Edwards*

Beware the fury of a patient man. *John Dryden*

An angry man opens his mouth and shuts up his eyes. *Cato*

Anger is seldom without argument but seldom with a good one. *Halifax*

> I was angry with my friend:
> I told my wrath, my wrath did end.
> I was angry with my foe:
> I told it not, my wrath did grow. *William Blake*

Anger and intolerance are the twin enemies of correct understanding.
Mahatma Gandhi

The flame of anger, bright and brief, sharpens the barb of love.
Walter S. Landor

Anger is as a stone cast into a wasp's nest. *Malabar Proverb*

An angry man is again angry with himself when he returns to reason.
Publilius Syrus

The intoxication of anger, like that of the grape, shows us to others, but hides us from ourselves. We injure our own cause in the opinion of the world when we too passionately defend it. *Charles Caleb Colton*

Wise anger is like fire from a flint: there is great ado to get it out; and when it does come, it is out again immediately. *Matthew Henry*

Anger is a momentary madness, so control your passion or it will control you. *Horace*

Anger begins with folly, and ends with repentance. *H. G. Bohn*

Keep cool; anger is not an argument. *Daniel Webster*

Anybody can become angry—that is easy; but to be angry with the right person, and to the right degree, and at the right time, and for the right purpose, and in the right way—that is not within everybody's power and is not easy. *Aristotle*

Whenever you are angry, be assured that it is not only a present evil, but that you have increased a habit. *Epictetus*

The greatest remedy for anger is delay. *Seneca*

When a man is wrong and won't admit it, he always gets angry. *Haliburton*

ANTICIPATION   *Also see:* ANXIETY, DISAPPOINTMENT, HOPE.

Nothing is so good as it seems beforehand.   *George Eliot*

If pleasures are greatest in anticipation, just remember that this is also true of trouble.   *Elbert Hubbard*

What we anticipate seldom occurs, what we least expected generally happens.   *Benjamin Disraeli*

Few enterprises of great labor or hazard would be undertaken if we had not the power of magnifying the advantages we expect from them.
Samuel Johnson

Our desires always disappoint us; for though we meet with something that gives us satisfaction, yet it never thoroughly answers our expectation.
François de La Rochefoucauld

A man's delight in looking forward to and hoping for some particular satisfaction is a part of the pleasure flowing out of it, enjoyed in advance. But this is afterward deducted, for the more we look forward to anything the less we enjoy it when it comes.   *Arthur Schopenhauer*

We love to expect, and when expectation is either disappointed or gratified, we want to be again expecting.   *Samuel Johnson*

Nothing is so wretched or foolish as to anticipate misfortunes. What madness is it to be expecting evil before it comes.   *Seneca*

ANXIETY   *Also see:* ANTICIPATION, FEAR, WORRY.

The natural role of twentieth-century man is anxiety.   *Norman Mailer*

The thinner the ice, the more anxious is everyone to see whether it will bear.   *Josh Billings*

Never trouble trouble till trouble troubles you.   *Anonymous*

Where everything is bad it must be good to know the worst.
Francis H. Bradley

We have a lot of anxieties, and one cancels out another very often.
Winston Churchill

Do not anticipate trouble, or worry about what may never happen. Keep in the sunlight.   *Benjamin Franklin*

God never built a Christian strong enough to carry today's duties and tomorrow's anxieties piled on the top of them.   *Theodore Ledyard Cuyler*

How much have cost us the evils that never happened!   *Thomas Jefferson*

The misfortunes hardest to bear are these which never came.
James Russell Lowell

Borrow trouble for yourself, if that's your nature, but don't lend it to your neighbors.   *Rudyard Kipling*

APATHY *Also see:* IDLENESS, NEGLECT, WORK.

Apathy is a sort of living oblivion.   *Horace Greeley*

There is no calamity which a great nation can invite which equals that which follows a supine submission to wrong and injustice.
Grover Cleveland

The apathy of the people is enough to make every statue leap from its pedestal and hasten the resurrection of the dead.   *William Lloyd Garrison*

The tyranny of a prince in an oligarchy is not so dangerous to the public welfare as the apathy of a citizen in a democracy.   *Montesquieu*

Most people are **on** the world, not in it—having no conscious sympathy or relationship to anything about them—undiffused, separate, and rigidly alone like marbles of polished stone, touching but separate.   *John Muir*

. . . indifference is a militant thing . . . when it goes away it leaves smoking ruins, where lie citizens bayonetted through the throat. It is not a children's pastime like mere highway robbery.   *Stephen Crane*

Nothing for preserving the body like having no heart.   *John Petit-Senn*

APPEARANCE   *Also see:* DRESS, FASHION, ILLUSION, REALITY.

How little do they see what is, who frame their hasty judgments upon that which seems.   *Robert Southey*

The world is governed more by appearances than by realities, so that it is fully as necessary to seem to know something as to know it.
Daniel Webster

Getting talked about is one of the penalties for being pretty, while being above suspicion is about the only compensation for being homely.
Kin Hubbard

You are only what you are when no one is looking.   *Robert C. Edwards*

The bosom can ache beneath diamond brooches; and many a blithe heart dances under coarse wool.   *Edwin Hubbel Chapin*

Half the work that is done in this world is to make things appear what they are not.   *Elias Root Beadle*

   The Devil hath power
   To assume a pleasing shape.   *William Shakespeare*

You may turn into an archangel, a fool, or a criminal—no one will see it. But when a button is missing—everyone sees that.   *Erich M. Remarque*

There are no greater wretches in the world than many of those whom people in general take to be happy.   *Seneca*

When I see a bird that walks like a duck and swims like a duck and quacks like a duck, I call that bird a duck.   *Richard Cardinal Cushing*

APPETITE   *Also see:* DESIRE, EATING, GLUTTON, HUNGER.

Reason should direct and appetite obey.   *Cicero*

Any young man with good health and a poor appetite can save up money.
J. M. Bailey

Let the stoics say what they please, we do not eat for the good of living, but because the meat is savory and the appetite is keen.
Ralph Waldo Emerson

Animals feed; man eats. Only the man of intellect and judgment knows how to eat.   *Anthelme Brillat-Savarin*

A well-governed appetite is a great part of liberty.   *Seneca*

ARGUMENT   *Also see:* DIFFERENCE, DISSENT, QUARREL.

Debate is the death of conversation.   *Emil Ludwig*

People generally quarrel because they cannot argue.   *Gilbert K. Chesterton*

A long dispute means both parties are wrong.   *Voltaire*

Behind every argument is someone's ignorance.   *Louis D. Brandeis*

> When much dispute has past,
> We find our tenets just the same as last.   *Alexander Pope*

The best way I know of to win an argument is to start by being in the right.   *Lord Hailsham*

He who establishes his argument by noise and command shows that his reason is weak.   *Michel de Montaigne*

In argument similes are like songs in love; they describe much, but prove nothing.   *Matthew Prior*

Weak arguments are often thrust before my path; but although they are most unsubstantial, it is not easy to destroy them. There is not a more difficult feat known than to cut through a cushion with a sword.
Richard Whately

Any fact is better established by two or three good testimonies than by a thousand arguments.   *Nathaniel Emmons*

The sounder your argument, the more satisfaction you get out of it. *Ed Howe*

Argument, as usually managed, is the worst sort of conversation, as in books it is generally the worst sort of reading.   *Jonathan Swift*

The purely agitational attitude is not good enough for a detailed consideration of a subject.   *Jawaharlal Nehru*

Agitation is the atmosphere of the brains.   *Wendell Phillips*

Never contend with one that is foolish, proud, positive, testy, or with a superior, or a clown, in matter of argument.   *Thomas Fuller*

ARISTOCRACY *Also see:* ANCESTRY, KING, RANK.

What is aristocracy? A corporation of the best, of the bravest.

Thomas Carlyle

I am an aristocrat. I love liberty; I hate equality.   *John Randolph*

Democracy means government by the uneducated, while aristocarcy means government by the badly educated.   *Gilbert K. Chesterton*

There is a natural aristocracy among men. The grounds of this are virtue and talent.   *Thomas Carlyle*

Noblesse oblige; or, superior advantages bind you to larger generosity.

Ralph Waldo Emerson

Aristocracy is always cruel.   *Wendell Phillips*

Some will always be above others. Destroy the equality today, and it will appear again tomorrow.   *Ralph Waldo Emerson*

A monied aristocracy in our country . . . has already set the government at defiance.   *Thomas Jefferson*

The aristocrat is the democrat ripe and gone to seed. *Ralph Waldo Emerson*

Authority forgets a dying king.   *Alfred, Lord Tennyson*

ART *Also see:* ARTIST.

If art is to nourish the roots of our culture, society must set the artist free to follow his vision wherever it takes him.   *John Fitzgerald Kennedy*

Art, like morality, consists in drawing the line somewhere.

Gilbert K. Chesterton

The people who make art their business are mostly imposters.

Pablo Picasso

Art is an effort to create, beside the real world, a more human world.

André Maurois

Art is the most intense mode of individualism that the world has known.

Oscar Wilde

The art of a people is a true mirror of their minds.   *Jawaharlal Nehru*

Art is the stored honey of the human soul, gathered on wings of misery and travail.   *Theodore Dreiser*

The course of Nature is the art of God.   *Edward Young*

Art is a jealous mistress, and if a man has a genius for painting, poetry, music, architecture or philosophy, he makes a bad husband and an ill provider.   *Ralph Waldo Emerson*

Art is a form of catharsis.   *Dorothy Parker*

25

ART (continued)

In art the hand can never execute anything higher than the heart can inspire.
Ralph Waldo Emerson

Classic art was the art of necessity: modern romantic art bears the stamp of caprice and chance.
Ralph Waldo Emerson

Science and art belong to the whole world, and before them vanish the barriers of nationality.
Johann Wolfgang von Goethe

Art is a collaboration between God and the artist, and the less the artist does the better.
André Gide

As long as art is the beauty parlor of civilization, neither art nor civilization is secure.
John Dewey

Supreme art is a traditional statement of certain heroic and religious truth, passed on from age to age, modified by individual genius, but never abandoned.
William Butler Yeats

There is no such thing as modern art. There is art—and there is advertising.
Albert Sterner

If my husband would ever meet a woman on the street who looked like the women in his paintings, he would fall over in a dead faint.
Mrs. Pablo Picasso

The true work of art is but a shadow of the divine perfection.
Michelangelo

All art is a revolt against man's fate.
André Malraux

Nothing is so poor and melancholy as art that is interested in itself and not in its subject.
George Santayana

Perpetual modernness is the measure of merit in every work of art.
Ralph Waldo Emerson

To my mind the old masters are not art; their value is in their scarcity.
Thomas A. Edison

Nature is a revelation of God;
Art a revelation of man.
Henry Wadsworth Longfellow

Art is the desire of a man to express himself, to record the reactions of his personality to the world he lives in.
Amy Lowell

We must never forget that art is not a form of propaganda, it is a form of truth.
John Fitzgerald Kennedy

Fashion is a potency in art, making it hard to judge between the temporary and the lasting.
E. C. Stedman

Great art is as irrational as great music. It is mad with its own loveliness.
George Jean Nathan

ARTIST   *Also see:* ART.

The artists must be sacrificed to their art. Like the bees, they must put their lives into the sting they give.   *Ralph Waldo Emerson*

An artist cannot speak about his art any more than a plant can discuss horticulture.   *Jean Cocteau*

The artist does not illustrate science (but) he frequently responds to the same interests that a scientist does.   *Lewis Mumford*

The defining function of the artist is to cherish consciousness.
Max Eastman

The work of art may have a moral effect, but to demand moral purpose from the artist is to make him ruin his work.   *Johann Wolfgang von Goethe*

One puts into one's art what one has not been capable of putting into one's existence. It is because he was unhappy that God created the world.
Henri de Montherlant

The true artist has the planet for his pedestal; the adventurer, after years of strife, has nothing broader than his shoes.   *Ralph Waldo Emerson*

Every artist dips his brush in his own soul, and paints his own nature into his pictures.   *Henry Ward Beecher*

The torpid artist seeks inspiration at any cost, by virtue or by vice, by friend or by fiend, by prayer or by wine.   *Ralph Waldo Emerson*

ASPIRATION . . . See AMBITION

ASSASSINATION   *Also see:* MURDER, SLANDER.

Assassination: the extreme form of censorship.   *George Bernard Shaw*

Assassination has never changed the history of the world.   *Benjamin Disraeli*

Woe to the hand that shed this costly blood.   *William Shakespeare*

I come fairly to kill him honestly.   *Beaumont and Fletcher*

> Yet each man kills the thing he loves,
> By each let this be heard,
> Some do it with a bitter look,
> Some with a flattering word,
> The coward does it with a kiss,
> The brave man with a sword!   *Oscar Wilde*

He'd make a lovely corpse.   *Charles Dickens*

Some men are alive simply because it is against the law to kill them.
Ed Howe

I'm proud of the fact that I never invented weapons to kill.
Thomas A. Edison

ATHEISM *Also see:* AGNOSTICISM, DOUBT, GOD, SKEPTICISM, SOUL.

I am an atheist, thank God! *Anonymous*

I don't believe in God because I don't believe in Mother Goose.
Clarence Darrow

Nobody talks so constantly about God as those who insist that there is no God. *Heywood Broun*

To be an atheist requires an infinitely greater measure of faith than to receive all the great truths which atheism would deny. *Joseph Addison*

There are no atheists in the foxholes of Bataan. *Douglas MacArthur*

Atheism is rather in the life than in the heart of man. *Francis Bacon*

The atheist has no hope. *J. F. Clarke*

An atheist is one who hopes the Lord will do nothing to disturb his disbelief. *Franklin P. Jones*

Infidelity does not consist in believing or in disbelieving: it consists in professing to believe what one does not believe. *Thomas Paine*

An atheist is a man who has no invisible means of support.
Fulton J. Sheen

AUTHORITY *Also see:* DEMOCRACY, GOVERNMENT, KING, POWER, PRESIDENT.

Nothing is more gratifying to the mind of man than power or dominion.
Joseph Addison

Every great advance in natural knowledge has involved the absolute rejection of authority. *Thomas Huxley*

The wisest have the most authority. *Plato*

All authority belongs to the people. *Thomas Jefferson*

He who is firmly seated in authority soon learns to think security, and not progress, the highest lesson of statecraft. *James Russell Lowell*

If you wish to know what a man is, place him in authority.
Yugoslav Proverb

All authority is quite degrading. *Oscar Wilde*

Who holds a power but newly gained is ever stern of mood. *Aeschylus*

Authority without wisdom is like a heavy ax without an edge, fitter to bruise than polish. *Anne Bradstreet*

The highest duty is to respect authority. *Leo XIII*

Authority is no stronger than the man who wields it. *Dolores E. McGuire*

AUTOMATION *Also see:* MACHINE, SCIENCE, WORK.

The Christian notion of the possibility of redemption is incomprehensible to the computer.
Vance Packard

If it keeps up, man will atrophy all his limbs but the push-button finger.
Frank Lloyd Wright

Jobs are physically easier, but the worker now takes home worries instead of an aching back.
Homer Bigart

We live in a time when automation is ushering in a second industrial revolution.
Adlai E. Stevenson

AVARICE *Also see:* GREED, MISER, MONEY, SELFISHNESS, WEALTH.

If you would abolish avarice, you must abolish its mother, luxury.
Cicero

Avarice increases with the increasing pile of gold.
Juvenal

. . . generally the last passion of those lives of which the first part has been squandered in pleasure, and the second devoted to ambition.
Samuel Johnson

Avarice in old age is foolish; for what can be more absurd than to increase our provisions for the road the nearer we approach to our journey's end.
Cicero

Poverty wants some things, luxury many, avarice all things.
Abraham Cowley

The avaricious man is like the barren sandy ground of the desert which sucks in all the rain and dew with greediness, but yields no fruitful herbs or plants for the benefit of others.
Zeno

Avarice is always poor.
Samuel Johnson

Avarice is the vice of declining years.
George Bancroft

AVERAGE *Also see:* CONFORMITY, MAJORITY, MODERATION.

The average person puts only 25% of his energy and ability into his work. The world takes off its hat to those who put in more than 50% of their capacity, and stands on its head for those few and far between souls who devote 100%.
Andrew Carnegie

I am only an average man but, by George, I work harder at it than the average man.
Theodore Roosevelt

Not doing more than the average is what keeps the average down.
William M. Winans

A jury is a group of twelve people of average ignorance.
Herbert Spencer

I consider myself an average man, except in the fact that I consider myself an average man.
Michel de Montaigne

B

BABY *Also see:* BIRTH, CHILDREN, FAMILY.

A baby is God's opinion that the world should go on.   *Carl Sandburg*

The worst feature of a new baby is its mother's singing.   *Kin Hubbard*

Babies are such a nice way to start people.   *Don Herold*

When the first baby laughed for the first time, the laugh broke into a thousand pieces and they all went skipping about, and that was the beginning of fairies.   *James Matthew Barrie*

BACHELOR

By persistently remaining single a man converts himself into a permanent public temptation.   *Oscar Wilde*

Bachelors know more about women than married men; if they didn't, they'd be married too.   *H. L. Mencken*

A bachelor never quite gets over the idea that he is a thing of beauty and a boy forever.   *Helen Rowland*

Bachelors have consciences, married men have wives.   *H. L. Mencken*

It is impossible to believe that the same God who permitted His own son to die a bachelor regards celibacy as an actual sin.   *H. L. Mencken*

The only good husbands stay bachelors: They're too considerate to get married.   *Finley Peter Dunne*

   I would be married, but I'd have no wife,
   I would be married to a single life.   *Richard Crashaw*

A single man has not nearly the value he would have in a state of union. He is an incomplete animal. He resembles the odd half of a pair of scissors.   *Benjamin Franklin*

A bachelor's life is a fine breakfast, a flat lunch, and a miserable dinner.   *Jean de La Bruyére*

BARGAIN *Also see:* ADVERTISING, ECONOMY, GAIN, SALESMANSHIP.

. . . anything a customer thinks a store is losing money on.   *Kin Hubbard*

Sometimes one pays most for the things one gets for nothing.   *Albert Einstein*

Nothing is cheap which is superfluous, for what one does not need, is dear at a penny.   *Plutarch*

There are very honest people who do not think that they have had a bargain unless they have cheated a merchant.   *Anatole France*

BEAUTY *Also see:* APPEARANCE, ART, ARTIST, BLUSH, CHARM.

. . . it's a sort of bloom on a woman. If you have it you don't need to have anything else; and if you don't have it, it doesn't much matter what else you have. *James Matthew Barrie*

Beauty is not caused. It is. *Emily Dickinson*

There is no cosmetic for beauty like happiness. *Countess of Blessington*

Nothing's beautiful from every point of view. *Horace*

Beauty is power; a smile is its sword. *Charles Reade*

Truth exists for the wise, beauty for the feeling heart. *Johann von Schiller*

Beauty is an outward gift which is seldom despised, except by those to whom it has been refused. *Edward Gibbon*

Beauty is the first present nature gives to women and the first it takes away. *George Brossin Méré*

In every man's heart there is a secret nerve that answers to the vibrations of beauty. *Christopher Morley*

Beauty is only skin deep, but it's a valuable asset if you're poor or haven't any sense. *Kin Hubbard*

BEHAVIOR *Also see:* CHARM, COURTESY, MANNERS, MORALITY.

Behavior is a mirror in which every one displays his image. *Johann Wolfgang von Goethe*

Live so that you can at least get the benefit of the doubt. *Kin Hubbard*

Be nice to people on your way up because you'll meet them on your way down. *Wilson Mizner*

As a rule, there is no surer way to the dislike of men than to behave well where they have behaved badly. *Lew Wallace*

I don't say we all ought to misbehave, but we ought to look as if we could. *Orson Welles*

With a gentleman I am always a gentleman and a half, and with a fraud I try to be a fraud and a half. *Otto von Bismarck*

The reason the way of the transgressor is hard is because it's so crowded. *Kin Hubbard*

When man learns to understand and control his own behavior as well as he is learning to understand and control the behavior of crop plants and domestic animals, he may be justified in believing that he has become civilized. *E. C. Stakman*

BELIEF
Also see: ATHEISM, BUSINESS, CALAMITY, CONFIDENCE, CREDULITY, FAITH, HOPE, OPINION, PREJUDICE, RELIGION, THEORY, TRUST.

We are born believing. A man bears beliefs, as a tree bears apples.
Ralph Waldo Emerson

Nothing is so firmly believed as that which we least know.
Michel de Montaigne

It is always easier to believe than to deny. Our minds are naturally affirmative.
John Burroughs

One person with a belief is equal to a force of ninety-nine who have only interests.
John Stuart Mill

Man can believe the impossible, but can never believe the improbable.
Oscar Wilde

Every time a child says "I don't believe in fairies" there is a little fairy somewhere that falls down dead.
James Matthew Barrie

Believe that life is worth living, and your belief will help create the fact.
William James

The practical effect of a belief is the real test of its soundness.
James A. Froude

BENEVOLENCE . . . See GENEROSITY

BIBLE
Also see: GOD.

The inspiration of the Bible depends upon the ignorance of the gentleman who reads it.
Robert Green Ingersoll

The Bible is a window in this prison of hope, through which we look into eternity.
John Sullivan Dwight

The total absence of humor from the Bible is one of the most singular things in all literature.
Alfred North Whitehead

All human discoveries seem to be made only for the purpose of confirming more and more strongly the truths that come on high and are contained in the sacred writings.
John F. Herschel

To say nothing of its holiness or authority, the Bible contains more specimens of genius and taste than any other volume in existence.
Walter S. Landor

Most people are bothered by those passages of Scripture they do not understand, but the passages that bother me are those I do understand.
Mark Twain

The Bible may be the truth, but it is not the whole truth and nothing but the truth.
Samuel Butler

BIGOTRY

Also see: INTOLERANCE, OPINION, PERSECUTION, PREJU DICE, RACE, REASON, ZEAL.

There is no bigotry like that of "free thought" run to seed.
Horace Greeley

Wisdom has never made a bigot, but learning has.   *Josh Billings*

A man must be both stupid and uncharitable who believes there is no virtue or truth but on his own side.   *Joseph Addison*

The mind of the bigot is like the pupil of the eye; the more light you pour upon it, the more it will contract.   *Oliver Wendell Holmes*

Bigotry murders religion to frighten fools with her ghost.
Charles Caleb Colton

Bigotry dwarfs the soul by shutting out the truth.   *Edwin Hubbel Chapin*

BIRTH

Also see: ANCESTRY, BABY, BIRTH CONTROL, CHILDREN, DEATH, FAMILY.

The moment you're born you're done for.   *Arnold Bennett*

About the only thing we have left that actually discriminates in favor of the plain people is the stork.   *Kin Hubbard*

Our birth is nothing but our death begun,
As tapers waste the moment they take fire.   *Edward Young*

There is (sic) two things in life for which we are never fully prepared, and that is—twins.   *Josh Billings*

The fate of nations is intimately bound up with their powers of reproduction. All nations and all empires first felt decadence gnawing at them when their birth rate fell off.   *Benito Mussolini*

If nature had arranged that husbands and wives should have children alternatively, there would never be more than three in a family.
Laurence Housman

To heir is human.   *Dolores E. McGuire*

BIRTH CONTROL

Also see: BIRTH, POPULATION, SEX.

Prevention of birth is a precipitation of murder.   *Tertullian*

There is an old saying here that a man must do three things during life: plant trees, write books and have sons. I wish they would plant more trees and write more books.   *Luis Muñoz Marin*

However we may pity the mother whose health and even life is imperiled by the performance of her natural duty, there yet remains no sufficient reason for condoning the direct murder of the innocent.   *Plus XI*

No woman can call herself free who does not own and control her body. No woman can call herself free until she can choose consciously whether she will or will not be a mother.   *Margaret H. Sanger*

BLINDNESS *Also see:* EYE.

In the country of the blind the one-eyed man is king.   *Erasmus*

A blind man will not thank you for a looking-glass.   *Thomas Fuller*

There's none so blind as they that won't see.   *Jonathan Swift*

My darkness has been filled with the light of intelligence, and behold, the outer day-lit world was stumbling and groping in social blindness.
Helen Keller

Hatred is blind, as well as love.   *Thomas Fuller*

What a blind person needs is not a teacher but another self.
Helen Keller

BLOOD *Also see:* ANCESTRY, CHILDREN, REVOLUTION, WAR.

Blood will tell, but often it tells too much.   *Don Marquis*

The best blood will at some time get into a fool or a mosquito.
Austin O'Malley

No one need think that the world can be ruled without blood. The civil sword shall and must be red and bloody.   *Martin Luther*

The future can be anything we want it to be, providing we have the faith and that we realize that peace, no less than war, required "blood and sweat and tears."   *Charles F. Kettering*

The blood of the martyrs is the seed of the church.   *Tertullian*

Peace, above all things, is to be desired, but blood must sometimes be spilled to obtain it on equable and lasting terms.   *Andrew Jackson*

Blood is a cleansing and sanctifying thing, and the nation that regards it as the final horror has lost its manhood . . . there are many things more horrible than bloodshed, and slavery is one of them!   *Padraic Pearse*

Blood alone moves the wheels of history.   *Benito Mussolini*

Young blood must have its course, lad, and every dog its day.
Charles Kingsley

BLUSH *Also see:* CRIME.

Man is the only animal that blushes. Or needs to.   *Mark Twain*

When a girl ceases to blush, she has lost the most powerful charm of her beauty.   *Gregory I*

The man that blushes is not quite a brute.   *Edward Young*

As blushing will sometimes make a whore pass for a virtuous woman, so modesty may make a fool seem a man of sense.   *Jonathan Swift*

BOASTING . . . See VANITY

BODY *Also see:* HEALTH, MORTALITY, SOUL.

A healthy body is a guest chamber for the soul: a sick body is a prison.
Francis Bacon

Our bodies are apt to be our autobiographies. *Frank Gelett Burgess*

A human being is an ingenious assembly of portable plumbing.
Christopher Morley

We are bound to our bodies like an oyster is to its shell. *Plato*

The human body is a magazine of inventions, the patent office, where are the models from which every hint is taken. All the tools and engines on earth are only extensions of its limbs and senses. *Ralph Waldo Emerson*

All of us have mortal bodies, composed of perishable matter, but the soul lives forever: it is a portion of the Deity housed in our bodies.
Flavius Josephus

Our body is a well-set clock, which keeps good time, but if it be too much or indiscreetly tampered with, the alarm runs out before the hour.
Joseph Hall

BOLDNESS *Also see:* CONFIDENCE, COURAGE, COWARDICE, GAL-LANTRY.

Fortune befriends the bold. *John Dryden*

Who bravely dares must sometimes risk a fall. *Tobias G. Smollett*

Fools rush in where angels fear to tread. *Alexander Pope*

When you cannot make up your mind which of two evenly balanced courses of action you should take—choose the bolder. *W. J. Slim*

Finite to fail, but infinite to venture. *Emily Dickinson*

Boldness is ever blind, for it sees not dangers and inconveniences; whence it is bad in council though good in execution. *Francis Bacon*

It is wonderful what strength of purpose and boldness and energy of will are roused by the assurance that we are doing our duty. *Walter Scott*

In great straits and when hope is small, the boldest counsels are the safest.
Livy

Boldness is a mask for fear, however great. *Lucan*

Boldness is a child of ignorance. *Francis Bacon*

BOOK *Also see:* BIBLE, CENSORSHIP, HISTORY, LEARNING, LITERATURE, READING, WORD.

If I have not read a book before, it is, for all intents and purposes, new to me whether it was printed yesterday or three hundred years ago.
William Hazlitt

That is a good book which is opened with expectation and closed in profit.
Amos Bronson Alcott

Some books leave us free and some books make us free.
Ralph Waldo Emerson

The books that help you the most are those which make you think the most.
Theodore Parker

A wicked book cannot repent.
Old Proverb

A room without books is like a body without a soul.
Cicero

The newest books are those that never grow old.
Holbrook Jackson

A book is a mirror: If an ass peers into it, you can't expect an apostle to look out.
G. C. Lichtenberg

A book is the only immortality.
Rufus Choate

Read the best books first, or you may not have a chance to read them all.
Henry David Thoreau

Books are not men and yet they stay alive.
Stephen Vincent Benét

My books are water; those of the great geniuses are wine—everybody drinks water.
Mark Twain

If a law were passed giving six months to every writer of a first book, only the good ones would do it.
Bertrand Russell

This is the best book ever written by any man on the wrong side of a question of which he is profoundly ignorant.
Thomas B. Macaulay

A house is not a home unless it contains food and fire for the mind as well as the body.
Margaret Fuller

Some books are to be tasted; others swallowed; and some to be chewed and digested.
Francis Bacon

Every man is a volume if you know how to read him.
William Ellery Channing

The man who does not read good books has no advantage over the man who can't read them.
Mark Twain

Books, like friends, should be few and well chosen.
Samuel Paterson

A real book is not one that we read, but one that reads us.
W. H. Auden

BORE and BOREDOM *Also see:* COMMUNICATION, CONVERSATION, LOQUACITY.

Bore, n. A person who talks when you wish him to listen.
Ambrose Bierce

There are few wild beasts more to be dreaded than a communicative man having nothing to communicate. *Christian Nestell Bovee*

The capacity of human beings to bore one another seems to be vastly greater than that of any other animal. *H. L. Mencken*

Any subject can be made interesting, and therefore any subject can be made boring. *Hilaire Belloc*

The man who lets himself be bored is even more contemptible than the bore. *Samuel Butler*

A man who spends so much time talking about himself that you can't talk about yourself. *Melville D. Landon*

A guy who wraps up a two-minute idea in a two-hour vocabulary.
Walter Winchell

Boredom is a vital problem for the moralist, since at least half of the sins of mankind are caused by the fear of it. *Bertrand Russell*

People always get tired of one another. I grow tired of myself whenever I am left alone for ten minutes, and I am certain that I am fonder of myself than anyone can be of another person. *George Bernard Shaw*

We always get bored with those whom we bore.
François de La Rochefoucauld

BORROWING *Also see:* CREDIT, DEBT.

The shoulders of a borrower are always a little straighter than those of a beggar. *Morris Leopold Ernst*

If you would know the value of money, go try to borrow some; for he that goes a-borrowing goes a-sorrowing. *Benjamin Franklin*

The human species, according to the best theory I can form of it, is composed of two distinct races: the men who borrow, and the men who lend.
Charles Lamb

Only an inventor knows how to borrow, and every man is or should be an inventor. *Ralph Waldo Emerson*

Live within your income, even if you have to borrow money to do so.
Josh Billings

Lots of fellows think a home is only good to borrow money on.
Kin Hubbard

He who borrows sells his freedom. *German Proverb*

Creditors have better memories than debtors. *Proverb*

BOYS Also see: AGE, BACHELOR, CHILDREN, GIRLS, YOUTH.

The fact that boys are allowed to exist at all is evidence of a remarkable Christian forbearance among men.   *Ambrose Bierce*

I am convinced that every boy, in his heart, would rather steal second base than an automobile.   *Thomas Cambell Clark*

When you can't do anything else to a boy, you can make him wash his face.   *Ed Howe*

Boys will be boys, and so will a lot of middle-aged men.   *Kin Hubbard*

There is nothing so aggravating as a fresh boy who is too old to ignore and too young to kick.   *Kin Hubbard*

Boys are beyond the range of anybody's sure understanding, at least when they are between the ages of 18 months and 90 years.   *James Thurber*

A man can never quite understand a boy, even when he has been a boy.   *Gilbert K. Chesterton*

The glory of the nation rests in the character of her men. And character comes from boyhood. Thus every boy is a challenge to his elders.   *Herbert Hoover*

Of all wild beasts, the most difficult to manage.   *Plato*

A boy is a magical creature—you can lock him out of your workshop, but you can't lock him out of your heart.   *Allan Beck*

———————

BREVITY Also see: CONVERSATION, LOQUACITY, SIMPLICITY, WORDS.

Never be so brief as to become obscure.   *Tryon Edwards*

The more you say, the less people remember. The fewer the words, the greater the profit.   *Fénelon*

Brevity is the best recommendation of speech, whether in a senator or an orator.   *Cicero*

If you would be pungent, be brief; for it is with words as with sunbeams—the more they are condensed, the deeper they burn.   *Robert Southey*

The fewer the words, the better the prayer.   *Martin Luther*

There's a great power in words, if you don't hitch too many of them together.   *Josh Billings*

It is my ambition to say in ten sentences what others say in a whole book.   *Nietzsche*

Brevity is a great charm of eloquence.   *Cicero*

Brevity and conciseness are the parents of correction.   *Hosea Ballou*

BROTHERHOOD Also see: CITIZENSHIP, EQUALITY, FAMILY, FRIENDSHIP, HUMANITY, MAN, SELFISHNESS.

On this shrunken globe, men can no longer live as strangers.
Adlai E. Stevenson

When man to man shall be friend and brother. *Gerald Massey*

We must learn to live together as brothers or perish together as fools.
Martin Luther King

We do not want the men of another color for our brothers-in-law, but we do want them for our brothers. *Booker T. Washington*

Brotherhood is the very price and condition of man's survival.
Carlos P. Romulo

Brotherhood is not just a Bible word. Out of comradeship can come and will come the happy life for all. *Heywood Broun*

We live in a world that has narrowed into a neighborhood before it has broadened into a brotherhood. *Lyndon Baines Johnson*

It is easier to love humanity than to love one's neighbor. *Eric Hoffer*

BUSINESS Also see: ACTION, ADVERTISING, EMPLOYMENT, INDUSTRY, FINANCE, PURSUIT, SPECULATION, WORK.

There are two times in a man's life when he should not speculate: when he can't afford it, and when he can. *Mark Twain*

All business proceeds on beliefs, or judgments of probabilities, and not on certainties. *Charles Eliot*

It is not the crook in modern business that we fear but the honest man who does not know what he is doing. *Owen D. Young*

The successful business man sometimes makes his money by ability and experience; but he generally makes it by mistake. *Gilbert K. Chesterton*

Business is a combination of war and sport. *André Maurois*

A man to carry on a successful business must have imagination. He must see things as in a vision, a dream of the whole thing.
Charles M. Schwab

Business is like riding a bicycle—either you keep moving or you fall down.
Anonymous

The best mental effort in the game of business is concentrated on the major problem of securing the consumer's dollar before the other fellow gets it.
Stuart Chase

A friendship founded on business is better than a business founded on friendship. *John D. Rockefeller*

BUSY *Also see:* BUSINESS, INDUSTRY, PERSEVERANCE, WORK.

It is not enough to be busy; so are the ants. The question is: What are we busy about? *Henry David Thoreau*

The busy have no time for tears. *Lord Byron*

Occupation is the scythe of time. *Napoleon Bonaparte*

A really busy person never knows how much he weighs. *Ed Howe*

Whoever admits that he is too busy to improve his methods has acknowledged himself to be at the end of his rope. And that is always the saddest predicament which anyone can get into. *J. Ogden Armour*

What we hope ever to do with ease, we must learn first to do with diligence. *Samuel Johnson*

The successful people are the ones who can think up things for the rest of the world to keep busy at. *Don Marquis*

Who makes quick use of the moment, is a genius of prudence. *Johann Kaspar Lavater*

Occupation is the necessary basis of all enjoyment. *Leigh Hunt*

The great happiness of life, I find, after all, to consist in the regular discharge of some mechanical duty. *Johann von Schiller*

Busy souls have no time to be busybodies. *Austin O'Malley*

C

CALAMITY *Also see:* ADVERSITY, AFFLICTION, ANTICIPATION, CRISIS, DEBT, MISERY, WAR.

Calamities are of two kinds. Misfortune to ourselves, and good fortune to others. *Ambrose Bierce*

He who forsees calamities, suffers them twice over. *Beilby Porteus*

Calamity is the perfect glass wherein we truly see and know ourselves. *William Davenant*

Calamity is the test of integrity. *Samuel Richardson*

Calamity is virtue's opportunity. *Seneca*

It is only from the belief of the goodness and wisdom of a supreme being, that our calamities can be borne in the manner which becomes a man. *Henry Mackenzie*

Calamity is man's true touchstone. *Beaumont and Fletcher*

CANDOR *Also see:* HONESTY, SINCERITY, TRUTH.

Candor is the brightest gem of criticism. *Benjamin Disraeli*

Examine what is said, not him who speaks. *Arabian Proverb*

Friends, if we be honest with ourselves, we shall be honest with each other.
George Macdonald

Frank and explicit—that is the right line to take when you wish to conceal your own mind and confuse the minds of others. *Benjamin Disraeli*

Candor is a proof of both a just frame of mind, and of a good tone of breeding. It is a quality that belongs equally to the honest man and to the gentleman. *James Fenimore Cooper*

Nothing astonishes men so much as common sense and plain dealing.
Ralph Waldo Emerson

Gracious to all, to none subservient, Without offense he spake the word he meant. *Thomas Bailey Aldrich*

There is no wisdom like frankness. *Benjamin Disraeli*

We want all our friends to tell us our bad qualities; it is only the particular ass that does so whom we can't tolerate. *William James*

A "No" uttered from deepest conviction is better and greater than a "Yes" merely uttered to please, or what is worse, to avoid trouble.
Mahatma Gandhi

CAPITALISM *Also see:* BUSINESS, FINANCE, MONEY.

The fundamental idea of modern capitalism is not the right of the individual to possess and enjoy what he has earned, but the thesis that the exercise of this right redounds to the general good. *Ralph Barton Perry*

Capital is that part of wealth which is devoted to obtaining further wealth.
Alfred Marshall

The dynamo of our economic system is self-interest which may range from mere petty greed to admirable types of self-expression. *Felix Frankfurter*

The inherent vice of capitalism is the unequal sharing of blessings; the inherent virtue of socialism is the equal sharing of miseries.
Winston Churchill

Capitalism and communism stand at opposite poles. Their essential difference is this: The communist, seeing the rich man and his fine home, says: "No man should have so much." The capitalist, seeing the same thing, says: "All men should have as much." *Phelps Adams*

CATASTROPHE . . . See CALAMITY

CAUSE *Also see:* EFFICIENCY, MOTIVE, PURPOSE, RESULT.

That cause is strong, which has not a multitude, but a strong man behind it.
James Russell Lowell

We are all ready to be savage in some cause. The difference between a good man and a bad one is the choice of the cause. *William James*

The little trouble in the world that is not due to love is due to friendship.
Ed Howe

No cause is helpless if it is just. Errors, no matter how popular, carry the seeds of their own destruction. *John W. Scoville*

No man is worth his salt who is not ready at all times to risk his well-being, to risk his body, to risk his life, in a great cause. *Theodore Roosevelt*

In war, events of importance are the result of trivial causes.
Julius Caesar

The humblest citizen of all the land, when clad in the armor of a righteous cause, is stronger than all the hosts of Error. *William Jennings Bryan*

A bad cause will never be supported by bad means and bad men.
Thomas Paine

The mark of the immature man is that he wants to die nobly for a cause, while the mark of a mature man is that he wants to live humbly for one.
Wilhelm Stekel

Great causes and little men go ill together. *Jawaharlal Nehru*

The probability that we may fail in the struggle ought not to deter us from the support of a cause we believe to be just. *Abraham Lincoln*

Ours is an abiding faith in the cause of human freedom. We know it is God's cause. *Thomas E. Dewey*

Men are blind in their own cause. *Heywood Broun*

It is not a field of a few acres of ground, but a cause, that we are defending, and whether we defeat the enemy in one battle, or by degrees, the consequences will be the same. *Thomas Paine*

It is only after an unknown number of unrecorded labors, after a host of noble hearts have succumbed in discouragement, convinced that their cause is lost; it is only then that cause triumphs. *Guizot*

Respectable men and women content with good and easy living are missing some of the most important things in life. Unless you give yourself to some great cause you haven't even begun to live. *William P. Merrill*

If you want to be an orator, first get your great cause. *Wendell Phillips*

CAUTION

Also see: ADVICE, COWARDICE, DISCRETION, PRUDENCE, SAFETY, VIGILANCE.

Hasten slowly.

Augustus Caesar

I don't like these cold, precise, perfect people, who, in order not to speak wrong, never speak at all, and in order not to do wrong, never do anything.

Henry Ward Beecher

Among mortals second thoughts are wisest.

Euripides

The chief danger in life is that you may take too many precautions.

Alfred Adler

Deliberate with caution, but act with decision; and yield with graciousness, or oppose with firmness.

Charles Hole

Be slow of tongue and quick of eye.

Miguel de Cervantes

It is a good thing to learn caution from the misfortunes of others.

Publilius Syrus

CENSORSHIP

Also see: ASSASSINATION, FREEDOM, FREEDOM of PRESS, FREEDOM of SPEECH, NEWSPAPER.

Only the suppressed word is dangerous.

Ludwig Börne

I am opposed to censorship. Censors are pretty sure fools. I have no confidence in the suppression of everyday facts.

James Robinson

Censorship reflects a society's lack of confidence in itself.

Potter Stewart

He is always the severest censor of the merit of others who has the least worth of his own.

Elias Lyman Maggon

Every burned book enlightens the world.

Ralph Waldo Emerson

Damn all expurgated books; the dirtiest book of all is the expurgated book.

Walt Whitman

Pontius Pilate was the first great censor, and Jesus Christ the first great victim of censorship.

Ben Lindsay

I am mortified to be told that, in the United States of America, the sale of a book can become a subject of inquiry, and of criminal inquiry too.

Thomas Jefferson

If there had been a censorship of the press in Rome we should have had today neither Horace nor Juvenal, nor the philosophical writings of Cicero.

Voltaire

As long as I don't write about the government, religion, politics, and other institutions, I am free to print anything.

Beaumarchais

CENSURE *Also see:* ABUSE, CRITICISM.

Censure is the tax a man pays to the public for being eminent.

Jonathan Swift

Few persons have sufficient wisdom to prefer censure, which is useful, to praise which deceives them. *François de La Rochefoucauld*

The readiest and surest way to get rid of censure, is to correct ourselves.

Demosthenes

He who would acquire fame must not show himself afraid of censure. The dread of censure is the death of genius. *William Gilmore Simms*

The censure of those who are opposed to us, is the highest commendation that can be given us. *Seigneur de Saint-Evremond*

It is folly for an eminent man to think of escaping censure, and a weakness to be affected with it. All the illustrious persons of antiquity, and indeed of every age in the world, have passed through this fiery persecution.

Joseph Addison

They have a right to censure that have a heart to help. *William Penn*

I find that the pain of a little censure, even when it is unfounded, is more acute than the pleasure of much praise. *Thomas Jefferson*

CERTAINTY *Also see:* CONFIDENCE, DOUBT, FACT, KNOWLEDGE,
QUESTION, SUCCESS.

To be absolutely certain about something, one must know everything or nothing about it. *Olin Miller*

Convictions are more dangerous foes of truth than lies. *Nietzsche*

In these matters the only certainty is that there is nothing certain.

Pliny the Elder

If we begin with certainties, we shall end in doubts; but if we begin with doubts, and are patient in them, we shall end in certainties.

Francis Bacon

There is nothing certain in a man's life but that he must lose it.

Owen Meredith

To be positive: to be mistaken at the top of one's voice.

Ambrose Bierce

Ah, what a dusty answer gets the soul when hot for certainties in this our life! *George Meredith*

When I was young I was sure of everything; in a few years, having been mistaken a thousand times, I was not half so sure of most things as I was before; at present, I am hardly sure of anything but what God has revealed to me. *John Wesley*

CHANGE *Also see:* IMPROVEMENT, PROGRESS, REFORM, REVOLUTION, VARIETY.

All change is not growth; all movement is not forward. *Ellen Glasgow*

Change is an easy panacea. It takes character to stay in one place and be happy there. *Elizabeth Clarke Dunn*

He that will not apply new remedies must expect new evils. *Francis Bacon*

The world hates change, yet it is the only thing that has brought progress. *Charles F. Kettering*

The problem is not whether business will survive in competition with business, but whether any business will survive at all in the face of social change. *Laurence Joseph McGinley*

Everyone thinks of changing the world, but no one thinks of changing himself. *Leo Tolstoi*

There is a certain relief in change, even though it be from bad to worse; as I have found in traveling in a stage-coach, that it is often a comfort to shift one's position and be bruised in a new place. *Washington Irving*

We are restless because of incessant change, but we would be frightened if change were stopped. *Lyman Lloyd Bryson*

There is nothing permanent except change. *Heraclitus*

Weep not that the world changes—did it keep a stable, changeless state, it were a cause indeed to weep. *William Cullen Bryant*

Things do not change, we do. *Henry David Thoreau*

Christians are supposed not merely to endure change, nor even to profit by it, but to cause it. *Harry Emerson Fosdick*

I've never met a person, I don't care what his condition, in whom I could not see possibilities. I don't care how much a man may consider himself a failure, I believe in him, for he can change the thing that is wrong in his life any time he is ready and prepared to do it. Whenever he develops the desire, he can take away from his life the thing that is defeating it. The capacity for reformation and change lies within. *Preston Bradley*

Life belongs to the living, and he who lives must be prepared for changes. *Johann Wolfgang von Goethe*

Never swap horses crossing a stream. *American Proverb*

We emphasize that we believe in change because we were born of it, we have lived by it, we prospered and grew great by it. So the status quo has never been our god, and we ask no one else to bow down before it. *Carl T. Rowan*

CHARACTER *Also see:* FAME, INDIVIDUALITY, MORALITY, PERSONALITY, QUALITY, REPUTATION, TEMPER.

Let us not say, Every man is the architect of his own fortune; but let us say, Every man is the architect of his own character.
George Dana Boardman

Weakness of character is the only defect which cannot be amended.
François de La Rochefoucauld

A person reveals his character by nothing so clearly as the joke he resents.
G. C. Lichtenberg

Characters do not change. Opinions alter, but characters are only developed.
Benjamin Disraeli

Man's character is his fate.
Heraclitus

You must look into people, as well as at them.
Lord Chesterfield

Make the most of yourself, for that is all there is of you.
Ralph Waldo Emerson

Character is not made in a crisis—it is only exhibited.
Robert Freeman

What you are thunders so that I cannot hear what you say to the contrary.
Ralph Waldo Emerson

A man never discloses his own character so clearly as when he describes another's.
Jean Paul Richter

The four cornerstones of character on which the structure of this nation was built are: Initiative, Imagination, Individuality and Independence.
Edward Rickenbacker

There is no such thing as a "self-made" man. We are made up of thousands of others. Everyone who has ever done a kind deed for us, or spoken one word of encouragement to us, has entered into the make-up of our character and of our thoughts, as well as our success.
George Matthew Adams

Every man has three characters—that which he exhibits, that which he has, and that which he thinks he has.
Alphonse Karr

Character is a victory, not a gift.
Anonymous

Instead of saying that man is the creature of circumstance, it would be nearer the mark to say that man is the architect of circumstance. It is character which builds an existence out of circumstance. From the same materials one man builds palaces, another hovels; one warehouses, another villas; bricks and mortar are mortar and bricks until the architect can make them something else.
Thomas Carlyle

CHARITY

Also see: GENEROSITY, HEART, HELP, HUMANITY, KINDNESS, LOVE, OSTENTATION, TOLERANCE.

Charity: a thing that begins at home, and usually stays there.
Elbert Hubbard

Not he who has much is rich, but he who gives much. *Erich Fromm*

As the purse is emptied, the heart is filled. *Victor Hugo*

He who waits to do a great deal of good at once, will never do anything.
Samuel Johnson

The truly generous is the truly wise, and he who loves not others, lives unblest.
Henry Home

A bone to the dog is not charity. Charity is the bone shared with the dog, when you are just as hungry as the dog. *Jack London*

Though I speak with the tongues of men and angels and have not charity, I am become as sounding brass, or a tinkling cymbal.
I Corinthians 13:1-3

Charity sees the need, not the cause. *German Proverb*

With malice toward none, with charity for all, with firmness in the right as God gives us to see the right, let us finish the work we are in.
Abraham Lincoln

Every charitable act is a stepping stone towards heaven.
Henry Ward Beecher

If you haven't got any charity in your heart, you have the worst kind of heart trouble. *Bob Hope*

What we frankly give, forever is our own. *George Granville*

Prayer carries us half way to God, fasting brings us to the door of His palace, and alms-giving procures us admission. *The Koran*

If you give money, spend yourself with it. *Henry David Thoreau*

Give no bounties: make equal laws: secure life and prosperity and you need not give alms. *Ralph Waldo Emerson*

One must be poor to know the luxury of giving. *George Eliot*

> They take the paper and they read the headlines,
> So they've heard of unemployment and they've heard of breadlines,
> And they philanthropically cure them all
> By getting up a costume charity ball. *Ogden Nash*

The highest exercise of charity is charity towards the uncharitable.
J. S. Buckminster

It is more blessed to give than to receive. *Acts. 20:35*

CHARM *Also see:* BEAUTY, BLUSH, GRACE.

There are charms made only for distant admiration. *Samuel Johnson*

A really plain woman is one who, however beautiful, neglects to charm.
Edgar Saltus

There is no personal charm so great as the charm of a cheerful temperament. *Henry Van Dyke*

Charm is more than beauty. *Yiddish Proverb*

CHEERFULNESS *Also see:* CHARM, HAPPINESS, HUMOR, JOY, OP-
TIMISM, SMILE.

A good laugh is sunshine in a house. *William Makepeace Thackeray*

The best way to cheer yourself up is to try to cheer somebody else up.
Mark Twain

Keep your face to the sunshine and you cannot see the shadow.
Helen Keller

So of cheerfulness, or a good temper, the more it is spent, the more it
remains. *Ralph Waldo Emerson*

The true source of cheerfulness is benevolence. *P. Godwin*

Let us be of good cheer, remembering that the misfortunes hardest to bear
are those which never happen. *James Russell Lowell*

Wondrous is the strength of cheerfulness, and its power of endurance—the
cheerful man will do more in the same time, will do it better, will preserve
it longer, than the sad or sullen. *Thomas Carlyle*

I feel an earnest and humble desire, and shall till I die, to increase the
stock of harmless cheerfulness. *Charles Dickens*

Cheerfulness in most cheerful people, is the rich and satisfying result of
strenuous discipline. *Edwin Percy Whipple*

Cheerfulness removes the rust from the mind, lubricates our inward ma-
chinery, and enables us to do our work with fewer creaks and groans. If
people were universally cheerful, probably there wouldn't be half the quar-
reling or a tenth part of the wickedness there is. Cheerfulness, too, promotes health and immortality. Cheerful people live longest here on earth,
afterward in our hearts. *Anonymous*

Health is the condition of wisdom, and the sign is cheerfulness,—an open
and noble temper. *Ralph Waldo Emerson*

Cheer up! The worst is yet to come! *Philander Johnson*

The cheerful live longest in years, and afterwards in our regards. Cheerfulness is the off-shoot of goodness. *Christian Nestell Bovee*

CHILDREN *Also see:* BIRTH, BOYS, FAMILY, FATHER, GIRLS, YOUTH.

It is dangerous to confuse children with angels.   *David Fyfe*

Childhood sometimes does pay a second visit to man; youth never.
Anna Jameson

It is a wise child that knows his own father.   *Homer*

It is a wise father that knows his own child.   *William Shakespeare*

The best way to make children good is to make them happy.   *Oscar Wilde*

The child is father of the man.   *William Wordsworth*

The potential possibilities of any child are the most intriguing and stimulating in all creation.   *Ray L. Wilbur*

Pretty much all the honest truth telling there is in the world is done by children.   *Oliver Wendell Holmes*

Don't take up a man's time talking about the smartness of your children; he wants to talk to you about the smartness of his children.   *Ed Howe*

Let the child's first lesson be obedience, and the second will be what thou wilt.   *Benjamin Franklin*

Children are our most valuable natural resource.   *Herbert Hoover*

Better to be driven out from among men than to be disliked of children.
Richard Henry Dana

My mother loved children—she would have given anything if I had been one.   *Groucho Marx*

A child is a curly, dimpled lunatic.   *Ralph Waldo Emerson*

Children in a family are like flowers in a bouquet: there's always one determined to face in an opposite direction from the way the arranger desires.
Marcelene Cox

We've had bad luck with our kids—they've all grown up. *Christopher Morley*

> Ah! what would the world be to us
>   If the children were no more?
> We should dread the desert behind us
>   Worse than the dark before.   *Henry Wadsworth Longfellow*

Children are poor men's riches.   *English Proverb*

If a child annoys you, quiet him by brushing his hair. If this doesn't work, use the other side of the brush on the other end of the child.   *Anonymous*

CHOICE *Also see:* DECISION, DESIRE, DESTINY, FREEDOM, LIBERTY.

Between two evils, choose neither; between two goods, choose both.
Tryon Edwards

In literature, as in love, we are astonished at the choice made by other people.
André Maurois

Life often presents us with a choice of evils rather than of goods.
Charles Caleb Colton

When you have to make a choice and don't make it, that in itself is a choice.
William James

He who chooses the beginning of a road chooses the place it leads to. It is the means that determine the end.
Harry Emerson Fosdick

A man is too apt to forget that in this world he cannot have everything. A choice is all that is left him.
H. Mathews

CHRISTIANITY *Also see:* BROTHERHOOD, CHURCH, FAITH, RELIGION.

Satan the envious said with a sigh: Christians know more about their hell than I.
Alfred Kreymborg

The trouble with some of us is that we have been inoculated with small doses of Christianity which keep us from catching the real thing.
Leslie Dixon Weatherhead

Christianity is a battle, not a dream.
Wendell Phillips

A Christian is a man who feels repentance on Sunday for what he did on Saturday and is going to do on Monday.
Thomas Ybarra

Christian: one who believes that the New Testament is a divinely inspired book admirably suited to the spiritual needs of his neighbors.
Ambrose Bierce

Christianity has not been tried and found wanting; it has been found difficult and not tried.
Gilbert K. Chesterton

There is one single fact which we may oppose to all the wit and argument of infidelity, namely, that no man ever repented of being a Christian on his death bed.
Hannah More

Christianity does not remove you from the world and its problems; it makes you fit to live in it, triumphantly and usefully.
Charles Templeton

If a man cannot be a Christian in the place where he is, he cannot be a Christian anywhere.
Henry Ward Beecher

Christianity is a missionary religion, converting, advancing, aggressive, encompassing the world; a non-missionary church is in the bands of death.
Friedrich Max Müller

CHURCH and STATE *Also see:* CHRISTIANITY, RELIGION.

The church is actually patronized by the social order as a means of stabilizing and perpetuating the existing system.   *C. C. Morrison*

In the relationship between man and religion, the state is firmly committed to a position of neutrality.   *Thomas Campbell Clark*

The church is the only place where someone speaks to me and I do not have to answer back.   *Charles deGaulle*

No religion can long continue to maintain its purity when the church becomes the subservient vassal of the state.   *Felix Adler*

The church is only a secular institution in which the half-educated speak to the half-converted.   *William Ralph Inge*

CITIZENSHIP *Also see:* AMERICA, COUNTRY, DUTY, HEROISM, PATRIOTISM, RIGHTS.

The most important office . . . that of private citizen.   *Louis D. Brandeis*

Citizenship consists in the service of the country.   *Jawaharlal Nehru*

Voting is the least arduous of a citizen's duties. He has the prior and harder duty of making up his mind.   *Ralph Barton Perry*

The first requisite of a good citizen in this republic of ours is that he should be able and willing to pull his weight.   *Theodore Roosevelt*

Citizenship comes first today in our crowded world. . . . No man can enjoy the privileges of education and thereafter with a clear conscience break his contract with society. To respect that contract is to be mature, to strengthen it is to be a good citizen, to do more than your share under it is to be noble.   *Isaiah Bowman*

Every good citizen makes his country's honor his own, and cherishes it not only as precious but as sacred. He is willing to risk his life in its defense and is conscious that he gains protection while he gives it.   *Andrew Jackson*

Let us at all times remember that all American citizens are brothers of a common country, and should dwell together in bonds of fraternal feeling.   *Abraham Lincoln*

Now the trumpet summons us again—not as a call to bear arms, though arms we need—not as a call to battle, though embattled we are—but a call to bear the burden of a long twilight struggle year in and year out, "rejoicing in hope, patient in tribulation"—a struggle against the common enemies of man: tyranny, poverty, disease and war itself.   *John Fitzgerald Kennedy*

If you will help run our government in the American way, then there will never be danger of our government running America in the wrong way.   *Omar N. Bradley*

CIVILIZATION *Also see:* ADVENTURE, BEHAVIOR, CULTURE, DOUBT, IMPROVEMENT, PROGRESS.

Civilization is not a burden. It is an opportunity.   *Alexander Meiklejohn*

Anyone can be a barbarian; it requires a terrible effort to remain a civilized man.   *Leonard Sidney Woolf*

The true test of civilization is, not the census, nor the size of the cities, nor the crops, but the kind of man that the country turns out.
Ralph Waldo Emerson

Civilization begins with order, grows with liberty, and dies with chaos.
Will Durant

The end of the human race will be that it will eventually die of civilization.
Ralph Waldo Emerson

Civilization is a limitless multiplication of unnecessary necessities.
Mark Twain

You can't say civilization isn't advancing: in every war, they kill you in a new way.   *Will Rogers*

The three great elements of modern civilization, Gunpowder, Printing, and the Protestant Religion.   *Thomas Carlyle*

Civilization is the order and freedom promoting cultural activity.
Will Durant

Mankind's struggle upwards, in which millions are trampled to death, that thousands may mount on their bodies.   *Clara Lucas Balfour*

In the advance of civilization, it is new knowledge which paves the way, and the pavement is eternal.   *W. R. Whitney*

Civilization ceases when we no longer respect and no longer put into their correct places the fundamental values, such as work, family and country; such as the individual, honor and religion.   *R. P. Lebret*

Every advance in civilization has been denounced as unnatural while it was recent.   *Bertrand Russell*

The true civilization is where every man gives to every other every right that he claims for himself.   *Robert Green Ingersoll*

Civilization is the process of reducing the infinite to the finite.
Oliver Wendell Holmes

All the things now enjoyed by civilization have been created by some man and sold by another man before anybody really enjoyed the benefits of them.   *James G. Daly*

CLASS *Also see:* ARISTOCRACY, ORDER, SOCIETY.

All mankind is divided into three classes: those that are immovable, those that are movable, and those that move.
Arabian Proverb

There is nothing to which men cling more tenaciously than the privileges of class.
Leonard Sidney Woolf

Let him who expects one class of society to prosper in the highest degree, while the other is in distress, try whether one side of the face can smile while the other is pinched.
Thomas Fuller

The distinctions separating the social classes are false; in the last analysis they rest on force.
Albert Einstein

The ignorant classes are the dangerous classes.
Henry Ward Beecher

I never would believe that Providence had sent a few men into the world, ready booted and spurred to ride, and millions ready saddled and bridled to be ridden.
Richard Rumbold

Other lands have their vitality in a few, a class, but we have it in the bulk of our people.
Walt Whitman

Mankind is divided into rich and poor, into property owners and exploited; and to abstract oneself from this fundamental division and from the antagonism between poor and rich means abstracting oneself from fundamental facts.
Joseph Stalin

CLEVERNESS *Also see:* CYNIC, INTELLIGENCE, WIT.

Clever men are good, but they are not the best.
Thomas Carlyle

A man likes his wife to be just clever enough to appreciate his cleverness, and just stupid enough to admire it.
Israel Zangwill

Cleverness is serviceable for everything, sufficient for nothing.
Amiel

The doctrine of human equality reposes on this: that there is no man really clever who has not found that he is stupid.
Gilbert K. Chesterton

Find enough clever things to say, and you're a Prime Minister; write them down and you're a Shakespeare.
George Bernard Shaw

Mother is far too clever to understand anything she does not like.
Arnold Bennett

Cleverness is not wisdom.
Euripides

The desire to seem clever often keeps us from being so.
François de La Rochefoucauld

It is great cleverness to know how to conceal our cleverness.
François de La Rochefoucauld

COMMITTEE

If you want to kill any idea in the world today, get a committee working on it.   *Charles F. Kettering*

When it comes to facing up to serious problems, each candidate will pledge to appoint a committee. And what is a committee? A group of the unwilling, picked from the unfit, to do the unnecessary. But it all sounds great in a campaign speech.   *Richard Long Harkness*

To get something done a committee should consist of three men, two of whom are absent.   *Anonymous*

A committee is a group that keeps minutes and loses hours.   *Milton Berle*

A cul-de-sac to which ideas are lured and then quietly strangled.
                                                              John A. Lincoln

---

COMMON SENSE   *Also see:* CANDOR, INTELLIGENCE, PRUDENCE, REASON, UNDERSTANDING.

Common sense is genius in homespun.   *Alfred North Whitehead*

Common sense is very uncommon.   *Horace Greeley*

Common sense is in spite of, not as the result of education.   *Victor Hugo*

Common sense is only a modification of talent. Genius is an exaltation of it. The difference is, therefore, in degree, not nature.
                                                          Edward G. Bulwer-Lytton

He was one of those men who possess almost every gift, except the gift of the power to use them.   *Charles Kingsley*

Common sense is instinct, and enough of it is genius.   *Josh Billings*

Common sense and nature will do a lot to make the pilgrimage of life not too difficult.   *W. Somerset Maugham*

Common sense is compelled to make its way without the enthusiasm of anyone.   *Ed Howe*

Nothing is more fairly distributed than common sense: no one thinks he needs more of it than he already has.   *Descartes*

Common sense is the knack of seeing things as they are, and doing things as they ought to be done.   *Josh Billings*

The two World Wars came in part, like much modern literature and art, because men, whose nature is to tire of everything in turn, . . . tired of common sense and civilization.   *F. L. Lucas*

COMMUNICATION
Also see: CONVERSATION, NEWSPAPER, TELEVISION.

A world community can exist only with world communication, which means something more than extensive shortwave facilities scattered about the globe. It means common understanding, a common tradition, common ideas, and common ideals.
Robert M. Hutchins

News is that which comes from the North, East, West and South, and if it comes from only one point on the compass, then it is a class publication and not news.
Benjamin Disraeli

Every improvement in communication makes the bore more terrible.
Frank Moore Colby

The fantastic advances in the field of electronic communication constitute a greater danger to the privacy of the individual.
Earl Warren

Each mind is pressed, and open every ear, to hear new tidings, though they no way joy us.
Edward Fairfax

We shall never be able to remove suspicion and fear as potential causes of war until communication is permitted to flow, free and open, across international boundaries.
Harry S. Truman

COMMUNISM
Also see: ARISTOCRACY, CAPITALISM, DEMOCRACY.

Communism is a society where each one works according to his abilities and gets according to his needs.
Pierre Joseph Proudhon

The theory of Communism may be summed up in one sentence: Abolish all private property.
Karl Marx

Communism possesses a language which every people can understand—its elements are hunger, envy, and death.
Heinrich Heine

A communist is like a crocodile: when it opens its mouth you cannot tell whether it is trying to smile or preparing to eat you up.
Winston Churchill

Communism is the death of the soul. It is the organization of total conformity—in short, of tyranny—and it is committed to making tyranny universal.
Adlai E. Stevenson

Communism has nothing to do with love. Communism is an excellent hammer which we use to destroy our enemy.
Mao Tse-tung

I never agree with Communists or any other kind of kept men.
H. L. Mencken

Communism means barbarism.
James Russell Lowell

What is a Communist? One who hath yearnings
For equal division of unequal earnings.
Idler or bungler, or both, he is willing
To fork out his copper and pocket a shilling.
Ebenezer Elliott

COMPASSION *Also see:* KINDNESS, MERCY, PITY, SYMPATHY.

The dew of compassion is a tear. *Lord Byron*

The mind is no match with the heart in persuasion; constitutionality is no match with compassion. *Everett M. Dirksen*

The value of compassion cannot be over-emphasized. Anyone can criticize. It takes a true believer to be compassionate. No greater burden can be borne by an individual than to know no one cares or understands. *Arthur H. Stainback*

Man may dismiss compassion from his heart, but God never will. *William Cowper*

COMPETITION . . . See RIVALRY

COMPLAINT *Also see:* DISCONTENT.

Had we not faults of our own, we should take less pleasure in complaining of others. *Fénelon*

Constant complaint is the poorest sort of pay for all the comforts we enjoy. *Benjamin Franklin*

I will not be as those who spend the day in complaining of headache, and the night in drinking the wine that gives it. *Johann Wolfgang von Goethe*

The usual fortune of complaint is to excite contempt more than pity. *Samuel Johnson*

Complaint is the largest tribute Heaven receives. *Jonathan Swift*

We have no more right to put our discordant states of mind into the lives of those around us and rob them of their sunshine and brightness than we have to enter their houses and steal their silverware. *Julia Moss Seton*

I believe in grumbling; it is the politest form of fighting known. *Ed Howe*

The wheel that squeaks the loudest is the one that gets the grease. *Josh Billings*

The wheel that squeaks the loudest is the first to be replaced. *Anonymous*

COMPLIMENT *Also see:* FLATTERY, PRAISE.

If you can't get a compliment any other way, pay yourself one. *Mark Twain*

When a man makes a woman his wife, it's the highest compliment he can pay her, and it's usually the last. *Helen Rowland*

I have been complimented many times and they always embarrass me; I always feel that they have not said enough. *Mark Twain*

Don't tell a woman she's pretty; tell her there's no other woman like her, and all roads will open to you. *Jules Renard*

COMPROMISE   *Also see:* AGREEMENT, EXPEDIENCY.

Better bend than break.   *Scottish Proverb*

Compromise is but the sacrifice of one right or good in the hope of retaining another—too often ending in the loss of both.   *Tryon Edwards*

An appeaser is one who feeds a crocodile—hoping it will eat him last.
Winston Churchill

Compromise is never anything but an ignoble truce between the duty of a man and the terror of a coward.   *Reginald Wright Kauffman*

Compromise makes a good umbrella, but a poor roof; it is temporary expedient, often wise in party politics, almost sure to be unwise in statesmanship.   *James Russell Lowell*

It is the weak man who urges compromise—never the strong man.
Elbert Hubbard

People talk about the middle of the road as though it were unacceptable. Actually, all human problems, excepting morals, come into the gray areas. Things are not all black and white. There have to be compromises. The middle of the road is all of the usable surface. The extremes, right and left, are in the gutters.   *Dwight D. Eisenhower*

From compromise and things half done,
   Keep me with stern and stubborn pride;
And when at last the fight is won,
   God, keep me still unsatisfied.   *Louis Untermeyer*

Life cannot subsist in society but by reciprocal concessions.
Samuel Johnson

Real life is, to most men, a long second-best, a perpetual compromise between the ideal and the possible; but the world of pure reason knows no compromise, no practical limitations, no barrier to the creative activity.
Bertrand Russell

From the beginning of our history the country has been afflicted with compromise. It is by compromise that human rights have been abandoned.
Charles Sumner

My candle burns at both ends;
   It will not last the night;
But, ah, my foes, and oh, my friends—
   It gives a lovely light.   *Edna St. Vincent Millay*

What are facts but compromises? A fact merely marks the point where we have agreed to let investigation cease.   *Bliss Carman*

All government, indeed every human benefit and enjoyment, every virtue, and every prudent act, is founded on compromise and barter.
Edmund Burke

CONCEIT . . . See VANITY

CONDUCT . . . See BEHAVIOR

CONFESSION *Also see:* CONSCIENCE, GUILT, SIN.

To confess a fault freely is the next thing to being innocent of it.

Publilius Syrus

Confession is good for the soul only in the sense that a tweed coat is good for dandruff—it is a palliative rather than a remedy. *Peter De Vries*

Nothing spoils a confession like repentance. *Anatole France*

It is the confession, not the priest, that gives us absolution. *Oscar Wilde*

Open confession is good for the soul. *Scottish Proverb*

The confession of evil works is the first beginning of good works.

St. Augustine

CONFIDENCE *Also see:* BELIEF, BOLDNESS, CENSORSHIP, DOUBT, FAITH, SECURITY, SELF-CONFIDENCE, TRUST.

The human heart, at whatever age, opens only to the heart that opens in return. *Marie Edgeworth*

I have great faith in fools—self-confidence my friends call it.

Edgar Allan Poe

For they conquer who believe they can. *John Dryden*

All you need in this life is ignorance and confidence, and then success is sure. *Mark Twain*

Have confidence that if you have done a little thing well, you can do a bigger thing well too. *Storey*

He who believes in nobody knows that he himself is not to be trusted.

Auerbach

If once you forfeit the confidence of your fellow-citizens, you can never regain their respect and esteem. *Abraham Lincoln*

Only trust thyself, and another shall not betray thee. *William Penn*

True prosperity is the result of well-placed confidence in ourselves and our fellow man. *Burt*

CONFORMITY *Also see:* ADAPTABILITY, AGREEMENT, CUSTOM, TRA-DITION.

Conform and be dull.   *J. Frank Doble*

Our wretched species is so made that those who walk on the well-trodden path always throw stones at those who are showing a new road.   *Voltaire*

The surest way to corrupt a youth is to instruct him to hold in higher esteem those who think alike than those who think differently.   *Nietzsche*

I was part of that strange race of people aptly described as spending their lives doing things they detest to make money they don't want to buy things they don't need to impress people they dislike.   *Emile Henry Gauvreau*

If a man does not keep pace with his companions, perhaps it is because he hears a different drummer. Let him step to the music which he hears, however measured or far away.   *Henry David Thoreau*

Singularity in the right hath ruined many; happy those who are convinced of the general opinion.   *Benjamin Franklin*

Most people can't understand how others can blow their noses differently than they do.   *Turgenev*

It gives me great pleasure indeed to see the stubbornness of an incorrigible nonconformist warmly acclaimed.   *Albert Einstein*

We are discreet sheep; we wait to see how the drove is going, and then go with the drove.   *Mark Twain*

CONSCIENCE *Also see:* HONOR, MORALITY, VIRTUE.

Conscience—the only incorruptible thing about us.   *Henry Fielding*

The only tyrant I accept in this world is the still voice within.
Mahatma Gandhi

Religions are the great fairy tales of conscience.   *George Santayana*

No ear can hear nor tongue can tell the tortures of the inward hell!
Lord Byron

Conscience is a mother-in-law whose visit never ends.   *H. L. Mencken*

Conscience is the mirror of our souls, which represents the errors of our lives in their full shape.   *George Bancroft*

A good conscience is a continued Christmas.   *Benjamin Franklin*

He who sacrifices his conscience to ambition burns a picture to obtain the ashes.   *Chinese Proverb*

'Tis the business of little minds to shrink; but he whose heart is firm, and whose conscience approves his conduct, will pursue his principles unto death.   *Thomas Paine*

CONSCIENTIOUS OBJECTION ... See DRAFT

CONSERVATION   *Also see:* NATURE, POLLUTION.

Conservation is ethically sound. It is rooted in our love of the land, our respect for the rights of others, our devotion to the rule of law.
Lyndon Baines Johnson

As soils are depleted, human health, vitality and intelligence go with them.
Louis Bromfield

Conservation means the wise use of the earth and its resources for the lasting good of men.
Gifford Pinchot

World-wide practice of Conservation and the fair and continued access by all nations to the resources they need are the two indispensable foundations of continuous plenty and of permanent peace.
Gifford Pinchot

CONTEMPT ... See HATE

CONTENTMENT   *Also see:* AMUSEMENT, ENJOYMENT, HAPPINESS, JOY, PEACE.

The secret of contentment is knowing how to enjoy what you have, and to be able to lose all desire for things beyond your reach.
Lin Yutang

Nothing contributes more to a person's peace of mind than having no opinions at all.
G. C. Lichtenberg

It is right to be contented with what we have, never with what we are.
James Mackintosh

Contentment is, after all, simply refined indolence.
Thomas C. Haliburton

Contentment is natural wealth, luxury is artificial poverty.
Socrates

One who is contented with what he has done will never become famous for what he will do. He has lain down to die, and the grass is already over him.
Christian Nestell Bovee

One should either be sad or joyful. Contentment is a warm sty for eaters and sleepers.
Eugene O'Neill

Since we cannot get what we like, let us like what we can get.
Spanish Proverb

My motto is: Contented with little, yet wishing for more.
Charles Lamb

Contentment is a pearl of great price, and whoever procures it at the expense of ten thousand desires makes a wise and a happy purchase.
John Balguy

If you are content, you have enough to live comfortably.
Plautus

CONTRAST *Also see:* DIFFERENCE.

The superiority of some men is merely local. They are great because their associates are little.   *Samuel Johnson*

Where there is much light, the shadow is deep.
Johann Wolfgang von Goethe

Joy and grief are never far apart. In the same street the shutters of one house are closed while the curtains of the next are brushed by the shadows of the dance. A wedding party returns from the church; and a funeral winds to its door. The smiles and sadness of life is the tragi-comedy of Shakespeare. Gladness and sighs brighten the dim mirror he beholds.
Robert Eldridge Willmott

The rose and the thorn, and sorrow and gladness are linked together.
Saadi

The lustre of diamonds is invigorated by the interposition of darker bodies; the lights of a picture are created by the shades; the highest pleasure which nature has indulged to sensitive perception is that of rest after fatigue.   *Samuel Johnson*

CONVERSATION *Also see:* ARGUMENT, GOSSIP, LOQUACITY.

Drawing on my fine command of language, I said nothing.
Robert Charles Benchley

Conversation is an art in which man has all mankind for competitors.
Ralph Waldo Emerson

Silence is one great art of conversation.   *William Hazlitt*

Not only to say the right thing in the right place, but far more difficult, to leave unsaid the wrong thing at the tempting moment.   *George Sala*

A good memory and a tongue tied in the middle is a combination which gives immortality to conversation.   *Mark Twain*

Conceit causes more conversation than wit.   *François de La Rochefoucauld*

Conversation would be vastly improved by the constant use of four simple words: I do not know.   *André Maurois*

Never hold anyone by the button or the hand in order to be heard out; for if people are unwilling to hear you, you had better hold your tongue than them.   *Lord Chesterfield*

Conversation should be pleasant without scurrility, witty without affectation, free without indecency, learned without conceitedness, novel without falsehood.   *William Shakespeare*

I attribute the little I know to my not having been ashamed to ask for information, and to my rule of conversing with all descriptions of men on those topics that form their own peculiar professions and pursuits.
John Locke

COUNTRY *Also see:* AMERICA, CITIZENSHIP, DEMOCRACY, NATION, PATRIOTISM.

Countries are well cultivated, not as they are fertile, but as they are free.
Montesquieu

So long as you are ready to die for humanity, the life of your country is immortal. *Giuseppe Mazzini*

I have no country to fight for: my country is the earth, and I am a citizen of the world. *Eugene V. Debs*

Our country. In her intercourse with foreign nations may she always be in the right; but our country right or wrong! *Stephen Decatur*

The world is my country, all mankind are my brethren, and to do good is my religion. *Thomas Paine*

How can a man be said to have a country when he has not right of a square inch of it. *Henry George*

There is no such thing as a little country. The greatness of a people is no more determined by their number than the greatness of a man is determined by his height. *Victor Hugo*

Indeed I tremble for my country when I reflect that God is just.
Thomas Jefferson

There ought to be a system of manners in every nation which a well-formed mind would be disposed to relish. To make us love our country, our country ought to be lovely. *Edmund Burke*

The most certain test by which we judge whether a country is really free is the amount of security enjoyed by minorities. *Lord Acton*

I offer neither pay, nor quarters, nor provisions; I offer hunger, thirst, forced marches, battles and death. Let him who loves his country in his heart and not with his lips only, follow me. *Giuseppe Garibaldi*

Let it be borne on the flag under which we rally in every exigency, that we have one country, one constitution, one destiny. *Daniel Webster*

Our country is the world—our countrymen are mankind.
William Lloyd Garrison

There is no greater sign of a general decay of virtue in a nation, than a want of zeal in its inhabitants for the good of their country.
Joseph Addison

My kind of loyalty was loyalty to one's country, not to its institutions or its officeholders. The country is the real thing, the substantial thing, the eternal thing; it is the thing to watch over, and care for, and be loyal to; institutions are extraneous, they are its mere clothing, and clothing can wear out, become ragged, cease to be comfortable, cease to protect the body from winter, disease, and death. *Mark Twain*

COURAGE *Also see:* BOLDNESS, COWARDICE, DANGER, DEFEAT, FIRMNESS, HEROISM, SPIRIT.

Courage is almost a contradiction in terms: it means a strong desire to live taking the form of readiness to die. *Gilbert K. Chesterton*

The greatest test of courage on earth is to bear defeat without losing heart. *Robert Green Ingersoll*

One man with courage makes a majority. *Andrew Jackson*

It takes vision and courage to create—it takes faith and courage to prove. *Owen D. Young*

I'd rather give my life than be afraid to give it. *Lyndon Baines Johnson*

Courage is resistance to fear, mastery of fear—not absence of fear. *Mark Twain*

This is no time for ease and comfort. It is the time to dare and endure. *Winston Churchill*

True courage is like a kite; a contrary wind raises it higher. *J. Petit-Senn*

Bravery has no place where it can avail nothing. *Samuel Johnson*

Far better it is to dare mighty things, to win glorious triumphs, even though checkered by failure, than to take rank with those poor spirits who neither enjoy much nor suffer much, because they live in the grey twilight that knows not victory nor defeat. *Theodore Roosevelt*

What a new face courage puts on everything! *Ralph Waldo Emerson*

Last, but by no means least, courage—moral courage, the courage of one's convictions, the courage to see things through. The world is in a constant conspiracy against the brave. It's the age-old struggle—the roar of the crowd on one side and the voice of your conscience on the other. *Douglas MacArthur*

Give us the fortitude to endure the things which cannot be changed, and the courage to change the things which should be changed, and the wisdom to know one from the other. *Oliver J. Hart*

Half a man's wisdom goes with his courage. *Ralph Waldo Emerson*

Courage that grows from constitution often forsakes a man when he has occasion for it; courage which arises from a sense of duty acts in a uniform manner. *Joseph Addison*

Courage is grace under pressure. *Ernest Hemingway*

No man in the world has more courage than the man who can stop after eating one peanut. *Channing Pollock*

COURT *Also see:* JUSTICE, LAW.

. . . a place where they dispense with justice. *Arthur Train*

A court is a place where what was confused before becomes more unsettled than ever. *Henry Waldorf Francis*

Dictum is what a court thinks but is afraid to decide. *Henry Waldorf Francis*

The place of justice is a hallowed place. *Francis Bacon*

The penalty for laughing in a courtroom is six months in jail; if it were not for this penalty, the jury would never hear the evidence. *H. L. Mencken*

COURTESY *Also see:* CHARM, CULTURE, GALLANTRY, MANNERS.

To speak kindly does not hurt the tongue. *Proverb*

Life is not so short but that there is always time for courtesy.
Ralph Waldo Emerson

It is better to have too much courtesy than too little, provided you are not equally courteous to all, for that would be injustice. *Baltasar Graclán*

Courtesies of a small and trivial character are the ones which strike deepest in the grateful and appreciating heart. *Henry Clay*

Nothing is ever lost by courtesy. It is the cheapest of the pleasures; costs nothing and conveys much. It pleases him who gives and him who receives, and thus, like mercy, it is twice blessed. *Erastus Wiman*

Courtesy is a science of the highest importance. It is . . . opening a door that we may derive instruction from the example of others, and at the same time enabling us to benefit them by our example, if there be anything in our character worthy of imitation. *Michel de Montaigne*

If a man be gracious and courteous to strangers, it shows he is a citizen of the world. *Francis Bacon*

Men, like bullets, go farthest when they are smoothest. *Jean Paul Richter*

The small courtesies sweeten life; the greater ennoble it.
Christian Nestell Bovee

We must be as courteous to a man as we are to a picture, which we are willing to give the advantage of a good light. *Ralph Waldo Emerson*

Politeness is the art of choosing among one's real thoughts. *Abel Stevens*

Intelligence and courtesy not always are combined;
Often in a wooden house a golden room we find.
Henry Wadsworth Longfellow

True politeness consists in being easy one's self, and in making every one about one as easy as one can. *Alexander Pope*

COWARDICE *Also see:* FEAR, SILENCE.

The cowards never started—and the weak died along the way. *Anonymous*

There are several good protections against temptation, but the surest is cowardice. *Mark Twain*

Great occasions do not make heroes or cowards; they simply unveil them to the eyes of men. *Bishop Westcott*

A coward is much more exposed to quarrels than a man of spirit. *Thomas Jefferson*

One who is in a perilous emergency thinks with his legs. *Ambrose Bierce*

At the bottom of a good deal of the bravery that appears in the world there lurks a miserable cowardice. Men will face powder and steel because they cannot face public opinion. *Edwin Hubbel Chapin*

Every hard-boiled egg is yellow inside. *Anonymous*

It is better to be the widow of a hero than the wife of a coward. *Dolores Ibarruri*

Fear has its use but cowardice has none. *Mahatma Gandhi*

To know what is right and not to do it is the worst cowardice. *Confucius*

The coward threatens when he is safe. *Johann Wolfgang von Goethe*

Cowards can never be moral. *Mahatma Gandhi*

The people to fear are not those who disagree with you, but those who disagree with you and are too cowardly to let you know. *Napoleon Bonaparte*

Faint heart ne'er won fair lady. *Miguel de Cervantes*

It is the coward who fawns upon those above him. It is the coward who is insolent whenever he dares be so. *Junius*

Cowardice . . . is almost always simply a lack of ability to suspend the functioning of the imagination. *Ernest Hemingway*

How many feasible projects have miscarried through despondency, and been strangled in their birth by a cowardly imagination. *Jeremy Collier*

Dishonesty, cowardice and duplicity are never impulsive. *George A. Knight*

A cowardly cur barks more fiercely than it bites. *Quintus Curtius Rufus*

Cowards die many times before their deaths;
The valiant never taste of death but once. *William Shakespeare*

CREATIVITY *Also see:* ACTION, ART, GOD, INVENTION, LITERATURE.

Ideas are the root of creation. *Ernest Dimnet*

Man was made at the end of the week's work when God was tired.

Mark Twain

It is wise to learn; it is God-like to create. *John Saxe*

Had I been present at the creation of the world I would have proposed some improvements. *Alfonso X*

> The world embarrasses me, and I cannot dream
> That this watch exists and has no watchmaker. *Voltaire*

Creation is a drug I can't do without. *Cecil B. DeMille*

. . . not picked from the leaves of any author, but bred amongst the weeds and tares of mine own brain. *Thomas Browne*

The merit of originality is not novelty; it is sincerity. *Thomas Carlyle*

CREDIT *Also see:* BORROWING, DEBT, REPUTATION.

The surest way to establish your credit is to work yourself into the position of not needing any. *Maurice Switzer*

The private control of credit is the modern form of slavery. *Upton Sinclair*

In God we trust; all others must pay cash. *Anonymous*

No man's credit is as good as his money. *Ed Howe*

Remember that credit is money. *Benjamin Franklin*

A pig bought on credit is forever grunting. *Spanish Proverb*

Nothing so cements and holds together all the parts of a society as faith or credit, which can never be kept up unless men are under some force or necessity of honestly paying what they owe to one another. *Cicero*

Men . . . are sent into the world with bills of credit, and seldom draw to their full extent. *Horace Walpole*

Credit is like a looking-glass, which when once sullied by a breath, may be wiped clear again; but if once cracked can never be repaired. *Walter Scott*

A person who can't pay, gets another person who can't pay, to guarantee that he can pay. *Charles Dickens*

Buying on trust is the way to pay double. *Anonymous*

Acquaintance: a person whom we know well enough to borrow from, but not well enough to lend to. *Ambrose Bierce*

CREDULITY *Also see:* BELIEF, DOUBT, FAITH, INNOCENCE, LYING.

Credulity is belief in slight evidence, with no evidence, or against evidence.
Tryon Edwards

The only disadvantage of an honest heart is credulity. *Philip Sidney*

You believe easily that which you hope for earnestly. *Terence*

The great masses of the people . . . will more easily fall victims to a great lie than to a small one. *Adolf Hitler*

I prefer credulity to skepticism and cynicism for there is more promise in almost anything than in nothing at all. *Ralph Barton Perry*

I cannot spare the luxury of believing that all things beautiful are what they seem. *Fitz-Greene Halleck*

Let us believe neither half of the good people tell us of ourselves, nor half the evil they say of others. *John Petit-Senn*

There's a sucker born every minute. *P. T. Barnum*

We believe at once in evil, we only believe in good upon reflection. Is this not sad? *Madame Dorothée Deluzy*

When people are bewildered they tend to become credulous.
Calvin Coolidge

The more gross the fraud, the more glibly will it go down and the more greedily will it be swallowed, since folly will always find faith wherever imposters will find impudence. *Christian Nestell Bovee*

CRIME *Also see:* DISHONESTY, FRAUD, GUILT, MURDER, RIOT, SIN, VICE, WICKEDNESS, WRONG.

All crime is a kind of disease and should be treated as such.
Mahatma Gandhi

Society prepares the crime; the criminal commits it.
Henry Thomas Buckle

We enact many laws that manufacture criminals, and then a few that punish them. *Allen Tucker*

We don't seem to be able to check crime, so why not legalize it and then tax it out of business. *Will Rogers*

And who are the greater criminals—those who sell the instruments of death, or those who buy them and use them? *Robert Emmet Sherwood*

Providence sees to it that no man gets happiness out of crime.
Vittorio Alfieri

CRIME *(continued)*

The real significance of crime is in its being a breach of faith with the community of mankind.
Joseph Conrad

Purposelessness is the fruitful mother of crime.
Charles H. Parkhurst

Crime is contagious. If the government becomes a lawbreaker, it breeds contempt for law.
Louis D. Brandeis

I have too great a soul to die like a criminal.
John Wilkes Booth

If you do big things they print your face, and if you do little things they print only your thumbs.
Arthur "Bugs" Baer

Whoever profits by the crime is guilty of it.
Anonymous

There is no den in the wide world to hide a rogue. Commit a crime and the earth is made of glass.
Ralph Waldo Emerson

What is crime amongst the multitude, is only vice among the few.
Benjamin Disraeli

It takes all sorts of people to make the underworld.
Don Marquis

Capital punishment is as fundamentally wrong as a cure for crime as charity is wrong as a cure for poverty.
Henry Ford

Crime is a product of social excess.
Lenin

If poverty is the mother of crimes, want of sense is the father.
Jean de La Bruyére

Few men have virtue to withstand the highest bidder.
George Washington

Set a thief to catch a thief.
Anonymous

Small crimes always precede great ones. Never have we seen timid innocence pass suddenly to extreme licentiousness.
Jean Baptiste Racine

Organized crime constitutes nothing less than a guerilla war against society.
Lyndon Baines Johnson

Men blush less for their crimes than for their weaknesses and vanity.
Jean de La Bruyére

Whenever man commits a crime heaven finds a witness.
Edward G. Bulwer-Lytton

Fear follows crime, and is its punishment.
Voltaire

We easily forget crimes that are known only to ourselves.
François de La Rochefoucauld

CRISIS *Also see:* CALAMITY, CHARACTER

Every little thing counts in a crisis.   *Jawaharlal Nehru*

Man is not imprisoned by habit. Great changes in him can be wrought by crisis—once that crisis can be recognized and understood. *Norman Cousins*

These are the times that try men's souls.   *Thomas Paine*

Every crisis offers you extra desired power. *William Moulton Marston*

Crises and deadlocks when they occur have at least this advantage, that they force us to think.   *Jawaharlal Nehru*

Crises refine life. In them you discover what you are. *Allan K. Chalmers*

The wise man does not expose himself needlessly to danger, since there are few things for which he cares sufficiently; but he is willing, in great crises, to give even his life—knowing that under certain conditions it is not worth-while to live.   *Aristotle*

. . . as we wake or sleep, we grow strong or we grow weak, and at last some crisis shows us what we have become.   *Bishop Westcott*

CRITICISM *Also see:* ADVICE, CENSURE, JUDGMENT, PRAISE.

I never give them hell; I just tell them the truth and they think it is hell.
Harry S. Truman

Blame is safer than praise.   *Ralph Waldo Emerson*

The strength of criticism lies in the weakness of the thing criticized.
Henry Wadsworth Longfellow

To avoid criticism do nothing, say nothing, be nothing. *Elbert Hubbard*

Even the lion has to defend himself against flies.   *Anonymous*

Remember that nobody will ever get ahead of you as long as he is kicking you in the seat of the pants.   *Walter Winchell*

Each generation produces its squad of "moderns" with peashooters to attack Gibraltar.   *Channing Pollock*

The rule in carving holds good as to criticism; never cut with a knife what you can cut with a spoon.   *Charles Buxton*

Criticism, as it was first instituted by Aristotle, was meant as a standard of judging well.   *Samuel Johnson*

It is much easier to be critical than to be correct. *Benjamin Disraeli*

The public is the only critic whose opinion is worth anything at all.
Mark Twain

CRUELTY   Also see: ABUSE, EVIL, INJURY, PUNISHMENT, VIOLENCE, WAR.

If it were absolutely necessary to choose, I would rather be guilty of an immoral act than of a cruel one.
Anatole France

One of the ill effects of cruelty is that it makes the bystanders cruel.
Thomas Fowell Buxton

All cruelty springs from hard-heartedness and weakness.
Seneca

Cruelty and fear shake hands together.
Honoré de Balzac

Man's inhumanity to man
Makes countless thousands mourn!
Robert Burns

Cruelty, like every other vice, requires no motive outside of itself; it only requires opportunity.
George Eliot

Cruelty is a part of nature, at least of human nature, but it is the one thing that seems unnatural to us.
Robinson Jeffers

When a man's dog turns against him it is time for a wife to pack her trunk and go home to mama.
Mark Twain

The difference between coarse and refined abuse is the difference between being bruised by a club and wounded by a poisoned arrow. *Samuel Johnson*

CULTURE   Also see: ART, CIVILIZATION, COURTESY, LITERATURE, MANNERS.

Culture is the habit of being pleased with the best and knowing why.
Henry Van Dyke

Every man's ability may be strengthened or increased by culture.
John Abbott

The acquiring of culture is the development of an avid hunger for knowledge and beauty.
Jesse Bennett

No culture can live, if it attempts to be exclusive.
Mahatma Gandhi

Culture is the widening of the mind and of the spirit.
Jawaharlal Nehru

Culture is one thing and varnish is another.
Ralph Waldo Emerson

That is true culture which helps us to work for the social betterment of all.
Henry Ward Beecher

Culture, with us, ends in headache.
Ralph Waldo Emerson

Culture of the mind must be subservient to the heart.
Mahatma Gandhi

The end of culture is right living.
W. Somerset Maugham

CUNNING . . . See DECEIT

CURIOSITY *Also see:* INTEREST, QUESTION, SCIENCE, SPECULATION, WONDER.

The first and simplest emotion which we discover in the human mind, is curiosity. *Edmund Burke*

One of the secrets of life is to keep our intellectual curiosity acute. *William Lyon Phelps*

Creatures whose mainspring is curiosity enjoy the accumulating of facts far more than the pausing at times to reflect on those facts. *Clarence Day*

It is a shameful thing to be weary of inquiry when what we search for is excellent. *Cicero*

The important thing is not to stop questioning. Curiosity has its own reason for existing. One cannot help but be in awe when he contemplates the mysteries of eternity, of life, of the marvelous structure of reality. It is enough if one tries merely to comprehend a little of this mystery every day. Never lose a holy curiosity. *Albert Einstein*

Curiosity is only vanity. Most frequently we wish not to know, but to talk. We would not take a sea voyage for the sole pleasure of seeing without hope of ever telling. *Blaise Pascal*

A person who is too nice an observer of the business of the crowd, like one who is too curious in observing the labor of bees, will often be stung for his curiosity. *Alexander Pope*

Curiosity is as much the parent of attention, as attention is of memory. *Richard Whately*

CUSTOM *Also see:* CONFORMITY, FASHION, HABIT, TRADITION.

Custom meets us at the cradle and leaves us only at the tomb. *Robert Green Ingersoli*

The old ways are the safest and surest ways. *Charles Caleb Colton*

The custom and fashion of today will be the awkwardness and outrage of tomorrow—so arbitrary are these transient laws. *Alexandre Dumas*

Take the course opposite to custom and you will almost always do well. *Jean-Jacques Rousseau*

Men will sooner surrender their rights than their customs. *Moritz Guedmann*

Custom governs the world; it is the tyrant of our feelings and our manners and rules the world with the hand of a despot. *J. Bartlett*

Custom is the plague of wise men and the idol of fools. *Thomas Fuller*

CUSTOM *(continued)*

Custom is the principle magistrate of man's life. *Francis Bacon*

There is nothing that strengthens a nation like reading of a nation's own history, whether that history is recorded in books or embodied in customs, institutions and monuments. *Joseph Anderson*

We do everything by custom, even believe by it; our very axioms, let us boast of free-thinking as we may, are oftenest simply such beliefs as we have never heard questioned. *Thomas Carlyle*

Men commonly think according to their inclinations, speak according to their learning and imbibed opinions, but generally act according to custom. *Francis Bacon*

Have a place for everything and keep the thing somewhere else; this is not advice, it is merely custom. *Mark Twain*

Custom has furnished the only basis which ethics have ever had. *Joseph Wood Krutch*

There is no tyrant like custom, and no freedom where its edicts are not resisted. *Christian Nestell Bovee*

Ancient custom has the force of law. *Legal Maxim*

CYNIC *Also see:* CREDULITY, DOUBT, PESSIMISM, PREJUDICE, SARCASM, SKEPTICISM.

A cynic is a man who looks at the world with a monocle in his mind's eye. *Carolyn Wells*

It takes a clever man to turn cynic and a wise man to be clever enough not to. *Fannie Hurst*

A cynic is a man who knows the price of everything, and the value of nothing. *Oscar Wilde*

A cynic is just a man who found out when he was ten that there wasn't any Santa Claus, and he's still upset. *J. G. Cozzens*

A cynic is a man who, when he smells flowers, looks around for a coffin. *H. L. Mencken*

A cynic can chill and dishearten with a single word. *Ralph Waldo Emerson*

The only deadly sin I know is cynicism. *Henry L. Stimson*

The cynic is one who never sees a good quality in a man, and never fails to see a bad one. He is the human owl, vigilant in darkness and blind to light, mousing for vermin, and never seeing noble game. *Henry Ward Beecher*

A cynic is a blackguard whose faulty vision sees things as they are, and not as they ought to be. *Ambrose Bierce*

D

DANGER *Also see:* ADVENTURE, BOLDNESS, CALAMITY, CAUTION, CENSORSHIP, COURAGE, FEAR.

As soon as there is life there is danger. *Ralph Waldo Emerson*

In this world there is always danger for those who are afraid of it.
George Bernard Shaw

There is nobody who is not dangerous for someone. *Marquise de Sévigné*

The most dangerous thing in the world is to try to leap a chasm in two jumps. *William Lloyd George*

If we survive danger it steels our courage more than anything else.
Reinhold Niebuhr

A timid person is frightened before a danger, a coward during the time, and a courageous person afterwards. *Jean Paul Richter*

There's nothing so comfortable as a small bankroll; a big one is always in danger. *Wilson Mizner*

This country has come to feel the same when Congress is in session as when the baby gets hold of a hammer. *Will Rogers*

We cannot banish dangers, but we can banish fears. We must not demean life by standing in awe of death. *David Sarnoff*

If a little knowledge is dangerous, where is the man who has so much as to be out of danger? *Thomas Huxley*

I saw a delicate flower had grown up two feet high between the horses' feet and the wheel track. An inch more to the right or left had sealed its fate, or an inch higher. Yet it lived to flourish, and never knew the danger it incurred. It did not borrow trouble, nor invite an evil fate by apprehending it. *Henry David Thoreau*

Don't play for safety—it's the most dangerous thing in the world.
Hugh Walpole

We triumph without glory when we conquer without danger. *Corneille*

The mere apprehension of a coming evil has put many into a situation of the utmost danger. *Lucan*

There is danger when a man throws his tongue into high gear before he gets his brain a-going. *C. C. Phelps*

The person who runs away exposes himself to that very danger more than a person who sits quietly. *Jawaharlal Nehru*

We are confronted by a first danger, the destructivness of applied atomic energy. And then we are confronted by a second danger, that we do not enough appreciate the first danger. *Raymond G. Swing*

DEATH

Also see: ABSENCE, BIRTH, CIVILIZATION, COMMUNISM, COWARDICE, DANGER, DEFEAT, DESPAIR, DESTINY, DISEASE, LIFE, IMMORTALITY.

To fear love is to fear life, and those who fear life are already three parts dead. *Bertrand Russell*

Nothing in this life became him like leaving it. *William Shakespeare*

I never think he is quite ready for another world who is altogether weary of this. *Hugh Hamilton*

All say, "How hard it is that we have to die"—a strange complaint to come from the mouths of people who have had to live. *Mark Twain*

He that lives to forever, never fears dying. *William Penn*

Some people are so afraid to die that they never begin to live. *Henry Van Dyke*

Most people would rather die than think: many do. *Bertrand Russell*

God's finger touched him, and he slept. *Alfred, Lord Tennyson*

Now comes the mystery. *Henry Ward Beecher*

The gods conceal from men the happiness of death, that they may endure life. *Lucan*

Men fear death, as if unquestionably the greatest evil, and yet no man knows that it may not be the greatest good. *William Mitford*

To stop sinning suddenly. *Elbert Hubbard*

Death is more universal than life; everyone dies but not everyone lives. *A. Sachs*

Death—the last sleep? No, it is the final awakening. *Walter Scott*

I look upon life as a gift from God. I did nothing to earn it. Now that the time is coming to give it back, I have no right to complain. *Joyce Cary*

Good men must die, but death cannot kill their names. *Proverb*

A punishment to some, to some a gift, and to many a favor. *Seneca*

I am ready to meet my maker, but whether my maker is prepared for the great ordeal of meeting me is another matter. *Winston Churchill*

Death is a very dull, dreary affair, and my advice to you is to have nothing whatever to do with it. *W. Somerset Maugham*

We owe a deep debt of gratitude to Adam, the first great benefactor of the human race: he brought death into the world. *Mark Twain*

DEBT   *Also see:* BORROWING, CREDIT, MONEY.

Some debts are fun when you are acquiring them, but none are fun when you set about retiring them.
Ogden Nash

Debt is a prolific mother of folly and of crime.
Benjamin Disraeli

Rather go to bed supperless than rise in debt.
Benjamin Franklin

A small debt produces a debtor; a large one, an enemy.
Publilius Syrus

A habit of debt is very injurious to the memory.
Austin O'Malley

Youth is in danger until it learns to look upon debts as furies.
Edward G. Bulwer-Lytton

Some people use one half their ingenuity to get into debt, and the other half to avoid paying it.
George D. Prentice

We often pay our debts not because it is only fair that we should, but to make future loans easier.
François de La Rochefoucauld

A church debt is the devil's salary.
Henry Ward Beecher

> Wilt thou seal up the avenues of ill?
> Pay every debt as if God wrote the bill.
Ralph Waldo Emerson

He who promises runs in debt.
The Talmud

'Tis against some men's principle to pay interest, and seems against others' interest to pay the principle.
Benjamin Franklin

Debt is the fatal disease of republics, the first thing and the mightiest to undermine governments and corrupt the people.
Wendell Phillips

Debt is the worst poverty.
Thomas Fuller

Speak not of my debts unless you mean to pay them.
George Herbert

Our national debt, after all, is an internal debt, owed not only by the nation but to the nation. If our children have to pay the interest they will pay that interest to themselves.
Franklin Delano Roosevelt

Do not accustom yourself to consider debt only as an inconvenience; you will find it a calamity.
Samuel Johnson

A man in debt is so far a slave.
Ralph Waldo Emerson

A mortgage casts a shadow on the sunniest field.
Robert Green Ingersoll

Never spend your money before you have it.
Thomas Jefferson

Debt is the slavery of the free.
Publilius Syrus

DECEIT *Also see:* FRAUD, SKEPTICISM.

You can fool some of the people all the time, and all of the people some of the time, but you cannot fool all of the people all the time.
Abraham Lincoln

The sure way to be cheated is to think one's self more cunning than others.
François de La Rochefoucauld

When a person cannot deceive himself the chances are against his being able to deceive other people.
Mark Twain

Every crowd has a silver lining.
P. T. Barnum

It is double the pleasure to deceive the deceiver.
Jean de la Fontaine

All deception in the course of life is indeed nothing else but a lie reduced to practice, and falsehood passing from words into things.
Robert South

Hateful to me as the gates of Hades is that man who hides one thing in his heart and speaks another.
Homer

DECENCY *Also see:* CENSORSHIP, MODESTY, MORALITY, VIRTUE.

Decency is the least of all laws, but yet it is the law which is most strictly observed.
François de La Rochefoucauld

Don't overestimate the decency of the human race.
H. L. Mencken

We are decent 99 percent of the time, when we could easily be vile.
R. W. Riis

No law reaches it, but all right-minded people observe it.
Chamfort

DECISION *Also see:* CHOICE.

The block of granite which was an obstacle in the pathway of the weak becomes a stepping-stone in the pathway of the strong.
Thomas Carlyle

It does not take much strength to do things, but it requires great strength to decide on what to do.
Elbert Hubbard

I hate to see things done by halves. If it be right, do it boldly,—if it be wrong leave it undone.
Bernard Gilpin

Perhaps no mightier conflict of mind occurs ever again in a lifetime than that first decision to unseat one's own tooth.
Gene Fowler

When possible make the decisions now, even if action is in the future. A reviewed decision usually is better than one reached at the last moment.
William B. Given, Jr.

All our final decisions are made in a state of mind that is not going to last.
Marcel Proust

DEFEAT *Also see:* COURAGE, FAILURE, VICTORY.

What is defeat? Nothing but education, nothing but the first step to something better.
Wendell Philips

There are some defeats more triumphant than victories.
Michel de Montaigne

It is defeat that turns bone to flint; it is defeat that turns gristle to muscle; it is defeat that makes men invincible.
Henry Ward Beecher

Politics has become so expensive that it takes a lot of money even to be defeated.
Will Rogers

Defeat is not the worst of failures. Not to have tried is the true failure.
George Edward Woodberry

Believe you are defeated, believe it long enough, and it is likely to become a fact.
Norman Vincent Peale

I would rather lose in a cause that I know some day will triumph than to triumph in a cause that I know some day will fail.
Wendell L. Willkie

Defeat never comes to any man until he admits it.
Josephus Daniels

Those who are prepared to die for any cause are seldom defeated.
Jawaharlal Nehru

Who asks whether the enemy were defeated by strategy or valor?
Vergil

The problems of victory are more agreeable than those of defeat, but they are no less difficult.
Winston Churchill

There are important cases in which the difference between half a heart and a whole heart makes just the difference between signal defeat and a splendid victory.
A. H. K. Boyd

Besides the practical knowledge which defeat offers, there are important personality profits to be taken. Defeat strips away false values and makes you realize what you really want. It stops you from chasing butterflies and puts you to work digging gold.
William Moulton Marston

Defeat should never be a source of courage, but rather a fresh stimulant.
Robert South

In War: Resolution. In Defeat: Defiance. In Victory: Magnanimity. In Peace: Goodwill.
Winston Churchill

Defeat is a school in which truth always grows strong.
Henry Ward Beecher

Many a good man I have seen go under.
Walt Whitman

DELIGHT ... See JOY

DELUSION Also see: REALITY, SELF-KNOWLEDGE.

No man is happy without a delusion of some kind. Delusions are as necessary to our happiness as realities.
Christian Nestell Bovee

The worst deluded are the self-deluded.
Christian Nestell Bovee

Love is the delusion that one woman differs from another.
H. L. Mencken

DEMOCRACY Also see: AMERICA, EQUALITY, FREEDOM, LIBERTY.

Democracy is good. I say this because other systems are worse.
Jawaharlal Nehru

Democracy is only a dream: it should be put in the same category as Arcadia, Santa Claus, and Heaven.
H. L. Mencken

Democracy is based upon the conviction that there are extraordinary possibilities in ordinary people.
Harry Emerson Fosdick

In a democracy, the individual enjoys not only the ultimate power but carries the ultimate responsibility.
Norman Cousins

Democracy is the art and science of running the circus from the monkey cage.
H. L. Mencken

Democracy . . . is a system of self-determination. It's the right to make the wrong choice.
John Patrick

Too many people expect wonders from democracy, when the most wonderful thing of all is just having it.
Walter Winchell

Democracy is the government of the people, by the people, for the people.
Abraham Lincoln

Democracy, I do not conceive that ever God did ordain as a fit government either for church or commonwealth. If the people be governors, who shall be governed?
John Cotton

As I would not be a slave, so I would not be a master. This expresses my idea of democracy.
Abraham Lincoln

. . . government that "substitutes election by the incompetent many for appointment by the corrupt few."
George Bernard Shaw

Democracy is the form of government that gives every man the right to be his own oppressor.
James Russell Lowell

Man's capacity for justice makes democracy possible, but man's inclination to injustice makes democracy necessary.
Reinhold Niebuhr

In free countries, every man is entitled to express his opinions—and every other man is entitled not to listen.
G. Norman Collie

DEPENDENCE *Also see:* FREEDOM, INDEPENDENCE.

There is no dependence that can be sure but a dependence upon one's self.
John Gay

He who imagines he can do without the world deceives himself much; but he who fancies the world cannot do without him is still more mistaken.
François de La Rochefoucauld

The ship of heaven guides itself and will not accept a wooden rudder.
Ralph Waldo Emerson

No degree of knowledge attainable by man is able to set him above the want of hourly assistance.
Samuel Johnson

Depend on no man, on no friend but him who can depend on himself. He only who acts conscientiously toward himself, will act so toward others.
Johann Kaspar Lavater

There is no one subsists by himself alone.
Owen Felltham

DESIRE *Also see:* AMBITION, LOVE, PASSION, WANT.

Desire is the essence of a man.
Benedict Spinoza

It is much easier to suppress a first desire than to satisfy those that follow.
François de La Rochefoucauld

What man knows is everywhere at war with what he wants.
Joseph Wood Krutch

There are two tragedies in life. One is not get your heart's desire. The other is to get it.
George Bernard Shaw

Some people wanted champagne and caviar when they should have had beer and hot dogs.
Dwight D. Eisenhower

The stoical scheme of supplying our wants by lopping off our desires is like cutting off our feet when we want shoes.
Jonathan Swift

By annihilating the desires, you annihilate the mind. Every man without passions has within him no principle of action, nor motive to act.
Claude Adrien Helvétius

All human activity is prompted by desire.
Bertrand Russell

We trifle when we assign limits to our desires, since nature hath set none.
Christian Nestell Bovee

Every human mind is a great slumbering power until awakened by a keen desire and by definite resolution to do.
Edgar F. Roberts

You will become as small as your controlling desire; as great as your dominant aspiration.
James Allen

While man's desires and aspirations stir he cannot choose but err.
Johann Wolfgang von Goethe

DESPAIR

Also see: DISAPPOINTMENT, HOPE, PAIN, POVERTY, SORROW.

What we call despair is often only the painful eagerness of unfed hope.
George Eliot

The man who lives only by hope will die with despair. *Italian Proverb*

When we are flat on our backs there is no way to look but up.
Roger W. Babson

Despair is the conclusion of fools. *Benjamin Disraeli*

Despair is like forward children, who, when you take away one of their playthings, throw the rest into the fire for madness. It grows angry with itself, turns its own executioner, and revenges its misfortunes on its own head. *Pierre Charron*

Despair ruins some, presumption many. *Benjamin Franklin*

It becomes no man to nurse despair, but, in the teeth of clenched antagonisms, to follow up the worthiest till he die. *Alfred, Lord Tennyson*

It is a miserable state of mind to have few things to desire, and many things to fear. *Francis Bacon*

The fact that God has prohibited despair gives misfortune the right to hope all things, and leaves hope free to dare all things. *Anne Sophie Swetchine*

The mass of men lead lives of quiet desperation. What is called resignation is confirmed desperation . . . A stereotyped but unconscious despair is concealed even under what are called the games and amusements of mankind. *Henry David Thoreau*

DESTINY

Also see: FATE, FORTUNE, FUTURE, GOD.

Destiny is no matter of chance. It is a matter of choice: It is not a thing to be waited for, it is a thing to be achieved. *William Jennings Bryan*

Lots of folks confuse bad management with destiny. *Kin Hubbard*

One meets his destiny often in the road he takes to avoid it.
French Proverb

If a man is destined to drown, he will drown even in a spoonful of water.
Yiddish Proverb

Destiny: A tyrant's authority for crime and a fool's excuse for failure.
Ambrose Bierce

Men heap together the mistakes of their lives, and create a monster they call Destiny. *John Oliver Hobbes*

Men are what their mothers made them. *Ralph Waldo Emerson*

Our destiny changes with our thought; we shall become what we wish to become, do what we wish to do, when our habitual thought corresponds with our desire. *Orison S. Marden*

DIFFERENCE *Also see:* ARGUMENT, CONTRAST, QUARREL, VARIETY.

The difference is no less real because it is of degree.
Benjamin Nathan Cardozo

The difference between a man and his valet: they both smoke the same cigars, but only one pays for them.
Robert Frost

The difference between the right word and the almost right word is the difference between lightning and the lightning bug.
Mark Twain

The difference between a moral man and a man of honor is that the latter regrets a discreditable act even when it has worked.
H. L. Mencken

If men would consider not so much wherein they differ, as wherein they agree, there would be far less of uncharitableness and angry feeling in the world.
Joseph Addison

Honest differences are often a healthy sign of progress.
Mahatma Gandhi

If by saying that all men are born equal, you mean that they are equally born, it is true, but true in no other sense; birth, talent, labor, virtue, and providence, are forever making differences.
Eugene Edwards

Where there is no difference, there is only indifference.
Louis Nizer

DIFFICULTY *Also see:* ADVERSITY, ANXIETY, LABOR.

Difficulties are meant to rouse, not discourage. The human spirit is to grow strong by conflict.
William Ellery Channing

No man who is occupied in doing a very difficult thing, and doing it very well, ever loses his self-respect.
George Bernard Shaw

The greatest difficulties lie where we are not looking for them.
Johann Wolfgang von Goethe

There are two ways of meeting difficulties: you alter the difficulties or you alter yourself meeting them.
Phyllis Bottome

Difficulties strengthen the mind, as labor does the body.
Seneca

Undertake something that is difficult; it will do you good. Unless you try to do something beyond what you have already mastered, you will never grow.
Ronald E. Osborn

Every difficulty slurred over will be a ghost to disturb your repose later on.
Chopin

We have inherited new difficulties because we have inherited more privileges.
Abram Sacher

DIGNITY
Also see: HONOR, PRIDE, RIGHTS, WORK.

True dignity is never gained by place, and never lost when honors are withdrawn.
Philip Massinger

There is a healthful hardiness about real dignity that never dreads contact and communion with others however humble.
Washington Irving

No race can prosper till it learns that there is as much dignity in tilling a field as in writing a poem.
Booker T. Washington

Dignity consists not in possessing honors, but in the consciousness that we deserve them.
Aristotle

When boasting ends, there dignity begins.
Owen D. Young

All celebrated people lose dignity on a close view.
Napoleon Bonaparte

Our dignity is not in what we do, but what we understand.
George Santayana

Dignity belongs to the conquered.
Kenneth Burke

Human rights rest on human dignity. The dignity of man is an ideal worth fighting for and worth dying for.
Robert Maynard

Dignity is a mask we wear to hide our ignorance.
Elbert Hubbard

The ultimate end of all revolutionary social change is to establish the sanctity of human life, the dignity of man, the right of every human being to liberty and well-being.
Emma Goldman

DILIGENCE
Also see: BUSY, EFFORT, INDUSTRY, LABOR, PERSEVERANCE, WORK.

The expectations of life depend upon diligence; the mechanic that would perfect his work must first sharpen his tools.
Confucius

Diligence is the mother of good luck.
Benjamin Franklin

He who labors diligently need never despair; for all things are accomplished by diligence and labor.
Menander of Athens

What we hope ever to do with ease, we must learn first to do with diligence.
Samuel Johnson

That which ordinary men are fit for, I am qualified in; and the best of me is diligence.
William Shakespeare

Few things are impossible to diligence and skill . . . Great works are performed, not by strength, but perseverance.
Samuel Johnson

When I was young I observed that nine out of every ten things I did were failures, so I did ten times more work.
George Bernard Shaw

Every noble work is at first impossible.
Thomas Carlyle

DIPLOMACY   *Also see:* DISCRETION, JUDGMENT, POLITICS, TACT.

I have discovered the art of deceiving diplomats. I speak the truth, and they never believe me.   *Camillo Di Cavour*

Diplomacy is to do and say the nastiest things in the nicest way.
Isaac Goldberg

To say nothing, especially when speaking, is half the art of diplomacy.
Will Durant

A diplomat is a person who can tell you to go to Hell in such a way that you actually look forward to the trip.   *Anonymous*

I never refuse. I contradict. I sometimes forget.   *Benjamin Disraeli*

The principle of give and take is the principle of diplomacy—give one and take ten.   *Mark Twain*

A diplomat is a man who remembers a lady's birthday but forgets her age.
Anonymous

Modern diplomats approach every problem with an open mouth.
Arthur J. Goldberg

Diplomacy: lying in state.   *Oliver Herford*

American diplomacy is easy on the brain but hell on the feet.
Charles G. Dawes

Diplomacy is the art of letting someone have your way.   *Daniele Vare*

Diplomacy is a disguised war, in which states seek to gain by barter and intrigue, by the cleverness of arts, the objectives which they would have to gain more clumsily by means of war.   *Randolph Bourne*

The only summit meeting that can succeed is the one that does not take place.   *Barry M. Goldwater*

Let us never negotiate out of fear. But let us never fear to negotiate.
John Fitzgerald Kennedy

This is the devilish thing about foreign affairs: they are foreign and will not always conform to our whims.   *James Reston*

A diplomat's life is made up of three ingredients: protocol, Geritol and alcohol.   *Adlai E. Stevenson*

A drop of honey catches more flies than a hogshead of vinegar.   *Proverb*

International arbitration may be defined as the substitution of many burning questions for a smouldering one.   *Ambrose Bierce*

DISAPPOINTMENT *Also see:* DEFEAT, FAILURE, HOPE.

Man must be disappointed with the lesser things of life before he can comprehend the full value of the greater. *Edward G. Bulwer-Lytton*

How disappointment tracks the steps of hope. *Letitia Elizabeth Landon*

Disappointment is often the salt of life. *Theodore Parker*

Disappointment is the nurse of wisdom. *Boyle Roche*

Too many people miss the silver lining because they're expecting gold. *Maurice Seitter*

Disappointment to a noble soul is what cold water is to burning metal; it strengthens, tempers, intensifies, but never destroys it. *Eliza Tabor*

What we anticipate seldom occurs; what we least expect generally happens. *Benjamin Disraeli*

The disappointment of manhood succeeds the delusion of youth. *Benjamin Disraeli*

If you expect perfection from people your whole life is a series of disappointments, grumblings and complaints. If, on the contrary, you pitch your expectations low, taking folks as the inefficient creatures which they are, you are frequently surprised by having them perform better than you had hoped. *Bruce Barton*

Mean spirits under disappointment, like small beer in a thunderstorm always turn sour. *John Randolph*

DISARMAMENT *Also see:* NUCLEAR WARFARE, WAR.

Moral disarmament is to safeguard the future; material disarmament is to save for the present, that there may be a future to safeguard. *Elihu Root*

The notion that disarmament can put a stop to war is contradicted by the nearest dogfight. *George Bernard Shaw*

Today, every inhabitant of this planet must contemplate the day when it may no longer be habitable. Every man, woman and child lives under a nuclear sword of Damocles, hanging by the slenderest of threads, capable of being cut at any moment by accident, miscalculation or madness. The weapons of war must be abolished before they abolish us. *John Fitzgerald Kennedy*

The best way to begin disarming is to begin—and the United States is ready to conclude firm agreements in these areas and to consider any other reasonable proposal. *Lyndon Baines Johnson*

There is no more dangerous misconception than this which misconstrues the arms race as the cause rather than a symptom of the tensions and divisions which theaten nuclear war. If the history of the past fifty years teaches us anything, it is that peace does not follow disarmament—disarmament follows peace. *Bernard M. Baruch*

DISCIPLINE *Also see:* CHEERFULNESS, ORDER, PARENTS.

To be in good moral condition requires at least as much training as to be in good physical condition. *Jawaharlal Nehru*

A stern discipline pervades all nature, which is a little cruel that it may be very kind. *Edmund Spenser*

In the order named, these are the hardest to control: Wine, women, and song. *Franklin P. Adams*

It is never wise to slip the hands of discipline. *Lew Wallace*

You never will be the person you can be if pressure, tension, and discipline are taken out of your life. *James G. Bilkey*

What we do on some great occasion will probably depend on what we already are; and what we are will be the result of previous years of self-discipline. *H. P. Liddon*

Man is still responsible. He must turn the alloy of modern experience into the steel of mastery and character. His success lies not with the stars but with himself. He must carry on the fight of self-correction and discipline. He must fight mediocrity as sin and live against the imperative of life's highest ideal. *Frank Curtis Williams*

He that has learned to obey will know how to command. *Solon*

If the self-discipline of the free cannot match the iron discipline of the mailed fist, in economic, scientific, and all other kinds of struggles as well as the military, then the peril of freedom will continue to rise. *John Fitzgerald Kennedy*

DISCONTENT *Also see:* ANXIETY, COMPLAINT, CONTENTMENT, DISSENT, REBELLION.

One thing only has been lent to youth and age in common—discontent. *Matthew Arnold*

Restlessness and discontent are the necessities of progress. *Thomas A. Edison*

That which makes people dissatisfied with their condition, is the chimerical idea they form of the happiness of others. *James Thomson*

Discontent is the first step in the progress of a man or a nation. *Oscar Wilde*

Discontent is something that follows ambition like a shadow. *Henry H. Haskins*

Who is not satisfied with himself will grow; who is not sure of his own correctness will learn many things. *Chinese Proverb*

The discontented man finds no easy chair. *Benjamin Franklin*

Who with a little cannot be content, endures an everlasting punishment. *Robert Herrick*

DISCOVERY *Also see:* INVENTION, ORIGINALITY.

All great discoveries are made by men whose feelings run ahead of their thinking.
Charles H. Parkhurst

What is wanted is not the will to believe but the wish to find out, which is the exact opposite.
Bertrand Russell

One of the advantages of being disorderly is that one is constantly making exciting discoveries.
A. A. Milne

If I have ever made any valuable discoveries, it has been owing more to patient attention, than to any other talent.
Isaac Newton

Great discoveries and improvements invariably involve the cooperation of many minds. I may be given credit for having blazed the trail but when I look at the subsequent developments I feel the credit is due to others rather than to myself.
Alexander Graham Bell

Through every rift of discovery some seeming anomaly drops out of the darkness, and falls, as a golden link, into the great chain of order.
Edwin Hubbel Chapin

DISCRETION *Also see:* CAUTION, COMMON SENSE, JUDGMENT, PRUDENCE.

Be discreet in all things, and so render it unnecessary to be mysterious about any.
First Duke of Wellington

I have never been hurt by anything I didn't say.
Calvin Coolidge

Discretion is the salt, and fancy the sugar of life; the one preserves, the other sweetens it.
Christian Nestell Bovee

If thou art a master, be sometimes blind; if a servant, sometimes deaf.
Thomas Fuller

Discretion in speech is more than eloquence.
Francis Bacon

Great ability without discretion comes almost invariably to a tragic end.
Gambetta

An ounce of discretion is worth a pound of learning.
Proverb

Philosophy is nothing but discretion.
John Selden

As a jewel of gold in a swine's snout, so is a fair woman which is without discretion.
Proverb

Abhor a knave and pity a fool in your heart, but let neither of them unnecessarily see that you do so.
Lord Chesterfield

Better lose the anchor than the whole ship.
Dutch Proverb

DISCUSSION . . . See CONVERSATION

DISEASE *Also see:* AFFLICTION, CRIME, DEATH, DEBT, HEALTH, MEDICINE, PAIN.

The fear of life is the favorite disease of the twentieth century.
William Lyon Phelps

Some remedies are worse than the diseases. *Publilius Syrus*

When the Czar has a cold all Russia coughs. *Russian Proverb*

Disease is a physical process that generally begins that equality which death completes. *Samuel Johnson*

We classify disease as error, which nothing but Truth or Mind can heal.
Mary Baker Eddy

Disease is the retribution of outraged Nature. *Hosea Ballou*

A bodily disease may be but a symptom of some ailment in the spiritual past. *Nathaniel Hawthorne*

The diseases of the present have little in common with the diseases of the past save that we die of them. *Agnes Repplier*

We are the carriers of health and disease—either the divine health of courage and nobility or the demonic diseases of hate and anxiety.
Joshua Loth Liebman

There are no such things as incurables; there are only things for which man has not found a cure. *Bernard M. Baruch*

It is dainty to be sick, if you have leisure and convenience for it.
Ralph Waldo Emerson

A person's age is not dependent upon the number of years that have passed over his head, but on the number of colds that have passed through it.
Shirley W. Wynne

Sickness and disease are in weak minds the sources of melancholy; but that which is painful to the body, may be profitable to the soul. Sickness puts us in mind of our mortality, and, while we drive on heedlessly in the full career of worldly pomp and jollity, kindly pulls us by the ear, and brings us to a proper sense of our duty. *Richard E. Burton*

If I had my way I'd make health catching instead of disease.
Robert Green Ingersoll

It is with disease of the mind, as with those of the body; we are half dead before we understand our disorder, and half cured when we do.
Charles Caleb Colton

DISHONESTY *Also see:* CRIME, DECEIT, FRAUD, HYPOCRISY, IN-JUSTICE, LYING.

If all mankind were suddenly to practice honesty, many thousands of people would be sure to starve. *G. C. Lichtenberg*

Honesty pays, but it doesn't seem to pay enough to suit some people. *Kin Hubbard*

Men are able to trust one another, knowing the exact degree of dishonesty they are entitled to expect. *Stephen Butler Leacock*

Dishonesty is so grasping it would deceive God himself, were it possible. *George Bancroft*

Don't place too much confidence in the man who boasts of being as honest as the day is long. Wait until you meet him at night. *Robert C. Edwards*

False words are not only evil in themselves, but they infect the soul with evil. *Socrates*

Hope of ill gain is the beginning of loss. *Democritus*

Dishonesty, cowardice and duplicity are never impulsive. *George A. Knight*

If you attempt to beat a man down and so get his goods for less than a fair price, you are attempting to commit burglary as much as though you broke into his shop to take the things without paying for them. There is cheating on both sides of the counter, and generally less behind it than before. *Henry Ward Beecher*

DISSENT *Also see:* ARGUMENT, DIFFERENCE, DIFFICULTY, QUARREL.

Dissent does not include the freedom to destroy the system of law which guarantees freedom to speak, assemble and march in protest. Dissent is not anarchy. *Seymour F. Simon*

The United States can . . . be proud that it has institutions and a structure that permit its citizens to express honest dissent, even though those who do so may be maligned by the highest official in the land. *New York Times*

In a number of cases dissenting opinions have in time become the law. *Charles Evans Hughes*

Those who begin coercive elimination of dissent soon find themselves exterminating dissenters. Compulsory unification of opinion achieves only the unanimity of the graveyard. *Felix Frankfurter*

Mere unorthodoxy or dissent from the prevailing mores is not to be condemned. The absence of such voices would be a symptom of grave illness in our society. *Earl Warren*

Thought that is silenced is always rebellious . . . Majorities, of course, are often mistaken. This is why the silencing of minorities is always dangerous. Criticism and dissent are the indispensable antidote to major delusions. *Alan Barth*

DISTRUST *Also see:* DOUBT, FAITH, FEAR, SUSPICION.

The feeling of mistrust is always the last which a great mind acquires.
Jean Baptiste Racine

On one issue at least, men and women agree: they both distrust women.
H. L. Mencken

The disease of mutual distrust among nations is the bane of modern civilization.
Franz Boas

However much we may distrust men's sincerity, we always believe they speak to us more sincerely than to others.   *François de La Rochefoucauld*

What loneliness is more lonely than distrust?   *George Eliot*

The man who trusts men will make fewer mistakes than he who distrusts them.   *Camillo di Cavour*

Never trust a man who speaks well of everybody.   *John Churton Collins*

DOUBT *Also see:* AGNOSTICISM, DISTRUST, FAITH, INCREDULITY, SKEPTICISM, SUSPICION, WISDOM.

To have doubted one's own first principles, is the mark of a civilized man.
Oliver Wendell Holmes

We know accurately only when we know little; with knowledge doubt enters.   *Johann Wolfgang von Goethe*

I respect faith, but doubt is what gets you an education.   *Wilson Mizner*

Men become civilized, not in proportion to their willingness to believe, but in proportion to their readiness to doubt.   *H. L. Mencken*

Doubt is a pain too lonely to know that faith is his twin brother.
Kahlil Gibran

Doubt is the beginning, not the end, of wisdom.   *George Iles*

Our doubts are traitors, and make us lose the good we oft might win by fearing to attempt.   *William Shakespeare*

Just think of the tragedy of teaching children not to doubt.
Clarence Darrow

Faith keeps many doubts in her pay. If I could not doubt, I should not believe.   *Henry David Thoreau*

In all affairs it's a healthy thing now and then to hang a question mark on the things you have long taken for granted.   *Bertrand Russell*

Modest doubt is called the beacon of the wise.   *William Shakespeare*

DRAFT *Also see:* SOLDIER, WAR.

Peacetime conscription is the greatest step toward regimentation and militarism ever undertaken by the Congress of the United States.

Burton Kendall Wheeler

A young man who does not have what it takes to perform military service is not likely to have what it takes to make a living.

John Fitzgerald Kennedy

Pressed into service means pressed out of shape. *Robert Frost*

People have not been horrified by war to a sufficient extent . . . War will exist until that distant day when the conscientious objector enjoys the same reputation and prestige as the warrior does today.

John Fitzgerald Kennedy

DREAM *Also see:* AMERICA, DEMOCRACY, ILLUSION, IMAGINATION, REVERIE.

Keep true to the dreams of thy youth. *Johann von Schiller*

Dreaming permits each and every one of us to be quietly and safely insane every night of our lives. *Charles William Dement*

The smaller the head, the bigger the dream. *Austin O'Malley*

Dreaming is an act of pure imagination, attesting in all men a creative power, which, if it were available in waking, would make every man a Dante or Shakespeare. *H. F. Hedge*

If one advances confidently in the directions of his dreams, and endeavors to live the life which he has imagined, he will meet with a success unexpected in common hours. *Henry David Thoreau*

Dreams are nothing but incoherent ideas, occasioned by partial or imperfect sleep. *Benjamin Rush*

All men of action are dreamers. *James G. Huneker*

The more a man dreams, the less he believes. *H. L. Mencken*

People who insist on telling their dreams are among the terrors of the breakfast table. *Max Beerbohm*

The end of wisdom is to dream high enough to lose the dream in the seeking of it. *William Faulkner*

Toil, feel, think, hope; you will be sure to dream enough before you die, without arranging for it. *John Sterling*

It is difficult to say what is impossible, for the dream of yesterday is the hope of today and the reality of tomorrow. *Robert H. Goddard*

A lost but happy dream may shed its light upon our waking hours, and the whole day may be infected with the gloom of a dreary or sorrowful one; yet of neither may we be able to recover a trace. *Walter de la Mare*

DRESS *Also see:* APPEARANCE, FASHION, TASTE.

Be careless in your dress if you must, but keep a tidy soul. *Mark Twain*

The body is the shell of the soul, and dress the husk of that shell; but the husk often tells what the kernel is. *Anonymous*

Eat to please thyself, but dress to please others. *Benjamin Franklin*

If honor be your clothing, the suit will last a lifetime; but if clothing be your honor, it will soon be worn threadbare. *William Arnot*

I say, beware of all enterprises that require new clothes, and not rather a wearer of new clothes. *Henry David Thoreau*

Clothes don't make the man, but clothes have got many a man a good job. *Herbert Harold Vreeland*

There is new strength, repose of mind, and inspiration in fresh apparel. *Ella Wheeler Wilcox*

The cat in gloves catches no mice. *Benjamin Franklin*

Many a one, for the sake of finery on the back, has gone with a hungry belly, and half-starved their families. "Silks and satins, scarlets and velvets, put out the kitchen fire," as Poor Richard says. *Benjamin Franklin*

Women dress alike all over the world: they dress to be annoying to other women. *Elsa Schiaparelli*

The well-dressed man is he whose clothes you never notice. *W. Somerset Maugham*

I'm a Hollywood writer, so I put on my sports jacket and take off my brain. *Ben Hecht*

Beauty when most unclothed is clothed best. *Phineas Fletcher*

No man is esteemed for gay garments but by fools and women. *Sir Walter Raleigh*

If a woman rebels against high-heeled shoes, she should take care to do it in a very smart hat. *George Bernard Shaw*

Good clothes open all doors. *Thomas Fuller*

Clothes make the man. *Latin Proverb*

Do not conceive that fine clothes make fine men, any more than fine feathers make fine birds. A plain, genteel dress is more admired, obtains more credit in the eyes of the judicious and sensible. *George Washington*

Keeping your clothes well pressed will keep you from looking hard pressed. *Coleman Cox*

DRUGS *Also see:* CRIME.

The time has come to stop the sale of slavery to the young.
Lyndon Baines Johnson

We have drugs to make women speak, but none to keep them silent.
Anatole France

O true apothecary! Thy drugs are quick. *William Shakespeare*

The young physician starts life with 20 drugs for each disease, and the old physician ends life with one drug for 20 diseases. *William Osler*

DRUNKENNESS *Also see:* ABSTINENCE, VICE.

The sight of a drunkard is a better sermon against that vice than the best that was ever preached on the subject. *John Faucit Saville*

Drunkenness is the ruin of a person. It is premature old age. It is temporary death. *St. Basil*

A drunkard is like a whiskey bottle, all neck and belly and no head.
Austin O'Malley

I drink to make other people interesting. *George Jean Nathan*

If we take habitual drunkards as a class, their heads and their hearts will bear advantageous comparison with those of any other class. There seems ever to have been a proneness in the brilliant and warm-blooded to fall into this vice. The demon of intemperance ever seems to have delighted in sucking the blood of genius and generosity. *Abraham Lincoln*

Alcoholism is tragically high on the list of our nation's health problems. Five million Americans are alcoholics. They bring incalculable grief to millions of families. They cost their families, their employers and society billions of dollars. *Lyndon Baines Johnson*

Extensive interviews show that not one alcoholic has ever actually seen a pink elephant. *Yale University, Center of Alcohol Studies*

Always remember, that I have taken more out of alcohol than alcohol has taken out of me. *Winston Churchill*

Drunkenness is temporary suicide: the happiness that it brings is merely negative, a momentary cessation of unhappiness. *Bertrand Russell*

There are more old drunkards than old doctors. *Benjamin Franklin*

Drunkenness is not a mere matter of intoxicating liquors; it goes deeper—far deeper. Drunkenness is the failure of a man to control his thoughts.
David Grayson

Drunkenness is nothing else but a voluntary madness. *Seneca*

DUTY *Also see:* AFFECTION, AUTHORITY, BOLDNESS, BUSY, RESPON-
SIBILITY, RIGHTS.

Only aim to do your duty, and mankind will give you credit where you fail.
Thomas Jefferson

Men do less than they ought, unless they do all that they can.
Thomas Carlyle

The reward of one duty is the power to fulfill another. *George Eliot*

Do something every day that you don't want to do; this is the golden rule
for acquiring the habit of doing your duty without pain. *Mark Twain*

. . . it is just as hard to do your duty when men are sneering at you as
when they are shooting at you. *Woodrow Wilson*

Duty is what one expects from others. *Oscar Wilde*

A duty dodged is like a debt unpaid; it is only deferred, and we must
come back and settle the account at last. *Joseph F. Newton*

Let us do our duty in our shop or our kitchen, in the market, the street,
the office, the school, the home, just as faithfully as if we stood in the
front rank of some great battle, and knew that victory for mankind depended on our bravery, strength and skill. When we do that, the humblest
of us will be serving in that great army which achieves the welfare of the
world. *Theodore Parker*

He who is false to the present duty breaks a thread in the loom, and you
will see the effect when the weaving of a lifetime is unravelled.
William Ellery Channing

Never mind your happiness; do your duty. *Will Durant*

For strength to bear is found in duty alone, and he is blest indeed who
learns to make the joy of others cure his own heartache. *Drake*

It is the duty of the government to make it difficult for people to do
wrong, easy to do right. *William E. Gladstone*

A man who neglects his duty as a citizen is not entitled to his rights as a
citizen. *Tiorio*

Knowledge of our duties is the most essential part of the philosophy of life.
If you escape duty you avoid action. The world demands results.
George W. Goethals

Sufficient to each day are the duties to be done and the trials to be endured. God never built a Christian strong enough to carry today's duties
and tomorrow's anxieties piled on top of them. *Theodore Ledyard Cuyler*

New occasions teach new duties. *James Russell Lowell*

Who escapes a duty, avoids a gain. *Theodore Parker*

E

EARTH *Also see:* NATURE, WORLD, UNIVERSE.

The earth is given as a common for men to labor and live in.
Thomas Jefferson

I don't know if there are men on the moon, but if there are they must be using the earth as their lunatic asylum. *George Bernard Shaw*

How far must suffering and misery go before we see that even in the day of vast cities and powerful machines, the good earth is our mother and that if we destroy her, we destroy ourselves? *Paul Bigelow Sears*

Man makes a great fuss about this planet which is only a ball-bearing in the hub of the universe. *Christopher Morley*

The earth and its resources belong of right to its people. *Gifford Pinchot*

There is enough for all. The earth is a generous mother; she will provide in plentiful abundance food for all her children if they will but cultivate her soil in justice and in peace. *Bourke Cockran*

Our earth is but a small star in a great universe. Yet of it we can make, if we choose, a planet unvexed by war, untroubled by hunger or fear, undivided by senseless distinctions of race, color or theory.
Stephen Vincent Benét

Earth is but the frozen echo of the silent voice of God. *Samuel M. Hageman*

I conjure you, my brethren, to remain faithful to earth, and do not believe those who speak unto you of superterrestrial hopes! Poisoners they are, whether they know it or not. *Nietzsche*

> The green earth sends her incense up
>   From many a mountain shrine;
> From folded leaf and dewey cup
>   She pours her sacred wine. *John Greenleaf Whittier*

Earth, thou great footstool of our God, who reigns on high; thou fruitful source of all our raiment, life, and food; our house, our parent, and our nurse. *Isaac Watts*

> The earth, that is sufficient,
>   I do not want the constellations any nearer,
> I know they are very well where they are,
>   I know they suffice for those who belong to them. *Walt Whitman*

The pagans do not know God, and love only the earth. The Jews know the true God, and love only the earth. The Christians know the true God, and do not love the earth. *Blaise Pascal*

"The earth is the Lord's fullness thereof": this is no longer a hollow dictum of religion, but a directive for economic action toward human brotherhood. *Lewis Mumford*

EATING *Also see:* GLUTTON.

Eat, drink, and be merry, for tomorrow ye diet.　　*William Gilmore Beymer*

To eat is human; to digest, divine.　　*C. T. Copeland*

The way to a man's heart is through his stomach.　　*Fanny Fern*

By eating what is sufficient man is enabled to work; he is hindered from working and becomes heavy, idle, and stupid if he takes too much. As to bodily distempers occasioned by excess, there is no end of them.
Thomas R. Jones

He who does not mind his belly will hardly mind anything else.
Samuel Johnson

There is no love sincerer than the love of food.　　*George Bernard Shaw*

When it comes to eating, you can sometimes help yourself more by helping yourself less.　　*Richard Armour*

I have been a success: for sixty years I have eaten, and have avoided being eaten.　　*Logan P. Smith*

Tell me what you eat, and I will tell you what you are.
Anthelme Brillat-Savarin

I saw few die of hunger; of eating, a hundred thousand.
Benjamin Franklin

We used to say "What's cooking?" when we came home from work. Now it's "What's thawing?"　　*Anonymous*

The proof of the pudding is in the eating.　　*Miguel de Cervantes*

　　Timid roach, why be so shy?
　　　We are brothers, thou and I.
　　In the midnight, like thyself,
　　　I explore the pantry shelf.　　*Christopher Morley*

Part of the secret of success in life is to eat what you like and let the food fight it out inside.　　*Mark Twain*

The difference between a rich man and a poor man is this—the former eats when he pleases, and the latter when he can get it.　　*Sir Walter Raleigh*

A fat kitchen, a lean will.　　*Benjamin Franklin*

In order to know whether a human being is young or old, offer it food of different kinds at short intervals. If young, it will eat anything at any hour of the day or night. If old, it observes stated periods.
Oliver Wendell Holmes

ECONOMY *Also see:* BARGAIN, MONEY, PRUDENCE.

There can be no economy where there is no efficiency. *Beaconsfield*

Without economy none can be rich, and with it few will be poor.
Samuel Johnson

Nothing is cheap which is superflous, for what one does not need, is dear at a penny. *Plutarch*

Beware of little expenses; a small leak will sink a great ship.
Benjamin Franklin

What this country needs is a good five-cent Nickel. *Franklin P. Adams*

Ere you consult your fancy, consult your purse. *Benjamin Franklin*

He who will not economize will have to agonize. *Confucius*

The man who will live above his present circumstances, is in great danger of soon living beneath them; or as the Italian proverb says, "The man that lives by hope, will die by despair." *Joseph Addison*

> A penny saved is two pence clear,
> A pin a day's a groat a year. *Benjamin Franklin*

The world abhors closeness, and all but admires extravagance; yet a slack hand shows weakness, and a tight hand strength. *Thomas Fowell Buxton*

I place economy among the first and most important virtues, and public debt as the greatest of dangers . . . We must make our choice between economy and liberty, or profusion and servitude. If we can prevent the government from wasting the labors of the people under the pretense of caring for them, they will be happy. *Thomas Jefferson*

> Have more than thou showest,
> Speak less than thou knowest. *William Shakespeare*

It is of no small commendation to manage a little well. To live well in abundance is the praise of the estate, not of the person. I will study more how to give a good account of my little, than how to make it more.
Joseph Hall

Economy is a way of spending money without getting any pleasure out of it.
Armand Salacrou

Economy is for the poor; the rich may dispense with it.
Christian Nestell Bovee

Let honesty and industry be thy constant companions, and spend one penny less than thy clear gains; then shall thy pocket begin to thrive; creditors will not insult, nor want oppress, nor hungerness bite, nor nakedness freeze thee. *Benjamin Franklin*

EDUCATION *Also see:* CULTURE, DEFEAT, DOUBT, READING, STUDY.

Only the educated are free.   *Epictetus*

Education is a better safeguard of liberty than a standing army.
                                                          Edward Everett

Education is a progressive discovery of our ignorance.   *Will Durant*

I have never let my schooling interfere with my education.   *Mark Twain*

Education makes people easy to lead, but difficult to drive; easy to govern,
but impossible to enslave.   *Henry Peter Brougham*

Education is an admirable thing, but nothing that is worth knowing can be
taught.   *Oscar Wilde*

Education is the process of driving a set of prejudices down your throat.
                                                        Martin H. Fischer

Nothing in education is so astonishing as the amount of ignorance it accumulates in the form of inert facts.   *Henry Brooks Adams*

If a man empties his purse into his head, no man can take it away from
him. An investment in knowledge always pays the best interest.
                                                        Benjamin Franklin

Education is a social process . . . Education is growth. . . . Education is,
not a preparation for life; education is life itself.   *John Dewey*

You can lead a boy to college, but you cannot make him think.
                                                          Elbert Hubbard

There is nothing so stupid as an educated man, if you get off the thing
that he was educated in.   *Will Rogers*

Education is the period during which you are being instructed by somebody
you do not know, about something you do not want to know.
                                                      Gilbert K. Chesterton

Education is that which discloses to the wise and disguises from the foolish
their lack of understanding.   *Ambrose Bierce*

Education is too important to be left solely to the educators.
                                                          Francis Keppel

He who opens a school door, closes a prison.   *Victor Hugo*

The best education in the world is that by struggling to get a living.
                                                        Wendell Phillips

My father must have had some elementary education for he could read and
write and keep accounts inaccurately.   *George Bernard Shaw*

Our progress as a nation can be no swifter than our progress in education.
                                                  John Fitzgerald Kennedy

EFFICIENCY *Also see:* ABILITY, DILIGENCE, GENIUS, INDUSTRY, ORDER, TECHNOLOGY.

It is more than probable that the average man could, with no injury to his health, increase his efficiency fifty percent. *Walter Scott*

A sense of the value of time—that is, of the best way to divide one's time into one's various activities—is an essential preliminary to efficient work; it is the only method of avoiding hurry. *Arnold Bennett*

In the old world that is passing, in the new world that is coming, national efficiency has been and will be a controlling factor in national safety and welfare. *Gifford Pinchot*

Loyal and efficient work in a great cause, even though it may not be immediately recognized, ultimately bears fruit. *Jawaharlal Nehru*

We want the spirit of America to be efficient; we want American character to be efficient; we want American character to display itself in what I may, perhaps, be allowed to call spiritual efficiency—clear disinterested thinking and fearless action along the right lines of thought. *Woodrow Wilson*

Obviously, the highest type of efficiency is that which can utilize existing material to the best advantage. *Jawaharlal Nehru*

EFFORT *Also see:* ACHIEVEMENT, ACTION, DILIGENCE, ENERGY, INDUSTRY, LABOR, PERSEVERANCE, WORK.

It is hard to fail, but it is worse never to have tried to succeed. In this life we get nothing save by effort. *Theodore Roosevelt*

Remember that the faith that moves mountains always carries a pick. *Anonymous*

The only method by which people can be supported is out of the effort of those who are earning their own way. We must not create a deterrent to hard work. *Robert A. Taft*

A law of nature rules that energy cannot be destroyed. You change its form from coal to steam, from steam to power in the turbine, but you do not destroy energy. In the same way, another law governs human activity and rules that honest effort cannot be lost, but that some day the proper benefits will be forthcoming. *Paul Speicher*

Things don't turn up in this world until somebody turns them up. *James A. Garfield*

Freedom from effort in the present merely means that there has been effort stored up in the past. *Theodore Roosevelt*

Many a man never fails because he never tries. *Norman MacEwan*

98

EGOTISM . . . See VANITY

ELOQUENCE *Also see:* LOQUACITY.

True eloquence consists in saying all that is proper, and nothing more.
François de La Rochefoucauld

False eloquence is exaggeration; true eloquence is emphasis.
William Rounseville Alger

It is of eloquence as of a flame; it requires matter to feed it, and motion to excite it; and it brightens as it burns. *Tacitus*

Eloquence is logic on fire. *Lyman Beecher*

Eloquence is the child of knowledge. *Benjamin Disraeli*

Noise proves nothing. Often a hen who has merely laid an egg cackles as if she had laid an asteroid. *Mark Twain*

There is no eloquence without a man behind it. *Ralph Waldo Emerson*

True eloquence does not consist in speech. Words and phrases may be marshalled in every way, but they cannot compass it. It must consist in the man, in the subject, and in the occasion. It comes, if at all, like the outbreaking of a fountain from the earth, or the bursting forth of volcanic fires, with spontaneous, original native force. *Daniel Webster*

EMINENCE . . . See ESTEEM

EMOTION *Also see:* CURIOSITY, PASSION, REASON, SENTIMENT.

When dealing with people remember you are not dealing with creatures of logic, but with creatures of emotion, creatures bristling with prejudice, and motivated by pride and vanity. *Dale Carnegie*

Emotion is not something shameful, subordinate, second-rate; it is a supremely valid phase of humanity at its noblest and most mature.
Joshua Loth Liebman

The young man who has not wept is a savage, and the old man who will not laugh is a fool. *George Santayana*

By starving emotions we become humorless, rigid and stereotyped; by repressing them we become literal, reformatory and holier-than-thou; encouraged, they perfume life; discouraged, they poison it. *Joseph Collins*

It is easier to manufacture seven facts out of whole cloth than one emotion.
Mark Twain

Emotion is the surest arbiter of a poetic choice, and it is the priest of all supreme unions in the mind. *Max Eastman*

Emotion turning back on itself, and not leading on to thought or action, is the element of madness. *John Sterling*

EMPLOYMENT *Also see:* BUSINESS, BUSY, EFFORT, WORK.

Not to enjoy life, but to employ life, ought to be our aim and inspiration.
John Ross Macduff

Each man's task is his life preserver.   *George B. Emerson*

When you hire people that are smarter than you are, you prove you are smarter than they are.   *R. H. Grant*

Employment gives health, sobriety and morals.   *Daniel Webster*

Early to bed and early to rise probably indicates unskilled labor.
John Ciardi

Employment, which Galen calls "nature's physician," is so essential to human happiness that indolence is justly considered as the mother of misery.   *Richard E. Burton*

The employer generally gets the employees he deserves.   *Walter Gilbey*

END and MEANS *Also see:* AIM, DEATH, PURPOSE, RESULT.

The end must justify the means.   *Matthew Prior*

Knowledge of means without knowledge of ends is animal training.
Everett Dean Martin

If well thou hast begun, go on; it is the end that crowns us, not the fight.
Robert Herrick

Freedom is only good as a means; it is no end in itself.   *Herman Melville*

The end justifies the means only when the means used are such as actually bring about the desired and desirable end.   *John Dewey*

If we are but sure the end is right, we are too apt to gallop over all bounds to compass it; not considering the lawful ends may be very unlawfully attained.   *William Penn*

In everything we ought to look to the end.   *Jean de La Fontaine*

ENDURANCE *Also see:* PATIENCE, STRENGTH, TOLERANCE, WILL.

To endure is the first thing that a child ought to learn, and that which he will have the most need to know.   *Jean Jacques Rousseau*

Whatever necessity lays upon thee, endure: whatever she commands, do.
Johann Wolfgang von Goethe

Endurance is patience concentrated.   *Thomas Carlyle*

Still achieving, still pursuing, learn to labor and to wait.
Henry Wadsworth Longfellow

There is a strength of quiet endurance as significant of courage as the most daring feats of prowess.   *Henry Theodore Tuckerman*

ENEMY *Also see:* CITIZENSHIP, DEBT, FORGIVENESS, FRIENDSHIP, QUARREL.

There is no little enemy. *Benjamin Franklin*

A man's greatness can be measured by his enemies. *Don Piatt*

Observe your enemies, for they first find out your faults. *Antisthenes*

A man cannot be too careful in the choice of his enemies. *Oscar Wilde*

If you have no enemies, you are apt to be in the same predicament in regard to friends. *Elbert Hubbard*

Our real enemies are the people who make us feel so good that we are slowly, but inexorably, pulled down into the quicksand of smugness and self-satisfaction. *Sydney Harris*

The man who ain't got an enemy is really poor. *Josh Billings*

Everyone needs a warm personal enemy or two to keep him free from rust in the movable parts of his mind. *Gene Fowler*

Man is his own worst enemy. *Cicero*

I wish my deadly foe no worse
Than want of friends, and empty purse. *Nicholas Breton*

In order to have an enemy, one must be somebody. One must be a force before he can be resisted by another force. A malicious enemy is better than a clumsy friend. *Anne Sophie Swetchine*

Nothing would more contribute to make a man wise than to have always an enemy in his view. *Lord Halifax*

An enemy is anyone who tells the truth about you. *Elbert Hubbard*

When you are ill make haste to forgive your enemies, for you may recover. *Ambrose Bierce*

You needn't love your enemy, but if you refrain from telling lies about him, you are doing well enough. *Ed Howe*

Five great enemies to peace inhabit with us: viz., avarice, ambition, envy, anger and pride. If those enemies were to be banished, we should infallibly enjoy perpetual peace. *Petrarch*

One very important ingredient of success is a good, wide-awake, persistent, tireless enemy. *Frank B. Shutts*

ENERGY *Also see:* AVERAGE, EFFICIENCY, EFFORT, FORCE, INDUSTRY, POWER, SPIRIT, STRENGTH, ZEAL.

The world belongs to the energetic.   *Ralph Waldo Emerson*

Energy and persistence conquer all things.   *Benjamin Franklin*

Goodwill is no easy symbol of good wishes. It is an immeasurable and tremendous energy, the atomic energy of the spirit.   *Eleanor Stock*

There is no genius in life like the genius of energy and industry.
Donald Grant Mitchell

Energy, like the biblical grain of the mustard-seed, will remove mountains.
Hosea Ballou

Energy will do anything that can be done in the world; and no talents, no circumstances, no opportunities will make a two-legged animal a man without it.   *Johann Wolfgang von Goethe*

The real difference between men is energy. A strong will, a settled purpose, an invincible determination, can accomplish almost anything; and in this lies the distinction between great men and little men.   *Thomas Fuller*

ENJOYMENT *Also see:* AMUSEMENT, CHEERFULNESS, CONTENTMENT, JOY, LEISURE, PLEASURE.

The first half of life consists of the capacity to enjoy without the chance; the last half consists of the chance without the capacity.   *Mark Twain*

No enjoyment, however inconsiderable, is confined to the present moment. A man is happier for life from having made once an agreeable tour, or lived for any length of time with pleasant people, or enjoyed any considerable interval of innocent pleasure.   *Sydney Smith*

True enjoyment comes from activity of the mind and exercise of the body; the two are ever united.   *Humboldt*

If your capacity to acquire has outstripped your capacity to enjoy, you are on the way to the scrap-heap.   *Glen Buck*

Temper your enjoyments with prudence, lest there be written on your heart that fearful word "satiety."   *Francis Quarles*

Only mediocrity of enjoyment is allowed to man.   *Hugh Blair*

May we never let the things we can't have, or don't have, or shouldn't have, spoil our enjoyment of the things we do have and can have. As we value our happiness let us not forget it, for one of the greatest lessons in life is learning to be happy without the things we cannot or should not have.   *Richard L. Evans*

ENTHUSIASM *Also see:* OPTIMISM, PASSION, ZEAL.

Mere enthusiasm is the all in all. *William Blake*

The enthusiasm of old men is singularly like that of infancy.
Gérard de Nerval

The worst bankrupt in the world is the man who has lost his enthusiasm.
H. W. Arnold

Every great and commanding movement in the annals of the world is the triumph of enthusiasm. Nothing great was ever achieved without it.
Ralph Waldo Emerson

No person who is enthusiastic about his work has anything to fear from life.
Samuel Goldwyn

Always exaggerate the importance of important things and overlook their deficiencies. *Hugh Stevenson Tigner*

Enthusiasm is nothing but moral inebriety. *Lord Byron*

EQUALITY *Also see:* ARISTOCRACY, CLEVERNESS, DEMOCRACY, DIFFERENCE, RACE, RIGHTS.

All human beings are born free and equal in dignity and rights.
U.N., Declaration of Human Rights, Art. 1.

Men are equal; it is not birth but virtue that makes the difference.
Voltaire

Equality is what does not exist among equals. *E. E. Cummings*

There are many humorous things in the world: among them the white man's notion that he is less savage than the other savages. *Mark Twain*

We hold these truths to be self-evident, that all men are created equal.
Thomas Jefferson

Complete equality means universal irresponsibility. *T. S. Eliot*

The only real equality is in the cemetery. *German Proverb*

The mass of mankind has not been born with saddles on their backs, nor a favored few booted and spurred, ready to ride them legitimately, by the grace of God. *Thomas Jefferson*

If there be a human being who is freer than I, then I shall necessarily become his slave. If I am freer than any other, then he will become my slave. Therefore equality is an absolutely necessary condition of freedom.
Mikhail A. Bakunin

ERROR *Also see:* CAUSE, TRUTH, WRONG.

It takes less time to do a thing right than it does to explain why you did it wrong.   *Henry Wadsworth Longfellow*

Men are apt to prefer a prosperous error to an afflicted truth.
Jeremy Taylor

The man who makes no mistakes does not usually make anything.
Edward Phelps

An error doesn't become a mistake until you refuse to correct it.
Orlando A. Battista

If I have erred, I err in company with Abraham Lincoln.
Theodore Roosevelt

Error is discipline through which we advance.   *William Ellery Channing*

Truth is immortal; error is mortal.   *Mary Baker Eddy*

To err is human, but when the eraser wears out ahead of the pencil, you're overdoing it.   *Josh Jenkins*

The proper method for hastening the decay of error is . . . by teaching every man to think for himself.   *William Godwin*

Sometimes we may learn more from a man's errors, than from his virtues.
Henry Wadsworth Longfellow

A man whose errors take ten years to correct is quite a man.
J. Robert Oppenheimer

ESTEEM *Also see:* ADMIRATION, HONOR.

The chief ingredients in the composition of those qualities that gain esteem and praise, are good nature, truth, good sense, and good breeding.
Joseph Addison

Oftentimes nothing profits more than self-esteem, grounded on what is just and right.   *John Milton*

Esteem has more engaging charms than friendship and even love. It captivates hearts better, and never makes ingrates.
François de La Rochefoucauld

ETERNITY *Also see:* BIBLE, FUTURE, GOD, HEAVEN, HELL, IMMORTALITY, TIME.

Eternity is not an everlasting flux of time, but time is a short parenthesis in a long period.   *John Donne*

Eternity is in love with the productions of time.   *William Blake*

All great natures delight in stability; all great men find eternity affirmed in the very promise of their faculties.   *Ralph Waldo Emerson*

Eternity has no gray hairs! The flowers fade, the heart withers, man grows old and dies, the world lies down in the sepulchre of ages, but time writes no wrinkles on the brow of eternity. *Reginald Heber*

The sum of all sums is eternity. *Lucretius*

The thought of eternity consoles for the shortness of life. *Luc de Clapiers*

I leave eternity to Thee; for what is man that he could live the lifetime of his God? *Herman Melville*

EVIL *Also see: CREDULITY, DANGER, VICE.*

It is a sin to believe evil of others, but it is seldom a mistake. *H. L. Mencken*

There is nothing evil save that which perverts the mind and shackles the conscience. *St. Ambrose*

I never wonder to see men wicked, but I often wonder to see them not ashamed. *Jonathan Swift*

He that will not apply new remedies must expect new evils. *Francis Bacon*

Evil often triumphs, but never conquers. *Joseph Roux*

The first lesson of history is the good of evil. *Ralph Waldo Emerson*

A person may cause evil to others not only by his actions but by his inaction, and in either case he is justly accountable to them for the injury. *John Stuart Mill*

A little evil is often necessary for obtaining a great good. *Voltaire*

There are a thousand hacking at the branches of evil to one who is striking at the root. *Henry David Thoreau*

Evil events from evil causes spring. *Aristophanes*

The mere apprehension of a coming evil has put many into a situation of the utmost danger. *Lucan*

It is privilege that causes evil in the world, not wickedness, and not men. *Lincoln Steffens*

It is the law of our humanity that man must know good through evil. No great principle ever triumphed but through much evil. No man ever progressed to greatness and goodness but through great mistakes. *Frederick W. Robertson*

All that is necessary for the triumph of evil is that good men do nothing. *Edmund Burke*

Evil unchecked grows, evil tolerated poisons the whole system. *Jawaharlal Nehru*

EVOLUTION   *Also see:* CHANGE.

Creative evolution is at last becoming conscious.   *E. E. Cummings*

All modern men are descended from a worm-like creature, but it shows more on some people.   *Will Cuppy*

Some call it evolution and others call it God.   *W. H. Carruth*

The question is this: is man an ape or an angel? I am on the side of the angels. I repudiate with indignation and abhorrence these new-fangled theories.   *Benjamin Disraeli*

One touch of Darwin makes the whole world kin.   *George Bernard Shaw*

We must remember that there are no shortcuts in evolution.   *Louis D. Brandeis*

There is no more reason to believe that man descended from some inferior animal than there is to believe that a stately mansion has descended from a small cottage.   *William Jennings Bryan*

Concerning what ultimately becomes of the individual it (evolution) has added nothing and subtracted nothing.   *Robert A. Millikan*

> Recall from time's abysmal chasm
>   That piece of Primal protoplasm;
> The first Amoeba, strangely splendid,
>   From whom we're all of us descended.   *Arthur Guiterman*

We are descended not only from monkeys, but also from monks.   *Elbert Hubbard*

EXAGGERATION   *Also see:* ELOQUENCE, LOQUACITY.

The speaking in a perpetual hyperbole is comely in nothing but love.   *Francis Bacon*

She felt in italics and thought in capitals.   *Henry James*

We always weaken whatever we exaggerate.   *Jean François de Laharpe*

Exaggeration is a blood relation to falsehood and nearly as blameable.   *Hosea Ballou*

There are people so addicted to exaggeration they can't tell the truth without lying.   *Josh Billings*

Exaggeration is truth that has lost its temper.   *Kahlil Gibran*

Some so speak in exaggerations and superlatives that we need to make a large discount from their statements before we can come at their real meaning.   *Tryon Edwards*

Exaggeration is a department of lying.   *Baltasar Gracián*

EXAMPLE *Also see:* CONFORMITY, INFLUENCE.

Example is not the main thing in life—it is the only thing.

Albert Schweitzer

Other men are lenses through which we read our own minds.

Ralph Waldo Emerson

None preaches better than the ant, and she says nothing. *Benjamin Franklin*

Old men are fond of giving good advice to console themselves for their inability to give bad examples. *François de La Rochefoucauld*

The first great gift we can bestow on others is a good example. *Morell*

Not the cry, but the flight of the wild duck, leads the flock to fly and follow. *Chinese Proverb*

Few things are harder to put up with than the annoyance of a good example. *Mark Twain*

The rotten apple spoils his companion. *Benjamin Franklin*

I have ever deemed it more honorable and more profitable, too, to set a good example than to follow a bad one. *Thomas Jefferson*

First find the man in yourself if you will inspire manliness in others.

Amos Bronson Alcott

Virtuous men do good by setting themselves up as models before the public, but I do good by setting myself up as a warning. *Michel de Montaigne*

EXCELLENCE . . . See PERFECTION

EXCUSES *Also see:* FAILURE, REGRET.

Don't make excuses, make good. *Elbert Hubbard*

An excuse is worse and more terrible than a lie; for an excuse is a lie guarded. *Alexander Pope*

He that is good for making excuses is seldom good for anything else.

Benjamin Franklin

Apologizing—a very desperate habit—one that is rarely cured. Apology is only egotism wrong side out. *Oliver Wendell Holmes*

We have forty million reasons for failure, but not a single excuse.

Rudyard Kipling

I don't trouble my spirit to vindicate itself or be understood; I see that the elementary laws never apologize. *Walt Whitman*

Stoop not then to poor excuse. *Sursum Corda*

Uncalled-for excuses are practical confessions. *Charles Simmons*

EXPECTATION . . . See ANTICIPATION

EXPEDIENCY   *Also see:* COMPROMISE, OPPORTUNITY.

I believe the moral losses of expediency always far outweigh the temporary gains.   *Wendell L. Willkie*

Modern man has developed a kind of Gallup-poll mentality, relying on quantity instead of quality and yielding to expediency instead of building a new faith.   *Walter Gropius*

When private virtue is hazarded on the perilous cast of expediency, the pillars of the republic, however apparent their stability, are infected with decay at the very center.   *Edwin Hubbel Chapin*

No man is justified in doing evil on the ground of expedience.
Theodore Roosevelt

Expedients are for the hour; principles for the ages.   *Henry Ward Beecher*

EXPERIENCE   *Also see:* AGE, THEORY.

One thorn of experience is worth a whole wilderness of warning.
James Russell Lowell

Men are wise in proportion, not to their experience, but to their capacity for experience.   *George Bernard Shaw*

Experience is a school where a man learns what a big fool he has been.
Josh Billings

Experience is a hard teacher because she gives the test first, the lesson after-wards.   *Vernon Sanders Law*

Experience is a comb that life gives you after you lose your hair.
Judith Stern

Nothing is a waste of time if you use the experience wisely.   *Rodin*

Experience is something you get too late to do anything about the mistakes you made while getting it.   *Anonymous*

    A sadder and a wiser man,
      He rose the morrow morn.   *Samuel Taylor Coleridge*

When I was a boy of fourteen, my father was so ignorant I could hardly stand to have the old man around. But when I got to be twenty-one, I was astonished at how much the old man had learned in seven years.
Mark Twain

Experience is one thing you can't get for nothing.   *Oscar Wilde*

Experience increases our wisdom but doesn't reduce our follies.
Josh Billings

A burnt child dreads the fire.   *English Proverb*

EXTRAVAGANCE *Also see:* DESIRE, ECONOMY.

Extravagance is the luxury of the poor; penury is the luxury of the rich.
Oscar Wilde

That is suitable to a man, in point of ornamental expense, not which he can afford to have, but which he can afford to lose. *Richard Whately*

An extravagance is anything you buy that is of no earthly use to your wife.
Franklin P. Jones

He who buys what he needs not, sells what he needs. *Japanese Proverb*

All decent people live beyond their incomes; those who aren't respectable live beyond other people's; a few gifted individuals manage to do both. *Saki*

EXTREMES *Also see:* EXTRAVAGANCE, RADICAL, REVERIE.

Mistrust the man who finds everything good; the man who finds everything evil; and still more the man who is indifferent to everything.
Johann Kaspar Lavater

Extremes meet and there is no better example than the haughtiness of humility. *Ralph Waldo Emerson*

Extremes, though contrary, have the like effects. Extreme heat kills, and so extreme cold: extreme love breeds satiety, and so extreme hatred; and too violent rigor tempts chastity, as does too much license. *George Chapman*

I would remind you that extremism in the defense of liberty is no vice. And let me also remind you that moderation in the pursuit of justice is no virtue. *Barry M. Goldwater*

In everything the middle course is best; all things in excess bring trouble.
Plautus

I never dared be radical when young for fear it would make me conservative when old. *Robert Frost*

Too austere a philosophy makes few wise men; too rigorous politics, few good subjects; too hard a religion, few persons whose devotion is of long continuance. *Seigneur de Saint-Evremond*

EYE *Also see:* ADVENTURE, BIGOTRY, ORIGINALITY, VISION.

Men are born with two eyes, but only one tongue, in order that they should see twice as much as they say. *Charles Caleb Colton*

One of the most wonderful things in nature is a glance of the eye; it transcends speech; it is the bodily symbol of identity. *Ralph Waldo Emerson*

The eye of the master will do more work than both his hands.
Benjamin Franklin

An eye can threaten like a loaded and levelled gun, or it can insult like hissing or kicking; or, in its altered mood, by beams of kindness, it can make the heart dance for joy. *Ralph Waldo Emerson*

F

FACTS *Also see:* ACCURACY, COMPROMISE, CURIOSITY, EMOTION, THEORY.

Get the facts, or the facts will get you. And when you get 'em, get 'em right, or they will get you wrong.
Thomas Fuller

Facts are facts and will not disappear on account of your likes.
Jawaharlal Nehru

A world of facts lies outside and beyond the world of words. *Thomas Huxley*

Get your facts first, and then you can distort them as much as you please.
Mark Twain

We should keep so close to facts that we never have to remember the second time what we said the first time.
F. Marion Smith

A fact in itself is nothing. It is valuable only for the idea attached to it, or for the proof which it furnishes.
Claude Bernard

If you get all the facts, your judgment can be right; if you don't get all the facts, it can't be right.
Bernard M. Baruch

A concept is stronger than a fact.
Charlotte P. Gillman

Comment is free but facts are sacred.
Charles P. Scott

FAILURE *Also see:* AMBITION, BOLDNESS, DEFEAT, DESPAIR, EFFORT, FATE, SUCCESS, WAR.

Show me a thoroughly satisfied man and I will show you a failure.
Thomas A. Edison

The only people who never fail are those who never try.
Ilka Chase

Failures are divided into two classes—those who thought and never did, and those who did and never thought.
John Charles Salak

Never give a man up until he has failed at something he likes.
Lewis E. Lawes

He's no failure. He's not dead yet.
William Lloyd George

The only time you don't fail is the last time you try anything—and it works.
William Strong

A failure is a man who has blundered but is not able to cash in on the experience.
Elbert Hubbard

Ninety-nine percent of the failures come from people who have the habit of making excuses.
George Washington Carver

A man can fail many times, but he isn't a failure until he begins to blame somebody else.
John Burroughs

FAITH
Also see: ATHEISM, BELIEF, CONFIDENCE, COURAGE, CREDIT, CRIME, DOUBT, EFFORT, FEAR, RELIGION.

The smallest seed of faith is better than the largest fruit of happiness.
Henry David Thoreau

Faith may be defined briefly as an illogical belief in the occurrence of the improbable.
H. L. Mencken

When faith is lost, when honor dies, the man is dead.
John Greenleaf Whittier

We have not lost faith, but we have transferred it from God to the medical profession.
George Bernard Shaw

It's not dying for faith that's so hard, it's living up to it.
William Makepeace Thackeray

I can believe anything provided it is incredible.
Oscar Wilde

Faith is love taking the form of aspiration.
William Ellery Channing

I always prefer to believe the best of everybody—it saves so much trouble.
Rudyard Kipling

FAME
Also see: ADMIRATION, ESTEEM, GLORY, HONOR, NAME, REPUTATION, VANITY.

Fame is proof that people are gullible.
Ralph Waldo Emerson

Fame usually comes to those who are thinking about something else.
Oliver Wendell Holmes

Fame is vapor, popularity an accident, riches take wings. Only one thing endures and that is character.
Horace Greeley

It often happens that those of whom we speak least on earth are best known in heaven.
Nicolas Caussin

The present condition of fame is merely fashion.
Gilbert K. Chesterton

Fame: an embalmer trembling with stage fright.
H. L. Mencken

The fame of great men ought to be judged always by the means they used to acquire it.
François de La Rochefoucauld

The lust of fame is the last that a wise man shakes off.
Tacitus

Fame is a fickle food
Upon a shifting plate.
Emily Dickinson

Even the best things are not equal to their fame.
Henry David Thoreau

The highest form of vanity is love of fame.
George Santayana

If fame is only to come after death, I am in no hurry for it.
Martial

FAMILIARITY *Also see:* FRIENDSHIP.

Familiarity is a magician that is cruel to beauty but kind to ugliness.

Ouida

All objects lose by too familiar a view.

John Dryden

Familiarity breeds contempt—and children.

Mark Twain

Familiar acts are beautiful through love.

Percy Bysshe Shelley

Though familiarity may not breed contempt, it takes off the edge of admiration.

William Hazlitt

When a man becomes familiar with his goddess, she quickly sinks into a woman.

Joseph Addison

Nothing is wonderful when you get used to it.

Ed Howe

Familiarity is the root of the closest friendships, as well as the intensest hatreds.

Antoine Rivarol

FAMILY *Also see:* ANCESTRY, BIRTH, CHILDREN.

If you cannot get rid of the family skeleton, you may as well make it dance.

George Bernard Shaw

A happy family is but an earlier heaven.

John Bowring

The greatest thing in family life is to take a hint when a hint is intended—and not to take a hint when a hint isn't intended.

Robert Frost

The family is one of nature's masterpieces.

George Santayana

None but a mule denies his family.

Anonymous

The family you come from isn't as important as the family you're going to have.

Ring Lardner

I would rather start a family than finish one.

Don Marquis

Families with babies and families without babies are sorry for each other.

Ed Howe

A family is a unit composed not only of children but of men, women, an occasional animal, and the common cold.

Ogden Nash

He that raises a large family does, indeed, while he lives to observe them, stand a broader mark for sorrow; but then he stands a broader mark for pleasure too.

Benjamin Franklin

Family life is too intimate to be preserved by the spirit of justice. It can be sustained by a spirit of love which goes beyond justice.

Reinhold Niebuhr

FANATICISM *Also see:* ENTHUSIASM, TYRANNY, ZEAL.

The downright fanatic is nearer to the heart of things than the cool and slippery disputant. *Edwin Hubbel Chapin*

Fanaticism consists in redoubling your efforts when you have forgotten your aim. *George Santayana*

A fanatic is one who can't change his mind and won't change the subject. *Winston Churchill*

The worst vice of the fanatic is his sincerity. *Oscar Wilde*

Fanaticism, the false fire of an overheated mind. *William Cowper*

There is no strong performance without a little fanaticism in the performer. *Ralph Waldo Emerson*

A fanatic is a man who does what he thinks the Lord would do if only He knew the facts of the case. *Finley Peter Dunne*

> Fanatics have their dreams, wherewith they weave
> A paradise for a sect. *John Keats*

What is fanaticism today is the fashionable creed tomorrow, and trite as the multiplication table a week after. *Wendell Phillips*

FASHION *Also see:* APPEARANCE, DRESS.

Fashion is a form of ugliness so intolerable that we have to alter it every six months. *Oscar Wilde*

Fashion is something barbarous, for it produces innovation without reason and imitation without benefit. *George Santayana*

Fashion must be forever new, or she becomes insipid. *James Russell Lowell*

Fashion is what one wears oneself. What is unfashionable is what other people wear. *Oscar Wilde*

Give feminine fashions time enough and they will starve all the moths to death. *Anonymous*

Every generation laughs at the old fashions, but follows religiously the new. *Henry David Thoreau*

Fashion is the science of appearances, and it inspires one with the desire to seem rather than to be. *Edwin Hubbel Chapin*

Ten years before its time, a fashion is indecent; ten years after, it is hideous; but a century after, it is romantic. *James Laver*

Be not too early in the fashion, nor too long out of it; nor at any time in the extremes of it. *Johann Kaspar Lavater*

FATE *Also see:* CHARACTER, DESTINY, FORTUNE.

I do not believe in the word Fate. It is the refuge of every self-confessed failure.
Andrew Soutar

If you believe in fate, believe in it, at least, for your good.
Ralph Waldo Emerson

What a man thinks of himself, that it is which determines, or rather indicates, his fate.
Henry David Thoreau

We make our own fortunes and we call them fate.
Benjamin Disraeli

There is no good arguing with the inevitable.
James Russell Lowell

What must be shall be; and that which is a necessity to him that struggles, is little more than choice to him that is willing.
Seneca

Fate! There is no fate. Between the thought and the success God is the only agent.
Edward G. Bulwer-Lytton

Fate is the friend of the good, the guide of the wise, the tyrant of the foolish, the enemy of the bad.
William Rounseville Alger

Fate often puts all the material for happiness and prosperity into a man's hands just to see how miserable he can make himself.
Don Marquis

FATHER *Also see:* CHILDREN, FAMILY, PARENT.

Paternity is a career imposed on you without any inquiry into your fitness.
Adlai E. Stevenson

The fundamental defect of fathers is that they want their children to be a credit to them.
Bertrand Russell

The words that a father speaks to his children in the privacy of home are not heard by the world, but, as in whispering-galleries, they are clearly heard at the end and by posterity.
Jean Paul Richter

No man is responsible for his father. That is entirely his mother's affair.
Margaret Turnbull

The worst misfortune that can happen to an ordinary man is to have an extraordinary father.
Austin O'Malley

I don't want to be a pal, I want to be a father.
Clifton Fadiman

There was a time when father amounted to something in the United States. He was held with some esteem in the community; he had some authority in his own household; his views were sometimes taken seriously by his children; and even his wife paid heed to him from time to time.
Adlai E. Stevenson

Every father expects his boy to do the things he wouldn't do when he was young.
Kin Hubbard

FAULT *Also see:* COMPLAINT, CONFESSION, ENEMY, WEAKNESS.

People who have no faults are terrible; there is no way of taking advantage of them.   *Anatole France*

To find a fault is easy; to do better may be difficult.   *Plutarch*

His only fault is that he has none.   *Pliny the Elder*

A benevolent man should allow a few faults in himself, to keep his friends in countenance.   *Benjamin Franklin*

If you are pleased at finding faults, you are displeased at finding perfections.   *Johann Kaspar Lavater*

We confess small faults, in order to insinuate that we have no great ones.   *François de La Rochefoucauld*

I like a friend better for having faults that one can talk about.   *William Hazlitt*

If the best man's faults were written on his forehead, he would draw his hat over his eyes.   *Thomas Gray*

The greatest of faults, I should say, is to be conscious of none.   *Thomas Carlyle*

His very faults smack of the raciness of his good qualities.   *Washington Irving*

FEAR *Also see:* BOLDNESS, COURAGE, COWARDICE, CRIME, CRUELTY, DANGER, DISEASE, SUPERSTITION.

The man who fears suffering is already suffering from what he fears.   *Michel de Montaigne*

There's nothing I'm afraid of like scared people.   *Robert Frost*

Nothing in life is to be feared. It is only to be understood.   *Marie Curie*

He who fears being conquered is sure of defeat.   *Napoleon Bonaparte*

The only thing we have to fear is fear itself.   *Franklin Delano Roosevelt*

Logic and cold reason are poor weapons to fight fear and distrust. Only faith and generosity can overcome them.   *Jawaharlal Nehru*

Fear is a kind of bell . . . it is the soul's signal for rallying.   *Henry Ward Beecher*

If a man harbors any sort of fear, it percolates through all his thinking, damages his personality, makes him landlord to a ghost.   *Lloyd Douglas*

Fear is the tax that conscience pays to guilt.   *George Sewell*

FEELINGS ... See EMOTION

FIDELITY *Also see:* LOYALTY.

Fidelity is seven-tenths of business success.
James Parton

Another of our highly prized virtues is fidelity. We are immensely pleased with ourselves when we are faithful.
Ida Ross Wylie

An ideal wife is one who remains faithful to you but tries to be just as charming as if she weren't.
Sacha Guitry

It is better to be faithful than famous.
Theodore Roosevelt

It goes far toward making a man faithful to let him understand that you think him so; and he that does but suspect I will deceive him gives me a sort of right to do it.
Seneca

Constancy is the complement of all other human virtues.
Giuseppe Mazzini

Nothing is more noble, nothing more venerable than fidelity. Faithfulness and truth are the most sacred excellences and endowments of the human mind.
Cicero

FINANCE *Also see:* BUSINESS, GAIN, MONEY, SPECULATION.

A holding company is a thing where you hand an accomplice the goods while the policeman searches you.
Will Rogers

High finance isn't burglary or obtaining money by false pretenses, but rather a judicious selection from the best features of those fine arts.
Finley Peter Dunne

A financier is a pawn-broker with imagination.
Arthur Wing Pinero

The way to stop financial joy-riding is to arrest the chauffeur, not the automobile.
Woodrow Wilson

Alexander Hamilton originated the put and take system in our national treasury: the taxpayers put it in, and the politicians take it out.
Will Rogers

There is no such thing as an innocent purchaser of stocks.
Louis D. Brandeis

One-third of the people in the United States promote, while the other two-thirds provide.
Will Rogers

The money-changers have fled from their high seats in the temple of our civilization. We may now restore that temple to the ancient truths.
Franklin Delano Roosevelt

Financial sense is knowing that certain men will promise to do certain things, and fail.
Ed Howe

FIRMNESS *Also see:* DECISION, RESOLUTION.

The greatest firmness is the greatest mercy.   *Henry Wadsworth Longfellow*

Firmness of purpose is one of the most necessary sinews of character, and one of the best instruments of success. Without it genius wastes its efforts in a maze of inconsistencies.   *Lord Chesterfield*

When firmness is sufficient, rashness is unnecessary.   *Napoleon Bonaparte*

Real firmness is good for anything; strut is good for nothing.
Alexander Hamilton

The purpose firm is equal to the deed.   *Edward Young*

The superior man is firm in the right way, and not merely firm.
Confucius

Steadfastness is a noble quality, but unguided by knowledge or humility it becomes rashness or obstinacy.   *J. Swartz*

That which is called firmness in a king is called obstinacy in a donkey.
Lord Erskine

It is only persons of firmness that can have real gentleness. Those who appear gentle are, in general, only a weak character, which easily changes into asperity.   *François de La Rochefoucauld*

FLATTERY *Also see:* COMPLIMENT, PRAISE.

Flattery is from the teeth out. Sincere appreciation is from the heart out.
Dale Carnegie

Just praise is only a debt, but flattery is a present.   *Samuel Johnson*

Always let your flattery be seen through for what really flatters a man is that you think him worth flattering.   *George Bernard Shaw*

None are more taken in with flattery than the proud, who wish to be the first and are not.   *Benedict Spinoza*

Flattery is a kind of bad money, to which our vanity gives us currency.
François de La Rochefoucauld

It is better to fall among crows than flatterers; for those devour only the dead—these the living.   *Antisthenes*

It is easy to flatter; it is harder to praise.   *Jean Paul Richter*

Avoid flatterers, for they are thieves in disguise.   *William Penn*

Flattery is like cologne water, to be smelt of, not swallowed.
Josh Billings

Knavery and flattery are blood relations.   *Abraham Lincoln*

FOOL *Also see:* ADMIRATION, BROTHERHOOD, DESPAIR, QUESTION.

The best way to convince a fool that he is wrong is to let him have his own way. *Josh Billings*

Let us be thankful for the fools; but for them the rest of us could not succeed. *Mark Twain*

No fools are so troublesome as those who have some wit. *François de La Rochefoucauld*

To be a man's own fool is bad enough; but the vain man is everybody's. *William Penn*

What the fool does in the end, the wise man does in the beginning. *Proverb*

A fool can no more see his own folly than he can see his ears. *William Makepeace Thackeray*

Fools grow without watering. *Thomas Fuller*

Nobody can describe a fool to the life, without much patient self-inspection. *Frank Moore Colby*

FORCE *Also see:* CUSTOM, POWER, REVOLUTION, VIOLENCE, WAR.

When force is necessary, it must be applied boldly, decisively and completely. But one must know the limitations of force; one must know when to blend force with a maneuver, the blow with an agreement. *Leon Trotsky*

Force is not a remedy. *John Bright*

Force rules the world, and not opinion; but opinion is that which makes use of force. *Blaise Pascal*

There is such a thing as a nation being so right that it does not need to convince others by force that it is right. *Woodrow Wilson*

Right reason is stronger than force. *James A. Garfield*

Force is all-conquering, but its victories are short-lived. *Abraham Lincoln*

We love force and we care very little how it is exhibited. *Ralph Waldo Emerson*

The power that is supported by force alone will have cause often to tremble. *Lajos Kossuth*

In this age of the rule of brute force, it is almost impossible for anyone to believe that any one else could possibly reject the law of the final supremacy of brute force. *Mahatma Gandhi*

FORGIVENESS *Also see:* MERCY.

The secret of forgiving everything is to understand nothing.
George Bernard Shaw

To err is human; to forgive, divine. *Alexander Pope*

The weak can never forgive. Forgiveness is the attribute of the strong.
Mahatma Gandhi

Forgive many things in others; nothing in yourself. *Ausonius*

It is easier to forgive an enemy than a friend. *Madame Dorothée Deluzy*

"I can forgive, but I cannot forget," is only another way of saying, "I will
not forgive." Forgiveness ought to be like a cancelled note—torn in two,
and burned up, so that it never can be shown against one.
Henry Ward Beecher

Humanity is never so beautiful as when praying for forgiveness, or else
forgiving another. *Jean Paul Richter*

Always forgive your enemies—nothing annoys them so much.
Oscar Wilde

A woman who can't forgive should never have more than a nodding acquaintance with a man. *Ed Howe*

There is no revenge so complete as forgiveness. *Josh Billings*

FORTUNE *Also see:* FATE, MERIT, PURSUIT, WEALTH.

Fortune is ever seen accompanying industry. *Oliver Goldsmith*

He that waits upon fortune, is never sure of a dinner. *Benjamin Franklin*

Fortune knocks at every man's door once in a life, but in a good many
cases the man is in a neighboring saloon and does not hear her.
Mark Twain

Fortune is the rod of the weak, and the staff of the brave.
James Russell Lowell

Fortunes made in no time are like shirts made in no time; it's ten to one
if they hang long together. *Douglas Jerrold*

Every man is the architect of his own fortune. *Sallust*

It is a madness to make fortune the mistress of events, because in herself
she is nothing, but is ruled by prudence. *John Dryden*

Fortune is a great deceiver. She sells very dear the things she seems to
give us. *Vincent Voiture*

Nature magically suits a man to his fortunes, by making them the fruit of
his character. *Ralph Waldo Emerson*

FRAUD *Also see:* DECEIT, DISHONESTY.

It is fraud to accept what you cannot repay.   *Publilius Syrus*

The first and worst of all frauds is to cheat oneself.   *Gamaliel Bailey*

For the most part fraud in the end secures for its companions repentance and shame.   *Charles Simmons*

Keep a cow, and the milk won't have to be watered but once.
                                                                  Josh Billings

The more gross the fraud the more glibly will it go down, and the more greedily be swallowed, since folly will always find faith where impostors will find imprudence.   *Charles Caleb Colton*

All frauds, like the wall daubed with untempered mortar . . . always tend to the decay of what they are devised to support.   *Richard Whately*

FREEDOM *Also see:* BOOK, BORROWING, COUNTRY, DISCIPLINE, EDUCATION, END and MEANS, EQUALITY, FREEDOM of PRESS, FREEDOM of SPEECH, INDEPENDENCE, LIBERTY, SECURITY.

I know but one freedom and that is the freedom of the mind.
                                                            Antoine de Saint-Exupéry

No man is free who is not a master of himself.   *Epictetus*

Freedom is not worth having if it does not connote freedom to err.
                                                                  Mahatma Gandhi

The unity of freedom has never relied on uniformity of opinion.
                                                          John Fitzgerald Kennedy

A hungry man is not a free man.   *Adlai E. Stevenson*

Only our individual faith in freedom can keep us free.
                                                            Dwight D. Eisenhower

The cost of freedom is always high, but Americans have always paid it. And one path we shall never choose, and that is the path of surrender, or submission.   *John Fitzgerald Kennedy*

We are not free; it was not intended we should be. A book of rules is placed in our cradle, and we never get rid of it until we reach our graves. Then we are free, and only then.   *Ed Howe*

Freedom rings where opinions clash.   *Adlai E. Stevenson*

Freedom is not an ideal, it is not even a protection, if it means nothing more than the freedom to stagnate.   *Adlai E. Stevenson*

Freedom suppressed and again regained bites with keener fangs than freedom never endangered.   *Cicero*

The basic test of freedom is perhaps less in what we are free to do than in what we are free not to do.   *Eric Hoffer*

FREEDOM of the PRESS *Also see:* CENSORSHIP, LIBERTY.

Our liberty depends on the freedom of the press, and that cannot be limited without being lost.
Thomas Jefferson

The liberty of the press is a blessing when we are inclined to write against others, and a calamity when we find ourselves overborne by the multitude of our assailants.
Samuel Johnson

The free press is the mother of all our liberties and of our progress under liberty.
Adlai E. Stevenson

The press is not only free, it is powerful. That power is ours. It is the proudest that man can enjoy.
Benjamin Disraeli

Let it be impressed upon your minds, let it be instilled into your children, that the liberty of the press is the palladium of all the civil, political, and religious rights.
Junius

FREEDOM of SPEECH *Also see:* CENSORSHIP, DISSENT, LIBERTY, FREEDOM of the PRESS.

I disapprove of what you say, but will defend to the death your right to say it.
Voltaire

I have always been among those who believed that the greatest freedom of speech was the greatest safety, because if a man is a fool the best thing to do is to encourage him to advertise the fact by speaking.
Woodrow Wilson

It is by the goodness of God that in our country we have these three unspeakably precious things: freedom of speech, freedom of conscience and the prudence never to practice either of them.
Mark Twain

People demand freedom of speech to make up for the freedom of thought which they avoid.
Sören Kierkegaard

I realize that there are certain limitations placed upon the right of free speech. I may not be able to say all I think, but I am not going to say anything I do not think.
Eugene V. Debs

Personally I have no enthusiam for organized jeering sections but I hold that the spontaneous right of raspberry should be denied to no one in America.
Heywood Broun

Free speech is to a great people what winds are to oceans and malarial regions, which waft away the elements of disease and bring new elements of health; and where free speech is stopped, miasma is bred, and death comes fast.
Henry Ward Beecher

Every man has a right to be heard, but no man has the right to strangle democracy with a single set of vocal chords.
Adlai E. Stevenson

Better a thousandfold abuse of free speech than denial of free speech. The abuse dies in a day, but the denial stays the life of the people, and entombs the hope of the race.
Charles Bradlaugh

FRIENDSHIP
Also see: AFFECTION, BROTHERHOOD, ENEMY, FAMILIARITY, LOVE, PRAISE.

The only way to have a friend is to be one.
Ralph Waldo Emerson

Friendship is neither a formality nor a mode: it is rather a life.
David Grayson

Friendship is always a sweet responsibility, never an opportunity.
Kahlil Gibran

If a man does not make new acquaintances as he advances through life, he will soon find himself left alone; one should keep his friendships in constant repair.
Samuel Johnson

Friendship is one mind in two bodies.
Mencius

Acquaintance: a degree of friendship called slight when its object is poor or obscure, and intimate when he is rich or famous.
Ambrose Bierce

A home-made friend wears longer than one you buy in the market.
Austin O'Malley

The best way to keep your friends is not to give them away.
Wilson Mizner

Friendship without self-interest is one of the rare and beautiful things of life.
James Francis Byrnes

Show me a genuine case of platonic friendship, and I shall show you two old or homely faces.
Austin O'Malley

Friendship is almost always the union of a part of one mind with a part of another: people are friends in spots.
George Santayana

Thy friendship oft has made my heart to ache; do be my enemy—for friendship's sake.
William Blake

FRUGALITY . . . See ECONOMY

FUTURE
Also see: PAST, PRESENT.

When all else is lost, the future still remains.
Christian Nestell Bovee

I never think of the future. It comes soon enough.
Albert Einstein

I like the dreams of the future better than the history of the past.
Patrick Henry

My interest is in the future because I am going to spend the rest of my life there.
Charles F. Kettering

The trouble with our times is that the future is not what it used to be.
Paul Valery

G

GAIN *Also see:* DUTY.

And gain is gain, however small.   *Robert Browning*

Sometimes the best gain is to lose.   *George Herbert*

For everything you have missed you have gained something.
Ralph Waldo Emerson

Gain cannot be made without some other person's loss.   *Publilius Syrus*

The true way to gain much, is never to desire to gain too much.
Francis Beaumont

No gain is so certain as that which proceeds from the economical use of what you already have.   *Latin Proverb*

It is always sound business to take any obtainable net gain, at any cost and at any risk to the rest of the community.   *Thornstein Veblen*

GALLANTRY *Also see:* COURTESY, FLATTERY.

Gallantry of the mind is saying the most empty things in an agreeable manner.   *François de la Rochefoucauld*

To give up your seat in a car to a woman, and tread on your neighbor's foot to get even.   *Elbert Hubbard*

Gallantry to women—the sure road to their favor—is nothing but the appearance of extreme devotion to all their wants and wishes, a delight in their satisfaction, and a confidence in yourself as being able to contribute toward it.   *William Hazlitt*

To do a perfectly unselfish act for selfish motives.   *Elbert Hubbard*

GENEROSITY *Also see:* ARISTOCRACY, CHARITY, FEAR, KINDNESS.

Generosity during life is a very different thing from generosity in the hour of death; one proceeds from genuine liberality and benevolence, the other from pride or fear.   *Horace Mann*

Generosity is giving more than you can, and pride is taking less than you need.   *Kahlil Gibran*

The more he cast away the more he had.   *John Bunyan*

What seems to be generosity is often no more than disguised ambition, which overlooks a small interest in order to secure a great one.
François de la Rochefoucauld

What I gave, I have; what I spent, I had; what I kept, I lost.   *Old Epitaph*

If there be any truer measure of a man than by what he does, it must be by what he gives.   *Robert South*

GENIUS *Also see:* ABILITY, ART, COMMON SENSE.

Genius does what it must, and talent does what it can.
Edward G. Bulwer-Lytton

When human power becomes so great and original that we can account for it only as a kind of divine imagination, we call it genius. *William Crashaw*

Genius is entitled to respect only when it promotes the peace and improves the happiness of mankind.
Lord Essex

One of the strongest characteristics of genius is the power of lighting its own fire. *John Watson Foster*

True genius sees with the eyes of a child and thinks with the brain of a genii. *Puzant Kevork Thomajan*

I don't want to be a genius—I have enough problems just trying to be a man. *Albert Camus*

Genius begins great works; labor alone finishes them. *Joseph Joubert*

Time, place, and action may with pains be wrought,
But Genius must be born; and never can be taught. *John Dryden*

Genius is one per cent inspiration and ninety-nine per cent perspiration.
Thomas A. Edison

To believe your own thought, to believe that what is true for you in your private heart is true for all men—that is genius. *Ralph Waldo Emerson*

Genius without education is like silver in the mine. *Benjamin Franklin*

Genius is the ability to act rightly without precedent—the power to do the right thing the first time. *Elbert Hubbard*

It is the privilege of genius that to it life never grows commonplace as to the rest of us. *James Russell Lowell*

When Nature has work to be done, she creates a genius to do it.
Ralph Waldo Emerson

No great genius is without an admixture of madness. *Aristotle*

Sometimes men come by the name of genius in the same way that certain insects come by the name of centipede—not because they have a hundred feet, but because most people can't count above fourteen.
G. C. Lichtenberg

Genius is an infinite capacity for taking life by the scruff of the neck.
Christopher Quill

When a true genius appears in this world you may know him by the sign that the dunces are all in confederacy against him. *Jonathan Swift*

GENTLEMAN *Also see:* COURTESY.

. . . one who never hurts anyone's feelings unintentionally.   *Oliver Herford*

We sometimes meet an original gentleman, who, if manners had not existed, would have invented them.   *Ralph Waldo Emerson*

This is the final test of a gentleman: his respect for those who can be of no possible service to him.   *William Lyon Phelps*

A true man of honor feels humbled himself when he cannot help humbling others.   *Robert E. Lee*

The true gentleman is subtly poised between an inner tact and an outer defense.   *Puzant Kevork Thomajan*

The man who is always talking about being a gentleman, never is one.   *Robert S. Surtees*

GIRLS *Also see:* WOMAN.

A homely girl hates mirrors.   *Proverb*

Little girls are the nicest things that happen to people.   *Allan Beck*

A girl is Innocence playing in the mud, Beauty standing on its head, and Motherhood dragging a doll by the foot.   *Allan Beck*

It is a common phenomenon that just the prettiest girls find it so difficult to get a man.   *Heinrich Heine*

I am fond of children—except boys.   *Lewis Carroll*

Some girls never know what they are going to do from one husband to another.   *Tom Masson*

I never expected to see the day when girls would get sunburned in the places they do now.   *Will Rogers*

GLORY *Also see:* FAME, HONOR.

For glory gives herself only to those who have always dreamed of her.   *Charles de Gaulle*

Glory built on selfish principles, is shame and guilt.   *William Cowper*

Our greatest glory consists not in never falling, but in rising every time we fall.   *Oliver Goldsmith*

Glory is the shadow of virtue.   *Latin Proverb*

Real glory springs from the silent conquest of ourselves.   *Joseph P. Thompson*

The fire of glory is the torch of the mind.   *Anonymous*

Glory paid to our ashes comes too late.   *Martial*

GLUTTON   *Also see:* ABSTINENCE, APPETITE, EATING.

The miser and the glutton are two facetious buzzards: one hides his store, and the other stores his hide.
Josh Billings

Their kitchen is their shrine, the cook their priest, the table their altar, and their belly their god.
Charles Buck

Glutton: one who digs his grave with his teeth.
French Proverb

A poor man who eats too much, as contradistinguished from a gourmand, who is a rich man who "lives well."
Elbert Hubbard

They whose sole bliss is eating can give but that one brutish reason why they live.
Juvenal

The pleasures of the palate deal with us like the Egyptian thieves, who strangle those whom they embrace.
Seneca

The fool that eats till he is sick must fast till he is well.
George W. Thornbury

One meal a day is enough for a lion, and it ought to be for a man.
George Fordyce

In general, mankind, since the improvement of cookery, eats twice as much as nature requires.
Benjamin Franklin

One should eat to live, not live to eat.
Benjamin Franklin

GOD   *Also see:* AGNOSTICISM, ARTIST, ATHEISM, BABY, CREATIVITY, DEMOCRACY, DISHONESTY, EARTH, FAITH, FREEDOM of the PRESS, HEAVEN, RELIGION.

I don't say what God is, but a name
That somehow answers us when we are driven
To feel and think how little we have to do
With what we are.
Edwin Arlington Robinson

I fear God, and next to God I chiefly fear him who fears Him not.
Saadi

If God did not exist it would be necessary to invent Him.
Voltaire

God, as some cynic has said, is always on the side which has the best football coach.
Heywood Broun

God enters by a private door into every individual.
Ralph Waldo Emerson

God is clever, but not dishonest.
Albert Einstein

God is not a cosmic bell-boy for whom we can press a button to get things.
Harry Emerson Fosdick

What is it: is man only a blunder of God, or God only a blunder of man?
Nietzsche

You must believe in God, in spite of what the clergy say.
Benjamin Jowett

GOD (continued)

If there is a God, atheism must seem to Him as less of an insult than religion.
Goncourt

Satan hasn't a single salaried helper; the Opposition employ a million.
Mark Twain

God never made His work for man to mend.
John Dryden

God sends us meat, the devil sends us cooks.
Proverb

God is more truly imagined than expressed, and He exists more truly than He is imagined.
St. Augustine

God is the brave man's hope, and not the coward's excuse.
Plutarch

God made the country and man made the town.
William Cowper

It's God—I'd have known Him by Blake's picture anywhere.
Robert Frost

If God has created us in His image, we have more than returned the compliment.
Voltaire

God created man in His own image, says the Bible; philosophers reverse the process: they create God in theirs.
G. C. Lichtenberg

When we know what God is, we shall be gods ourselves.
George Bernard Shaw

There cannot be a God because if there were one, I could not believe that I was not He.
Nietzsche

We love the Lord, of course, but we often wonder what He finds in us.
Ed Howe

An honest God is the noblest work of man.
Robert Green Ingersoll

You can believe in God without believing in immortality, but it is hard to see how anyone can believe in immortality and not believe in God.
Ernest Dimnet

The best way to know God is to love many things.
Vincent van Gogh

Two men please God—who serves Him with all his heart because he knows Him; who seeks Him with all his heart because he knows Him not.
Nikita Ivanovich Panin

Men talk of "finding God," but no wonder it is difficult; He is hidden in that darkest hiding-place, your heart. You yourself are a part of Him.
Christopher Morley

Man is, and always has been, a maker of gods. It has been the most serious and significant occupation of his sojourn in the world.
John Burroughs

In the faces of men and women I see God.
Walt Whitman

GOLD *Also see:* AVARICE, MISER.

Gold like the sun, which melts wax, but hardens clay, expands great souls.
Antoine Rivarol

The man who works for the gold in the job rather than for the money in the pay envelope, is the fellow who gets on.   *Joseph French Johnson*

Gold will be slave or master.   *Horace*

A mask of gold hides all deformities.   *Thomas Dekker*

It is much better to have your gold in the hand than in the heart.
Thomas Fuller

Gold's father is dirt, yet it regards itself as noble.   *Yiddish Proverb*

Curst greed of gold, what crimes thy tyrant power has caused.   *Vergil*

Gold has worked down from Alexander's time . . . When something holds good for two thousand years I do not believe it can be so because of prejudice or mistaken theory.   *Bernard M. Baruch*

There is thy gold; worse poison to men's souls,
Doing more murther in this loathsome world,
Than these poor compounds that thou mayst not sell:
William Shakespeare

GOSSIP *Also see:* CONVERSATION, SLANDER.

Of every ten persons who talk about you, nine will say something bad, and the tenth will say something good in a bad way.   *Antoine Rivarol*

Gossip is always a personal confession either of malice or imbecility.
Josiah Gilbert Holland

The only time people dislike gossip is when you gossip about them.
Will Rogers

Gossip is the art of saying nothing in a way that leaves practically nothing unsaid.   *Walter Winchell*

Truth is not exciting enough to those who depend on the characters and lives of their neighbors for all their amusement.   *George Bancroft*

Knowledge is power if you know about the right person.
Ethel Watts Mumford

There isn't much to be seen in a little town, but what you hear makes up for it.   *Kin Hubbard*

A cruel story runs on wheels, and every hand oils the wheels as they run.
Ouida

That which is everybody's business is nobody's business.   *Izaak Walton*

None are so fond of secrets as those who do not mean to keep them.
Charles Caleb Colton

GOVERNMENT *Also see:* AUTHORITY, CITIZENSHIP, COMPROMISE, DEMOCRACY, PARTY, POLITICS.

The best of all governments is that which teaches us to govern ourselves.
Johann Wolfgang von Goethe

Good government is no substitute for self-government. *Mahatma Gandhi*

Government is a kind of legalized pillage. *Elbert Hubbard*

The government is us; we are the government, you and I.
Theodore Roosevelt

You can't run a government solely on a business basis . . . Government should be human. It should have a heart. *Herbert Henry Lehman*

All free governments are managed by the combined wisdom and folly of the people. *James A. Garfield*

A government is the only known vessel that leaks from the top.
James Reston

No man is good enough to govern another man without that other's consent. *Abraham Lincoln*

My experience in government is that when things are non-controversial and beautifully coordinated, there is not much going on.
John Fitzgerald Kennedy

He mocks the people who proposes that the government shall protect the rich that they in turn may care for the laboring poor. *Grover Cleveland*

GRACE

Beauty and grace command the world. *Park Benjamin*

A graceful and pleasing figure is a perpetual letter of recommendation.
Francis Bacon

Gracefulness has been defined to be the outward expression of the inward harmony of the soul. *William Hazlitt*

He does it with a better grace, but I do it more natural. *William Shakespeare*

Grace is to the body, what good sense is to the mind.
François de La Rochefoucauld

Grace is savage and must be savage in order to be perfect.
Charles A. Stoddard

God appoints our graces to be nurses to other men's weaknesses.
Henry Ward Beecher

How inimitably graceful children are before they learn to dance.
Samuel Taylor Coleridge

Do you know that the ready concession of minor points is a part of the grace of life? *Henry Harland*

GRATITUDE

Gratitude is one of the least articulate of the emotions, especially when it is deep.   *Felix Frankfurter*

Gratitude is the heart's memory.   *French Proverb*

Gratitude is a duty which ought to be paid, but which none have a right to expect.   *Jean Jacques Rousseau*

Gratitude is one of those things that cannot be bought. It must be born with men, or else all the obligations in the world will not create it.   *Lord Halifax*

If you pick up a starving dog and make him prosperous, he will not bite you. This is the principal difference between a dog and a man.   *Mark Twain*

Gratitude is the fairest blossom which springs from the soul.   *Henry Ward Beecher*

Gratitude is not only the greatest of virtues, but the parent of all the others.   *Cicero*

Nothing tires a man more than to be grateful all the time.   *Ed Howe*

There is as much greatness of mind in acknowledging a good turn, as in doing it.   *Seneca*

GRAVE *Also see:* DEATH, MONUMENT.

The only difference between a rut and a grave is their dimensions.   *Ellen Glasgow*

He spake well who said that graves are the footprints of angels.   *Henry Wadsworth Longfellow*

O how small a portion of earth will hold us when we are dead, who ambitiously seek after the whole world while we are living.   *Philip II*

An angel's arm can't snatch me from the grave; legions of angels can't confine me there.   *Edward Young*

A grave, wherever found, preaches a short and pithy sermon to the soul.   *Nathaniel Hawthorne*

The grave is still the best shelter against the storms of destiny.   *G. C. Lichtenberg*

There is but one easy place in this world, and that is the grave.   *Henry Ward Beecher*

We weep over the graves of infants and the little ones taken from us by death; but an early grave may be the shortest way to heaven.   *Tryon Edwards*

GRAVITY   *Also see:* SORROW.

There is gravity in wisdom, but no particular wisdom in gravity.
Josh Billings

Too much gravity argues a shallow mind.   *Johann Kaspar Lavater*

Gravity is a trick of the body devised to conceal deficiencies of the mind.
François de La Rochefoucauld

Those wanting wit affect gravity, and go by the name of solid men.
John Dryden

Gravity is only the bark of wisdom; but it preserves it.   *Confucius*

GREED   *Also see:* AVARICE, DESIRE, MISER, SELFISHNESS.

The most pitiful human ailment is a birdseed heart.   *Wilson Mizner*

The greed of gain has no time or limit to its capaciousness. Its one object is to produce and consume. It has pity neither for beautiful nature nor for living human beings. It is ruthlessly ready without a moment's hesitation to crush beauty and life out of them, molding them into money.
Rabindranath Tagore

The covetous man pines in plenty, like Tantalus up to the chin in water, and yet thirsty.   *Thomas Adams*

It is economic slavery, the savage struggle for a crumb, that has converted mankind into wolves and sheep . . . My prison-house . . . is but the intensified replica of the world beyond, the larger prison locked with the levers of Greed, guarded by the spawn of Hunger.   *Alexander Berkman*

There is no fire like passion, there is no shark like hatred, there is no snare like folly, there is no torrent like greed.   *Buddha*

GRIEF   *Also see:* AFFLICTION, MISERY, SORROW.

It is foolish to tear one's hair in grief, as though sorrow would be made less by baldness.   *Cicero*

The only cure for grief is action.   *George Henry Lewes*

Excess of grief for the dead is madness; for it is an injury to the living, and the dead know it not.   *Xenophon*

Grief is the agony of an instant; the indulgence of grief the blunder of a life.   *Benjamin Disraeli*

While grief is fresh, every attempt to divert only irritates. You must wait till it be digested, and then amusement will dissipate the remains of it.
Samuel Johnson

There is no grief like the grief that does not speak.
Henry Wadsworth Longfellow

GUEST

Nobody can be as agreeable as an uninvited guest. *Kin Hubbard*

No one can be so welcome a guest that he will not annoy his host after three days. *Plautus*

Every guest hates the others, and the host hates them all.
Albanian Proverb

The first day, a guest; the second, a burden; the third, a pest.
Edouard R. Laboulaye

Visitors are insatiable devourers of time, and fit only for those who, if they did not visit, would do nothing. *William Cowper*

A civil guest will no more talk all, than eat all the feast. *George Herbert*

GUILT *Also see:* CONSCIENCE, CRIME, REPENTANCE.

Every man is guilty of all the good he didn't do. *Voltaire*

The guilty is he who meditates a crime; the punishment is his who lays the plot. *Conte Vittorio Alfieri*

The greatest incitement to guilt is the hope of sinning with impunity.
Cicero

Guilt once harbored in the conscious breast, intimidates the brave, degrades the great. *Samuel Johnson*

From the body of one guilty deed a thousand ghostly fears and haunting thoughts proceed. *William Wordsworth*

Action and care will in time wear down the strongest frame, but guilt and melancholy are poisons of quick dispatch. *Thomas Paine*

> Guilt is the source of sorrow, 'tis the fiend,
> Th' avenging fiend, that follows us behind
> With whips and stings. *Nicholas Rowe*

He who flees from trial confesses his guilt. *Publilius Syrus*

It is base to filch a purse, daring to embezzle a million, but it is great beyond measure to steal a crown. The sin lessens as the guilt increases.
Johann von Schiller

Suspicion always haunts the guilty mind. *William Shakespeare*

Men's minds are too ready to excuse guilt in themselves. *Livy*

Every guilty person is his own hangman. *Seneca*

Guilt is always jealous. *John Ray*

H

HABIT *Also see:* DEBT, DUTY, TRADITION.

Each year, one vicious habit rooted out, in time ought to make the worst man good. *Benjamin Franklin*

Habit, if not resisted, soon becomes necessity. *St. Augustine*

A single bad habit will mar an otherwise faultless character, as an ink-drop soileth the pure white page. *Hosea Ballou*

The unfortunate thing about this world is that the good habits are much easier to give up than the bad ones. *W. Somerset Maugham*

Cultivate only the habits that you are willing should master you. *Elbert Hubbard*

The chains of habit are too weak to be felt until they are too strong to be broken. *Samuel Johnson*

> Sow an act and you reap a habit.
> Sow a habit and you reap a character.
> Sow a character and you reap a destiny. *Charles Reade*

Habit is habit and not to be flung out of the window by any man, but coaxed downstairs a step at a time. *Mark Twain*

Habit converts luxurious enjoyments into dull and daily necessities. *Aldous Huxley*

Good habits result from resisting temptation. *Ancient Proverb*

Habits are to the soul what the veins and arteries are to the blood, the courses in which it moves. *Horace Bushnell*

Good habits, which bring our lower passions and appetites under automatic control, leave our natures free to explore the larger experiences of life. Too many of us divide and dissipate our energies in debating actions which should be taken for granted. *Ralph W. Sockman*

HAIR

By common consent gray hairs are a crown of glory; the only object of respect that can never excite envy. *George Bancroft*

Gray hair is a sign of age, not of wisdom. *Greek Proverb*

Gray hairs are death's blossoms. *English Proverb*

The hair is the richest ornament of women. *Martin Luther*

> Babies haven't any hair;
>   Old men's heads are just as bare;—
> Between the cradle and the grave
>   Lies a haircut and a shave. *Samuel Hoffenstein*

HAPPINESS

Also see: APPEARANCE, BEAUTY, CHEERFULNESS, DUTY, ENJOYMENT, FAITH, FATE, PLEASURE, SECURITY, ZEST.

It is pretty hard to tell what does bring happiness; poverty and wealth have both failed. *Kin Hubbard*

Happiness is not a reward—it is a consequence. Suffering is not a punishment—it is a result. *Robert Green Ingersoll*

Happiness is not a destination. It is a method of life. *Burton Hillis*

Be happy while you're living, for you're a long time dead. *Scottish Proverb*

To fill the hour—that is happiness. *Ralph Waldo Emerson*

A person is never happy except at the price of some ignorance. *Anatole France*

Happiness makes up in height for what it lacks in length. *Robert Frost*

The foolish man seeks happiness in the distance, the wise grows it under his feet. *James Oppenheim*

The grand essentials of happiness are: something to do, something to love, and something to hope for. *Allan K. Chalmers*

Happiness is the harvest of a quiet eye. *Austin O'Malley*

Happiness is like a sunbeam, which the least shadow intercepts, while adversity is often as the rain of spring. *Chinese Proverb*

Happiness isn't something you experience; it's something you remember. *Oscar Levant*

HARDSHIP ... See ADVERSITY

HASTE

No man who is in a hurry is quite civilized. *Will Durant*

Manners require time, and nothing is more vulgar than haste. *Ralph Waldo Emerson*

Though I am always in haste, I am never in a hurry. *John Wesley*

Take time for all things: great haste makes great waste. *Benjamin Franklin*

Make haste slowly. *Latin Proverb*

Rapidity does not always mean progress, and hurry is akin to waste. The old fable of the hare and the tortoise is just as good now, and just as true, as when it was first written. *Charles A. Stoddard*

Haste and rashness are storms and tempests, breaking and wrecking business; but nimbleness is a full, fair wind, blowing it with speed to the heaven. *Thomas Fuller*

HATE *Also see:* BLINDNESS, ENEMY.

Hatred does not cease by hatred, but only by love; this is the eternal rule.
Buddha

Hatred is the madness of the heart. *Lord Byron*

Heaven has no rage like love to hatred turned. *William Congreve*

A man who lives, not by what he loves but what he hates, is a sick man.
Archibald MacLeish

When our hatred is violent, it sinks us even beneath those we hate.
François de La Rochefoucauld

To hate fatigues. *Jean Rostand*

It is better to be hated for what you are than to be loved for what you are not. *André Gide*

There is no faculty of the human soul so persistent and universal as that of hatred. *Henry Ward Beecher*

Hatred is self-punishment. *Hosea Ballou*

I shall never permit myself to stoop so low as to hate any man.
Booker T. Washington

National hatred is something peculiar. You will always find it strongest and most violent where there is the lowest degree of culture.
Johann Wolfgang von Goethe

HEALTH *Also see:* BODY, CHEERFULNESS, DISEASE.

He who has health, has hope; and he who has hope, has everything.
Arabian Proverb

To become a thoroughly good man is the best prescription for keeping a sound mind and a sound body. *Francis Bowen*

Some people think that doctors and nurses can put scrambled eggs back into the shell. *Dorothy Canfield Fisher*

It is a wearisome disease to preserve health by too strict a regimen.
François de La Rochefoucauld

If I had my own way I'd make health catching instead of disease.
Robert Green Ingersoll

The only way to keep your health is to eat what you don't want, drink what you don't like, and do what you'd rather not. *Mark Twain*

There's a lot of people in this world who spend so much time watching their health that they haven't the time to enjoy it. *Josh Billings*

HEART *Also see:* CHARITY, COMPASSION, CONFIDENCE, COURAGE, GREED, GOVERNMENT, LOVE.

The head learns new things, but the heart forever more practices old experiences. *Henry Ward Beecher*

Wealth and want equally harden the human heart. *Theodore Parker*

The heart has reasons that reason does not understand. *Jacques Bènigne Bossuet*

There is no instinct like that of the heart. *Lord Byron*

The heart seldom feels what the mouth expresses. *Jean Galbert de Campistron*

The heart is forever making the head its fool. *François de La Rochefoucauld*

The heart of a fool is in his mouth, but the mouth of the wise man is in his heart. *Benjamin Franklin*

As the arteries grow hard, the heart grows soft. *H. L. Mencken*

Nothing is less in our power than the heart, and far from commanding we are forced to obey it. *Jean Jacques Rousseau*

Two things are bad for the heart—running up stairs and running down people. *Bernard M. Baruch*

———————

HEAVEN *Also see:* AMBITION, DEMOCRACY, FAMILY, HELL, HOME.

What a man misses mostly in heaven is company. *Mark Twain*

Heaven will be inherited by every man who has heaven in his soul. *Henry Ward Beecher*

To be with God. *Confucius*

What a pity the only way to heaven is in a hearse. *Stanislaw J. Lec*

The few men who have managed to reach heaven must be terribly spoiled by this time. *Ed Howe*

On earth there is no heaven, but there are pieces of it. *Jules Renard*

I don't like to commit myself about heaven and hell—you see, I have friends in both places. *Mark Twain*

To get to heaven, turn right and keep straight. *Anonymous*

The main object of religion is not to get a man into heaven, but to get heaven into him. *Thomas Hardy*

HELL
Also see: CHRISTIANITY, DECEIT, DIPLOMACY, HEAVEN.

Hell is truth seen too late—duty neglected in its season.   *Tryon Edwards*

There may be some doubt about hell beyond the grave but there is no doubt about there being one on this side of it.   *Ed Howe*

I never give them hell; I just tell the truth and they think it's hell.
Harry S. Truman

If there is no hell, a good many preachers are obtaining money under false pretenses.   *William A. Sunday*

The wicked work harder to reach hell than the righteous to reach heaven.
Josh Billings

The road to hell is thick with taxicabs.   *Don Herold*

To be in hell is to drift; to be in heaven is to steer.
George Bernard Shaw

> It doesn't matter what they preach,
>   Of high or low degree;
> The old Hell of the Bible
>   Is hell enough for me.   *Frank L. Stanton*

The road to Hell is paved with good intentions.   *Karl Marx*

HELP
Also see: CHARITY, GENEROSITY.

If you're in trouble, or hurt or need—go to the poor people. They're the only ones that'll help—the only ones.   *John Steinbeck*

He stands erect by bending over the fallen. He rises by lifting others.
Robert Green Ingersoll

God helps them that help themselves.   *Proverb*

Nothing makes one feel so strong as a call for help.   *George MacDonald*

Give me the ready hand rather than the ready tongue.   *Giuseppi Garibaldi*

Light is the task where many share the toil.   *Homer*

Every great man is always being helped by everybody; for his gift is to get good out of all things and all persons.   *John Ruskin*

When a person is down in the world, an ounce of help is better than a pound of preaching.   *Edward G. Bulwer-Lytton*

The race of mankind would perish did they cease to aid each other. We cannot exist without mutual help. All therefore that need aid have a right to ask it from their fellow-men; and no one who has the power of granting can refuse it without guilt.   *Walter Scott*

HEROISM *Also see:* COURAGE.

Self-trust is the essence of heroism. *Ralph Waldo Emerson*

The world's battlefields have been in the heart chiefly; more heroism has been displayed in the household and the closet, than on the most memorable battlefields in history. *Henry Ward Beecher*

Heroes are not known by the loftiness of their carriage; the greatest braggarts are generally the merest cowards. *Jean Jacques Rousseau*

A hero is no braver than an ordinary man, but he is braver five minutes longer. *Ralph Waldo Emerson*

Hero worship is strongest where there is least regard for human freedom. *Herbert Spencer*

The main thing about being a hero is to know when to die. *Will Rogers*

We can't all be heroes because someone has to sit on the curb and clap as they go by. *Will Rogers*

In war the heroes always outnumber the soldiers ten to one. *H. L. Mencken*

Hero-worship is mostly idol gossip. *Anonymous*

Every hero becomes at last a bore. *Ralph Waldo Emerson*

A boy doesn't have to go to war to be a hero; he can say he doesn't like pie when he sees there isn't enough to go around. *Ed Howe*

HISTORY *Also see:* CUSTOM, SPIRIT, TRADITION.

History is bunk. *Henry Ford*

What is history but a fable agreed upon? *Napoleon Bonaparte*

History is little more than the register of the crimes, follies and misfortunes of mankind. *Edward Gibbon*

The men who make history have not time to write it. *Metternich*

The main thing is to make history, not to write it. *Otto von Bismarck*

No historian can take part with—or against—the forces he has to study. To him even the extinction of the human race should merely be a fact to be grouped with other vital statistics. *Henry Brooks Adams*

God cannot alter the past, but historians can. *Samuel Butler*

Fellow citizens, we cannot escape history. *Abraham Lincoln*

History repeats itself, and that's one of the things that's wrong with history. *Clarence Darrow*

History is nothing but a pack of tricks that we play upon the dead. *Voltaire*

HOME *Also see:* FAMILY, FATHER.

My precept to all who build is, that the owner should be an ornament to the house, and not the house to the owner. *Cicero*

A hundred men may make an encampment, but it takes a woman to make a home. *Chinese Proverb*

Home is where the heart is. *Pliny the Elder*

Home is the place where, when you have to go there, they have to take you in. *Robert Frost*

Home is the most popular, and will be the most enduring of all earthly establishments. *Channing Pollock*

Home interprets heaven. Home is heaven for beginners. *Charles H. Parkhurst*

He is the happiest, be he king or peasant, who finds peace in his home. *Johann Wolfgang von Goethe*

Home life is no more natural to us than a cage is to a cockatoo. *George Bernard Shaw*

Home, the spot of earth supremely blest,
A dearer, sweeter spot than all the rest. *Robert Montgomery*

The worst feeling in the world is the homesickness that comes over a man occasionally when he is at home. *Ed Howe*

HONESTY *Also see:* ACCURACY, CANDOR, DISHONESTY, DISTRUST, TRUTH.

I would give no thought of what the world might say of me, if I could only transmit to posterity the reputation of an honest man. *Sam Houston*

Honesty is the rarest wealth anyone can possess, and yet all the honesty in the world ain't lawful tender for a loaf of bread. *Josh Billings*

Honesty pays, but it don't seem to pay enough to suit some people. *Kin Hubbard*

We must make the world honest before we can honestly say to our children that honesty is the best policy. *George Bernard Shaw*

Make yourself an honest man, and then you may be sure there is one less rascal in the world. *Thomas Carlyle*

Men are able to trust one another, knowing the exact degree of dishonesty they are entitled to expect. *Stephen Butler Leacock*

Some persons are likeable in spite of their unswerving integrity. *Don Marquis*

Honesty is the best policy—when there is money in it. *Mark Twain*

An honest man's the noblest work of God. *Alexander Pope*

HONOR *Also see:* DIGNITY, DRESS, ESTEEM, GLORY, RESPECT.

All honor's wounds are self-inflicted.   *Andrew Carnegie*

It is better to deserve honors and not have them than to have them and not deserve them.   *Mark Twain*

Woman's honor is nice as ermine; it will not bear a soil.   *John Dryden*

The difference between a moral man and a man of honor is that the latter regrets a discreditable act even when it has worked.   *H. L. Mencken*

Honor lies in honest toil.   *Grover Cleveland*

Better to die ten thousand deaths than wound my honor.   *Joseph Addison*

When a virtuous man is raised, it brings gladness to his friends, grief to his enemies, and glory to his posterity.   *Ben Jonson*

The louder he talked of his honor, the faster we counted our spoons.
Ralph Waldo Emerson

When faith is lost, when honor dies, the man is dead!
John Greenleaf Whittier

HOPE *Also see:* ANTICIPATION, ATHEISM, BELIEF, BIBLE, CREDULITY, DESPAIR, DISAPPOINTMENT, FAITH, TRUST.

To the sick, while there is life there is hope.   *Cicero*

Hope for the best, but prepare for the worst.   *English Proverb*

A woman's hopes are woven of sunbeams; a shadow annihilates them.
George Eliot

We should not expect something for nothing but we all do, and we call it hope.   *Ed Howe*

Every cloud has a silver lining, but it is sometimes difficult to get it to the mint.   *Don Marquis*

He that lives upon hope will die fasting.   *Benjamin Franklin*

Hope is the only universal liar who never loses his reputation for veracity.
Robert Green Ingersoll

Hope is the struggle of the soul, breaking loose from what is perishable, and attesting her eternity.   *Herman Melville*

A misty morning does not signify a cloudy day.   *Ancient Proverb*

In all things it is better to hope than to despair.
Johann Wolfgang von Goethe

Hope is the parent of faith.   *Cyrus A. Bartol*

HUMANITY
Also see: AMERICA, BROTHERHOOD, EMOTION, FOR-
GIVENESS, HUMILITY.

We cannot despair of humanity, since we ourselves are human beings.
Albert Einstein

There are times when one would like to hang the whole human race, and
finish the farce.
Mark Twain

Humanity is the sin of God.
Theodore Parker

There is nothing on earth divine except humanity.
Walter Savage Landor

The true grandeur of humanity is in moral elevation, sustained, enlightened
and decorated by the intellect of man.
Charles Sumner

Humanity to me is not a mob. A mob is a degeneration of humanity. A
mob is humanity going the wrong way.
Frank Lloyd Wright

HUMAN NATURE
Also see: BROTHERHOOD, LIFE, MAN, SOCIETY.

We have provided for the survival of man against all enemies except his
fellow man.
Lyman Lloyd Bryson

It is human nature to think wisely and act foolishly.
Anatole France

It is easier to love humanity as a whole than to love one's neighbor.
Eric Hoffer

Some of us are like wheelbarrows—only useful when pushed, and very
easily upset.
Jack Herbert

Every so often, we pass laws repealing human nature.
Howard Lindsay

There is a great deal of human nature in people.
Mark Twain

It will be very generally found that those who will sneer habitually at
human nature, and affect to despise it, are among its worst and least pleasant samples.
Charles Dickens

HUMILITY
Also see: MODESTY.

I feel coming on a strange disease—humility.
Frank Lloyd Wright

The first of all other virtues—for other people.
Oliver Wendell Holmes

Extremes meet and there is no better example than the haughtiness of humility.
Ralph Waldo Emerson

It was pride that changed angels into devils; it is humility that makes men
as angels.
St. Augustine

Without humility there can be no humanity.
John Buchan

HUMOR *Also see:* BIBLE, JESTING, WIT.

If I had no sense of humor, I would long ago have committed suicide.
Mahatma Gandhi

A man isn't poor if he can still laugh.
Raymond Hitchcock

Good humor is one of the best articles of dress one can wear in society.
William Makepeace Thackeray

If I studied all my life, I couldn't think up half the number of funny things passed in one session of congress.
Will Rogers

The satirist shoots to kill while the humorist brings his prey back alive and eventually releases him again for another chance.
Peter de Vries

Men will confess to treason, murder, arson, false teeth, or a wig. How many of them will own up to a lack of humor?
Frank Moore Colby

Humor is merely tragedy standing on its head with its pants torn.
Irvin S. Cobb

Everything is funny as long as it is happening to somebody else.
Will Rogers

Whenever you find humor, you find pathos close by his side.
Edwin Percy Whipple

Good humor isn't a trait of character, it is an art which requires practice.
David Seabury

There are very few good judges of humor, and they don't agree.
Josh Billings

HUNGER *Also see:* APPETITE, CULTURE, FREEDOM, GLUTTON, POPULATION.

An empty stomach is not a good political advisor.
Albert Einstein

Hunger does not breed reform; it breeds madness, and all the ugly distempers that make an ordered life impossible.
Woodrow Wilson

A hungry man is not a free man.
Adlai E. Stevenson

A hungry people listens not to reason, nor cares for justice, nor is bent by any prayers.
Seneca

No clock is more regular than the belly.
Rabelais

We can plant wheat every year, but the people who are starving die only once.
Fiorello H. La Guardia

No one can worship God or love his neighbor on an empty stomach.
Woodrow Wilson

HUSBAND *Also see:* GIRLS, MARRIAGE.

All husbands are alike, but they have different faces so you can tell them apart.
Anonymous

An archaeologist is the best husband any woman can have: the older she gets, the more interested he is in her.
Agatha Christie

The husband who wants a happy marriage should learn to keep his mouth shut and his checkbook open.
Groucho Marx

Husbands never become good; they merely become proficient.
H. L. Mencken

Husband: what is left of the lover after the nerve has been extracted.
Helen Rowland

A good husband should be deaf and a good wife should be blind.
French Proverb

Fat generally tends to make a man a better husband. His wife is happy in the knowledge she is not married to a woman chaser. Few fat men chase girls, because they get winded too easily.
Hal Boyle

HYPOCRISY *Also see:* DECEIT, LYING, OSTENTATION.

A hypocrite is the kind of politician who would cut down a redwood tree, then mount the stump and make a speech for conservation.
Adlai E. Stevenson

A bad man is worse when he pretends to be a saint.
Francis Bacon

It is with pious fraud as with a bad action; it begets a calamitous necessity of going on.
Thomas Paine

Hypocrite: the man who murdered both his parents . . . pleaded for mercy on the grounds that he was an orphan.
Abraham Lincoln

Where there is no religion, hypocrisy becomes good taste.
George Bernard Shaw

Every man alone is sincere; at the entrance of a second person hypocrisy begins.
Ralph Waldo Emerson

No man, for any considerable period, can wear one face to himself, and another to the multitude, without finally getting bewildered as to which may be the true.
Nathaniel Hawthorne

If it were not for the intellectual snobs who pay, the arts would perish with their starving practitioners—let us thank heaven for hypocrisy.
Aldous Huxley

He knows much of what men paint themselves would blister in the light of what they are.
Edwin Arlington Robinson

Hypocrisy is the homage that vice pays to virtue.
François de La Rochefoucauld

I

IDEA *Also see:* ACTION, COMMITTEE, COMMUNICATION, CREATIVITY, FACTS, THOUGHT.

If you want to get across an idea, wrap it up in a person. *Ralph Bunche*

Ideas are the root of creation. *Ernest Dimnet*

Man's fear of ideas is probably the greatest dike holding back human knowledge and happiness. *Morris Leopold Ernst*

An idea that is not dangerous is unworthy of being called an idea at all. *Elbert Hubbard*

Ideas are the factors that lift civilization. They create revolutions. There is more dynamite in an idea than in many bombs. *John H. Vincent*

There is one thing stronger than all the armies in the world, and that is an idea whose time has come. *Victor Hugo*

Many ideas grow better when transplanted into another mind than in the one where they sprung up. *Oliver Wendell Holmes*

There is no adequate defense, except stupidity, against the impact of a new idea. *P. W. Bridgman*

The vitality of thought is in adventure. *Ideas won't keep.* Something must be done about them. When the idea is new, its custodians have fervor, live for it, and if need be, die for it. *Alfred North Whitehead*

IDEAL *Also see:* AMERICA, COMMUNICATION.

The attainment of an ideal is often the beginning of a disillusion. *Stanley Baldwin*

Words without actions are the assassins of idealism. *Herbert Hoover*

Some men see things as they are and say why. I dream things that never were and say, why not? *Robert F. Kennedy*

We build statues out of snow, and weep to see them melt. *Walter Scott*

What we need most, is not so much to realize the ideal as to idealize the real. *H. F. Hedge*

Some men can live up to their loftiest ideals without ever going higher than a basement. *Theodore Roosevelt*

Ideals are like the stars: we never reach them, but like the mariners of the sea, we chart our course by them. *Carl Schurz*

The true ideal is not opposed to the real but lies in it; and blessed are the eyes that find it. *James Russell Lowell*

IDLENESS *Also see:* ACTION, LEISURE.

Sloth, like rust, consumes faster than labor wears, while the used key is always bright.
Benjamin Franklin

To do nothing at all is the most difficult thing in the world, the most difficult and the most intellectual.
Oscar Wilde

Prolonged idleness paralyzes initiative.
Anonymous

Laziness grows on people; it begins in cobwebs and ends in iron chains.
Thomas Fowell Buxton

The way to be nothing is to do nothing.
Nathaniel Howe

It is impossible to enjoy idling thoroughly unless one has plenty of work to do.
Jerome K. Jerome

That man is idle who can do something better.
Ralph Waldo Emerson

Idleness is the stupidity of the body, and stupidity is the idleness of the mind.
Johann G. Seume

Idleness is an inlet to disorder, and makes way for licentiousness. People who have nothing to do are quickly tired of their own company.
Jeremy Collier

An idle brain is the devil's workshop.
English Proverb

Purity of mind and idleness are incompatible.
Mahatma Gandhi

IDOLATRY *Also see:* GOD.

'Tis mad idolatry
To make the service greater than the god.
William Shakespeare

We boast our emancipation from many superstitions; but if we have broken any idols, it is through a transfer of idolatry.
Ralph Waldo Emerson

The idol is the measure of the worshipper.
James Russell Lowell

Idolatry is in a man's own thought, not in the opinion of another.
John Selden

Belief in a cruel God makes a cruel man.
Thomas Paine

Rapine, avarice, expense,
This is idolatry; and these we adore;
Plain living and high thinking are no more.
William Wordsworth

Whatever a man seeks, honors, or exalts more than God, this is the god of his idolatry.
William B. Ullathorne

When men have gone so far as to talk as though their idols have come to life, it is time that someone broke them.
Richard H. Tawney

IGNORANCE
Also see: DIGNITY, FOOL, HAPPINESS, KNOWLEDGE, MYSTERY, PREJUDICE.

Ignorance is the night of the mind, but a night without moon or star.
Confuclus

He knows so little and knows it so fluently.
Ellen Glasgow

Ignorance is a voluntary misfortune.
Nicholas Ling

Have the courage to be ignorant of a great number of things, in order to avoid the calamity of being ignorant of everything.
Sydney Smith

The older we grow the greater becomes our wonder at how much ignorance one can contain without bursting one's clothes.
Mark Twain

Everybody is ignorant, only on different subjects.
Will Rogers

There is nothing more frightful than ignorance in action.
Johann Wolfgang von Goethe

Where ignorance is bliss 'tis folly to be wise.
Thomas Gray

Most ignorance is vincible ignorance. We don't know because we don't want to know.
Aldous Huxley

I honestly believe it is better to know nothing than to know what ain't so.
Josh Billings

Ignorance breeds monsters to fill up the vacancies of the soul that are unoccupied by the verities of knowledge.
Horace Mann

ILLNESS . . . See DISEASE

ILLUSION
Also see: IMAGINATION, REVERIE.

A pleasant illusion is better than a harsh reality.
Christian Nestell Bovee

Nothing is more sad than the death of an illusion.
Arthur Koestler

Better a dish of illusion and a hearty appetite for life, than a feast of reality and indigestion therewith.
Harry A. Overstreet

Don't part with your illusions. When they are gone you may still exist, but you have ceased to live.
Mark Twain

It is respectable to have no illusions, and safe, and profitable—and dull.
Joseph Conrad

The one person who has more illusions than the dreamer is the man of action.
Oscar Wilde

Therefore trust to thy heart, and to what the world calls illusions.
Henry Wadsworth Longfellow

IMAGINATION *Also see:* BUSINESS, COWARDICE, CREATIVITY, DREAM, GENIUS, MOB.

You cannot depend on your eyes when your imagination is out of focus.
Mark Twain

He who has imagination without learning has wings and no feet.
Joseph Joubert

Imagination rules the world. *Napoleon Bonaparte*

Often it is just lack of imagination that keeps a man from suffering very much. *Marcel Proust*

The quality of the imagination is to flow and not to freeze.
Ralph Waldo Emerson

Imagination is not a talent of some men but is the health of every man.
Ralph Waldo Emerson

Imagination disposes of everything; it creates beauty, justice, and happiness, which are everything in this world. *Blaise Pascal*

Imagination is a quality given a man to compensate him for what he is not, and a sense of humor was provided to console him for what he is.
Oscar Wilde

Science does not know its debt to imagination. *Ralph Waldo Emerson*

IMITATION *Also see:* ADAPTABILITY, CONFORMITY, ORIGINALITY.

Imitation belittles. *Christian Nestell Bovee*

When people are free to do as they please, they usually imitate each other.
Eric Hoffer

There is much difference between imitating a good man and counterfeiting him. *Benjamin Franklin*

The only good imitations are those that poke fun at bad originals.
François de La Rochefoucauld

To copy others is necessary, but to copy oneself is pathetic. *Pablo Picasso*

Insist on yourself; never imitate. *Ralph Waldo Emerson*

Example has more followers than reason. We unconsciously imitate what pleases us, and approximate to the characters we most admire.
Christian Nestell Bovee

Men are so constituted that every one undertakes what he sees another successful in, whether he has aptitude for it or not.
Johann Wolfgang von Goethe

IMMORTALITY *Also see:* CONVERSATION, ETERNITY, GOD, LIFE.

The average man does not know what to do with this life, yet wants another one which will last forever.   *Anatole France*

Only the actions of the just smell sweet and blossom in the dust.
James Shirley

The first requisite for immortality is death.   *Stanislaw J. Lec*

The best argument I know for an immortal life is the existence of a man who deserves one.   *William James*

Immortality is the genius to move others long after you yourself have stopped moving.   *Frank Rooney*

One has to pay dearly for immortality; one has to die several times while one is still alive.   *Nietzsche*

If your contribution has been vital there will always be somebody to pick up where you left off, and that will be your claim to immortality.
Walter Gropius

Those who hope for no other life are dead even for this.
Johann Wolfgang von Goethe

The reward of great men is that, long after they have died, one is not quite sure that they are dead.   *Jules Renard*

___

IMPOSSIBILITY *Also see:* PERFECTION.

The Difficult is that which can be done immediately; the Impossible that which takes a little longer.   *George Santayana*

Apparently there is nothing that cannot happen today.   *Mark Twain*

Most of the things worth doing in the world had been declared impossible before they were done.   *Louis D. Brandeis*

Impossibility: a word only to be found in the dictionary of fools.
Napoleon Bonaparte

To the timid and hesitating everything is impossible because it seems so.
Walter Scott

Nothing is impossible; there are ways that lead to everything, and if we had sufficient will we should always have sufficient means. It is often merely for an excuse that we say things are impossible.
François de La Rochefoucauld

It is difficult to say what is impossible, for the dream of yesterday is the hope of today and the reality of tomorrow.   *Robert H. Goddard*

IMPROVEMENT *Also see:* PROGRESS, SELF-IMPROVEMENT.

People seldom improve when they have no other model but themselves to copy after.   *Oliver Goldsmith*

He who stops being better stops being good.   *Oliver Cromwell*

Acorns were good until bread was found.   *Francis Bacon*

Where we cannot invent, we may at least improve.   *Charles Caleb Colton*

As long as I can conceive something better than myself I cannot be easy unless I am striving to bring it into existence or clearing the way for it.
George Bernard Shaw

Undoubtedly a man is to labor to better his condition, but first to better himself.   *William Ellery Channing*

If a better system is thine, impart it; if not, make use of mine.   *Horace*

Much of the wisdom of one age, is the folly of the next.   *Charles Simmons*

INACTIVITY ... See IDLENESS

INCONSISTENCY *Also see:* CHANGE.

Every sweet has its sour; every evil its good.   *Ralph Waldo Emerson*

No author ever drew a character consistent to human nature, but he was forced to ascribe to it many inconsistencies.   *Edward G. Bulwer-Lytton*

Mutability of temper and inconsistency with ourselves is the greatest weakness of human nature.   *Joseph Addison*

Some persons do first, think afterward, and then repent forever.
Thomas Secker

A foolish consistency is the hobgoblin of little minds.   *Ralph Waldo Emerson*

All concord's born of contraries.   *Ben Jonson*

INCREDULITY *Also see:* AGNOSTICISM, DISTRUST, DOUBT, SKEPTICISM.

Incredulity robs us of many pleasures, and gives us nothing in return.
James Russell Lowell

The amplest knowledge has the largest faith. Ignorance is always incredulous.   *Robert Eldridge Willmott*

The curse of man, and the cause of nearly all his woe, is his stupendous capacity for believing the incredible.   *H. L. Mencken*

Incredulity is the wisdom of the fool.   *Josh Billings*

More persons, on the whole, are humbugged by believing in nothing than by believing in too much.   *P. T. Barnum*

INDECISION

There is no more miserable human being than one in whom nothing is habitual but indecision.   *William James*

The wavering mind is but a base possession.   *Euripides*

When a man has not a good reason for doing a thing, he has one good reason for letting it alone.   *Thomas Scott*

While the mind is in doubt it is driven this way and that by a slight impulse.   *Terence*

He is no wise man who will quit a certainty for an uncertainty.   *Samuel Johnson*

A man without decision can never be said to belong to himself.   *John Watson Foster*

Indecision is debilitating; it feeds upon itself; it is, one might almost say, habit-forming. Not only that, but it is contagious; it transmits itself to others.   *H. A. Hopf*

Indecision has often given an advantage to the other fellow because he did his thinking beforehand.   *Maurice Switzer*

Once I make up my mind, I'm full of indecision.   *Oscar Levant*

INDEPENDENCE   *Also see:* DEPENDENCE, FREEDOM, INDIVIDUALITY, LIBERTY.

No one can build his security upon the nobleness of another person.   *Willa Cather*

Without moral and intellectual independence, there is no anchor for national independence.   *David Ben-Gurion*

It is not the greatness of a man's means that makes him independent, so much as the smallness of his wants.   *William Cobbett*

I would rather sit on a pumpkin and have it all to myself than be on a crowded velvet cushion.   *Henry David Thoreau*

So live that you can look any man in the eye and tell him to go to hell.   *Anonymous*

There is no more independence in politics than there is in jail.   *Will Rogers*

I do desire we may be better strangers.   *William Shakespeare*

Can anything be so elegant as to have few wants, and to serve them one's self?   *Ralph Waldo Emerson*

(I am) lord of myself, accountable to none.   *Benjamin Franklin*

INDIVIDUALITY *Also see:* CHARACTER, ORIGINALITY, PERSONALITY, PROPERTY.

Individuality is either the mark of genius or the reverse. Mediocrity finds safety in standardization. *Frederick E. Crane*

The worth of the state, in the long run, is the worth of the individuals composing it. *John Stuart Mill*

The whole theory of the universe is directed unerringly to one single individual. *Walt Whitman*

An institution is the lengthened shadow of one man. *Ralph Waldo Emerson*

Men acquire a particular quality by constantly acting in a particular way. *Aristotle*

That so few now dare to be eccentric marks the chief danger of the time. *John Stuart Mill*

Individuality is founded in feeling; and the recesses of feeling, the darker, blinder strata of character, are the only places in the world in which we catch real fact in the making. *William James*

Individuality is the aim of political liberty. *James Fenimore Cooper*

INDOLENCE . . . See IDLENESS

INDUSTRY *Also see:* BUSINESS, BUSY, DILIGENCE, FORTUNE, LABOR.

No thoroughly occupied man was ever yet very miserable. *Letitia Landon*

It is better to wear out than to rust out. *Richard Cumberland*

The sleeping fox catches no poultry. *Benjamin Franklin*

The more we do, the more we can do. *William Hazlitt*

Like the bee, we should make our industry our amusement. *Oliver Goldsmith*

A man who gives his children habits of industry provides for them better than by giving them a fortune. *Richard Whately*

Industry need not wish, and he that lives upon Hope will die fasting. *Benjamin Franklin*

If you have great talents, industry will improve them; if moderate abilities, industry will supply their deficiencies. Nothing is denied to well-directed labor; nothing is ever to be attained without it. *Joshua Reynolds*

Industry is the soul of business and the keystone of prosperity. *Charles Dickens*

In the ordinary business of life, industry can do anything which genius can do, and very many things which it cannot. *Henry Ward Beecher*

INEQUALITY *Also see:* DIFFERENCE, EQUALITY.

One half of the world must sweat and groan that the other half may dream.
Henry Wadsworth Longfellow

No amount of artificial reinforcement can offset the natural inequalities of human individuals. *Henry P. Fairchild*

Some men must follow, and some command, though all are made of clay.
Henry Wadsworth Longfellow

There is always inequity in life. Some men are killed in a war, and some men are wounded, and some men are stationed in the Antarctic and some are stationed in San Francisco. It's very hard in military or personal life to assure complete equality. Life is unfair. *John Fitzgerald Kennedy*

Can one preach at home inequality of races and nations and advocate abroad good-will towards all men? *Dorothy Thompson*

People differ in capacity, skill, health, strength; and unequal fortune is a necessary result of unequal condition. Such inequality is far from being disadvantageous either to individuals or to the community. *Leo XIII*

INFERIORITY *Also see:* IGNORANCE, INEQUALITY, RACE.

The surrender of life is nothing to sinking down into acknowledgment of inferiority. *John C. Calhoun*

No man likes to have his intelligence or good faith questioned, especially if he has doubts about it himself. *Henry Brooks Adams*

We must interpret a bad temper as a sign of inferiority. *Alfred Adler*

No one can make you feel inferior without your consent. *Eleanor Roosevelt*

The superior man understands what is right; the inferior man understands what will sell. *Confucius*

Inferiority is what you enjoy in your best friends. *Lord Chesterfield*

Exaggerated sensitiveness is an expression of the feeling of inferiority.
Alfred Adler

Let a man once overcome his selfish terror at his own finitude, and his finitude is, in one sense, overcome. *George Santayana*

No two men can be half an hour together but one shall acquire an evident superiority over the other. *Samuel Johnson*

The greater the feeling of inferiority that has been experienced, the more powerful is the urge to conquest and the more violent the emotional agitation. *Alfred Adler*

INFLUENCE *Also see:* AUTHORITY, POWER.

Every life is a profession of faith, and exercises an inevitable and silent influence.   *Amiel*

The humblest individual exerts some influence, either for good or evil, upon others.   *Henry Ward Beecher*

No man should think himself a zero, and think he can do nothing about the state of the world.   *Bernard M. Baruch*

Blessed is the influence of one true, loving human soul on another.   *George Eliot*

The least movement is of importance to all nature. The entire ocean is affected by a pebble.   *Blaise Pascal*

We perceive and are affected by changes too subtle to be described.   *Henry David Thoreau*

He is greatest whose strength carries up the most hearts by the attraction of his own.   *Henry Ward Beecher*

Every thought which genius and piety throw into the world alters the world.   *Ralph Waldo Emerson*

I am a part of all that I have met.   *Alfred, Lord Tennyson*

Let him that would move the world, first move himself.   *Socrates*

INGRATITUDE *Also see:* GRATITUDE, SELFISHNESS.

Next to ingratitude the most painful thing to bear is gratitude.   *Henry Ward Beecher*

Nothing more detestable does the earth produce than an ungrateful man.   *Ausonius*

Ingratitude is treason to mankind.   *James Thomson*

A proud man is seldom a grateful man, for he never thinks he gets as much as he deserves.   *Henry Ward Beecher*

How sharper than a serpent's tooth it is
To have a thankless child!   *William Shakespeare*

Too great haste to repay an obligation is a kind of ingratitude.   *François de La Rochefoucauld*

When I'm not thanked at all I'm thanked enough.   *Henry Fielding*

One ungrateful man does an injury to all who stand in need of aid.   *Publilius Syrus*

We seldom find people ungrateful so long as it is thought we can serve them.   *François de La Rochefoucauld*

INHERITANCE

We pay for the mistakes of our ancestors, and it seems only fair that they should leave us the money to pay with. *Don Marquis*

Who comes for the inheritance is often made to pay for the funeral. *Yiddish Proverb*

To inherit property is not to be born—it is to be still-born, rather. *Henry David Thoreau*

Never say you know a man till you have divided an inheritance with him. *Johann Kaspar Lavater*

What madness it is for a man to starve himself to enrich his heir, and so turn a friend into an enemy! For his joy at your death will be proportioned to what you leave him. *Seneca*

I have also seen children successfully surmounting the effects of an evil inheritance. That is due to purity being an inherent attribute of the soul. *Mahatma Gandhi*

Enjoy what thou has inherited from thy sires if thou wouldst really possess it. What we employ and use is never an oppressive burden; what the moment brings forth, that only can it profit by. *Johann Wolfgang von Goethe*

INJURY *Also see:* ABUSE, JUSTICE, SLANDER, VENGEANCE.

No man is hurt but by himself. *Diogenes*

No man ever did a designed injury to another, but at the same time he did a greater to himself. *Lord Kames*

It is more noble by silence to avoid an injury than by argument to overcome it. *Francis Beaumont*

If the other person injures you, you may forget the injury; but if you injure him you will always remember. *Kahlil Gibran*

The natural principle of war is to do the most harm to our enemy with the least harm to ourselves; and this of course is to be effected by strategem. *Washington Irving*

Never does the human soul appear so strong as when it foregoes revenge and dares to forgive an injury. *Edwin Hubbel Chapin*

The injury we do and the one we suffer are not weighed in the same scale. *Aesop*

If an injury has to be done to a man it should be so severe that his vengeance need not be feared. *Niccolò Machiavelli*

Slight small injuries, and they will become none at all. *Thomas Fuller*

INJUSTICE *Also see:* JUSTICE.

No one will dare maintain that it is better to do injustice than to bear it.
Aristotle

If thou suffer injustice, console thyself; the true unhappiness is in doing it.
Democritus

Those who commit injustice bear the greatest burden.   *Hosea Ballou*

A book might be written on the injustice of the just.   *Anthony Hope*

He who commits injustice is ever made more wretched than he who suffers it.   *Plato*

Whatever the human law may be, neither an individual nor a nation can commit the least act of injustice against the obscurest individual without having to pay the penalty for it.   *Henry David Thoreau*

INNOCENCE *Also see:* GUILT, IGNORANCE, JUSTICE.

Innocence most often is a good fortune and not a virtue.   *Anatole France*

They that know no evil will suspect none.   *Ben Jonson*

Innocence is like polished armor; it adorns and defends.   *Robert South*

The innocence that feels no risk and is taught no caution, is more vulnerable than guilt, and oftener assailed.   *Nathaniel P. Willis*

He is armed without who is innocent within, be this thy screen, and this thy wall of brass.   *Horace*

To be innocent is to be not guilty; but to be virtuous is to overcome our evil inclinations.   *William Penn*

It is better that ten guilty persons escape than that one innocent suffer.
William Blackstone

INSANITY *Also see:* ACCURACY.

Insanity destroys reason, but not wit.   *Nathaniel Emmons*

Insanity is often the logic of an accurate mind overtaxed.
Oliver Wendell Holmes

There is no insanity so devastating in man's life as utter sanity.
William Allen White

I teach that all men are mad.   *Horace*

We do not have to visit a madhouse to find disordered minds; our planet is the mental institution of the universe.   *Johann Wolfgang von Goethe*

When we remember we are all mad, the mysteries disappear and life stands explained.   *Mark Twain*

Insanity is hereditary: you can get it from your children.   *Sam Levenson*

INSTINCT *Also see:* COMMON SENSE.

Instinct is the nose of the mind.   *Madame de Girardin*

Instinct is action taken in pursuance of a purpose, but without conscious perception of what the purpose is.   *Van Hartmann*

There is not, in my opinion, anything more mysterious in nature than this instinct in animals, which thus rise above reason, and yet fall infinitely short of it.   *Joseph Addison*

A goose flies by a chart which the Royal Geographical Society could not mend.   *Oliver Wendell Holmes*

Instinct is untaught ability.   *Alexander Bain*

The active part of man consists of powerful instincts, some of which are gentle and continuous; others violent and short; some baser, some nobler, and all necessary.   *Francis W. Newman*

It is the rooted instinct in men to admire what is better and more beautiful than themselves.   *James Russell Lowell*

A few strong instincts and a few plain rules suffice us.   *Ralph Waldo Emerson*

INSULT *Also see:* ABUSE, INJURY, IRONY.

A gentleman will not insult me, and no man not a gentleman can insult me.   *Frederick Douglass*

He who puts up with insult invites injury.   *Proverb*

The best way to procure insults is to submit to them.   *William Hazlitt*

If you can't ignore an insult, top it; if you can't top it, laugh it off; and if you can't laugh it off, it's probably deserved.   *Russell Lynes*

It is often better not to see an insult than to avenge it.   *Seneca*

There are two insults no human being will endure: that he has no sense of humor, and that he has never known trouble.   *Sinclair Lewis*

The slight that can be conveyed in a glance, in a gracious smile, in a wave of the hand, is often the *ne plus ultra* of art. What insult is so keen or so keenly felt, as the polite insult which it is impossible to resent?   *Julia Kavanagh*

A graceful taunt is worth a thousand insults.   *Louis Nizer*

It is not he who gives abuse that affronts, but the view that we take of it as insulting; so that when one provokes you it is your own opinion which is provoking.   *Epictetus*

INTEGRITY . . . See HONESTY

INTELLIGENCE *Also see:* COMMON SENSE, JUDGMENT, KNOWLEDGE, PERCEPTION, PRUDENCE.

It is impossible to underrate human intelligence—beginning with one's own.
Henry Brooks Adams

When you don't have an education, you've got to use your brains.
Anonymous

There is nobody so irritating as somebody with less intelligence and more sense than we have.
Don Herold

It is not the insurrections of ignorance that are dangerous, but the revolts of the intelligence.
James Russell Lowell

A weak mind is like a microscope, which magnifies trifling things but cannot receive great ones.
Lord Chesterfield

There is no such thing as an underestimate of average intelligence.
Henry Brooks Adams

The test of a first-rate intelligence is the ability to hold two opposed ideas at the same time, and still retain the ability to function.
F. Scott Fitzgerald

Intellect annuls fate. So far as a man thinks, he is free.
Ralph Waldo Emerson

INTEREST *Also see:* GAIN.

Interest makes some people blind, and others quick-sighted.
Francis Beaumont

There are no uninteresting things, there are only uninterested people.
Gilbert K. Chesterton

The virtues and vices are all put in motion by interest.
François de La Rochefoucauld

A man's interest in the world is only an overflow from his interest in himself.
George Bernard Shaw

I don't believe in principle, but I do in interest.   *James Russell Lowell*

Only free peoples can hold their purpose and their honor steady to a common end and prefer the interest of mankind to any narrow interest of their own.
Woodrow Wilson

It is a cursed evil to any man to become as absorbed in any subject as I am in mine.
Charles Darwin

I take it to be a principle rule of life, not to be too much addicted to any one thing.
Terence

INTOLERANCE *Also see:* ANGER, BIGOTRY, PREJUDICE.

Intolerance is a form of egotism, and to condemn egotism intolerantly is to share it.
George Santayana

Nothing dies so hard, or rallies so often as intolerance. *Henry Ward Beecher*

Intolerance has been the curse of every age and state. *Samuel Davies*

Whoever kindles the flames of intolerance in America is lighting a fire underneath his own home.
Harold E. Stassen

The closed mind, if closed long enough, can be opened by nothing short of dynamite.
Gerald W. Johnson

Bigotry and intolerance, silenced by argument, endeavors to silence by persecution, in old days by fire and sword, in modern days by the tongue.
Charles Simmons

In the blood of the martyrs to intolerance are the seeds of unbelief.
Walter Lippmann

INVENTION *Also see:* DISCOVERY.

Invention is the talent of youth, as judgment is of age. *Jonathan Swift*

Only an inventor knows how to borrow, and every man is or should be an inventor.
Ralph Waldo Emerson

The march of invention has clothed mankind with powers of which a century ago the boldest imagination could not have dreamt. *Henry George*

A tool is but the extension of a man's hand, and a machine is but a complex tool. And he that invents a machine augments the power of a man and the well-being of mankind.
Henry Ward Beecher

The universe is full of magical things patiently waiting for our wits to grow sharper.
Eden Phillpotts

Great discoveries and improvements invariably involve the cooperation of many minds. I may be given credit for having blazed the trail but when I look at the subsequent developments I feel the credit is due to others rather than to myself.
Alexander Graham Bell

We owe to the Middle Ages the two worst inventions of humanity—gunpowder and romantic love.
André Maurois

IRONY *Also see:* BOOK, HUMOR, WIT.

Irony is the gaity of reflection and the joy of wisdom. *Anatole France*

A taste for irony has kept more hearts from breaking than a sense of humor for it takes irony to appreciate the joke which is on oneself. *Jessamyn West*

Irony is jesting behind hidden gravity. *John Weiss*

Irony is an insult conveyed in the form of a compliment.
Edwin Percy Whipple

J

JAZZ *Also see:* MUSIC.

Jazz will endure as long as people hear it through their feet instead of their brains.　　　　　　　　　　　　　　　　　*John Philip Sousa*

The chief trouble with jazz is that there is not enough of it; some of it we have to listen to twice.　　　　　　　　　　　　　　　*Don Herold*

Jazz is the folk music of the machine age.　　　　　　*Paul Whiteman*

Jazz may be a thrilling communion with the primitive soul; or it may be an ear-splitting bore.　　　　　　　　　　　　　*Winthrop Sargeant*

Jazz tickles your muscles, symphonies stretch your soul.　*Paul Whiteman*

JEALOUSY *Also see:* RIVALRY, SARCASM.

There is never jealousy where there is not strong regard.　*Washington Irving*

Jealousy lives upon doubts. It becomes madness or ceases entirely as soon as we pass from doubt to certainty.　　　*François de La Rochefoucauld*

Jealousy is the injured lover's hell.　　　　　　　　　*John Milton*

Jealousy is . . . a tiger that tears not only its prey but also its own raging heart.　　　　　　　　　　　　　　　　　　　*Michael Beer*

What frenzy dictates, jealousy believes.　　　　　　　*John Gay*

The way to hold a husband is to keep him a little jealous; the way to lose him is to keep him a little more jealous.　　　*H. L. Mencken*

In jealousy there is more of self-love than of love to another.
　　　　　　　　　　　　　　　　François de La Rochefoucauld

Lots of people know a good thing the minute the other fellow sees it first.
　　　　　　　　　　　　　　　　　　　　Job E. Hedges

O, beware, my lord, of jealousy;
It is the green-eyed monster which doth mock
The meat it feeds on.　　　　　　　　　*William Shakespeare*

And oft, my jealousy shapes faults that are not.　*William Shakespeare*

JESTING *Also see:* HUMOR, WIT.

Many a true word is spoken in jest.　　　　　　　　*English Proverb*

Jesting is often only indigence of intellect.　　　*Jean de La Bruyére*

Judge of a jest when you have done laughing.　　　*William Lloyd*

The jest loses its point when he who makes it is the first to laugh.
　　　　　　　　　　　　　　　　　　Johann von Schiller

Jests that give pains are no jests.　　　　　　*Miguel de Cervantes*

JOURNALISM *Also see:* NEWSPAPER.

Journalists do not live by words alone, although sometimes they have to eat them.
Adlai E. Stevenson

Journalism is unreadable, and literature is unread.
Oscar Wilde

Get your facts first, and then you can distort 'em as you please.
Mark Twain

A news sense is really a sense of what is important, what is vital, what has color and life—what people are interested in. That's journalism.
Burton Rascoe

A journalist is a grumbler, a censurer, a giver of advice, a regent of sovereigns, a tutor of nations. Four hostile newspapers are more to be feared than a thousand bayonets.
Napoleon Bonaparte

Half my lifetime I have earned my living by selling words, and I hope thoughts.
Winston Churchill

Many a good newspaper story has been ruined by oververification.
James Gordon Bennett

Journalism is literature in a hurry.
Matthew Arnold

JOY *Also see:* ENJOYMENT, HAPPINESS, PLEASURE, SMILE.

Tranquil pleasures last the longest; we are not fitted to bear the burden of great joys.
Christian Nestell Bovee

One can endure sorrow alone, but it takes two to be glad.   *Elbert Hubbard*

Joys divided are increased.
Josiah Gilbert Holland

The most profound joy has more of gravity than of gaiety in it.
Michel de Montaigne

In this world, full often, our joys are only the tender shadows which our sorrows cast.
Henry Ward Beecher

Great joy, especially after a sudden change of circumstances, is apt to be silent, and dwells rather in the heart than on the tongue.   *Henry Fielding*

> All human joys are swift of wing,
> For heaven doth so allot it;
> That when you get an easy thing,
> You find you haven't got it.
>
> *Eugene Field*

There are joys which long to be ours. God sends ten thousands truths, which come about us like birds seeking inlet; but we are shut up to them, and so they bring us nothing, but sit and sing awhile upon the roof, and then fly away.
Henry Ward Beecher

JUDAISM *Also see:* RELIGION.

The builders of Judaism utilized emotion in order to sublimate the passions, the angers, the dreams, of the people. *Joshua Loth Liebman*

To be a Jew is a destiny. *Vicki Baum*

Judaism lives not in an abstract creed, but in its institutions. *Auerbach*

The religion of the Jews is, indeed, a light; but it is as the light of the glow-worm, which gives no heat, and illumines nothing but itself. *Samuel Taylor Coleridge*

Passover affirms the great truth that liberty is the inalienable right of every human being. *Morris Joseph*

Historically the profoundest meaning of Passover is something which sets Judaism apart from other religions. It marks the birth of a nation. Out of a mass of slaves, Moses fashioned a nation and gave them a faith. From that day to this, Jews have never ceased to be a people. *Philip S. Bernstein*

JUDGMENT *Also see:* DECISION, PRUDENCE, WISDOM.

You shall judge of a man by his foes as well as by his friends. *Joseph Conrad*

We judge ourselves by what we feel capable of doing; others judge us by what we have done. *Henry Wadsworth Longfellow*

Everyone complains of the badness of his memory, but nobody of his judgment. *François de La Rochefoucauld*

I mistrust the judgment of every man in a case in which his own wishes are concerned. *First Duke of Wellington*

One cool judgment is worth a thousand hasty councils. The thing to do is to supply light and not heat. *Woodrow Wilson*

Hesitancy in judgment is the only true mark of the thinker. *Dagobert D. Runes*

The average man's judgment is so poor, he runs a risk every time he uses it. *Ed Howe*

When you meet a man, you judge him by his clothes; when you leave, you judge him by his heart. *Russian Proverb*

It is with our judgments as with our watches: no two go just alike, yet each believes his own. *Alexander Pope*

Less judgment than wit is more sail than ballast. *William Penn*

Outward judgment often fails, inward judgment never. *Theodore Parker*

JUSTICE *Also see:* CAUSE, COURT, EQUALITY, LAW, RIGHTS.

Justice is the great interest of man on earth.   *Daniel Webster*

Justice is the bread of the nation; it is always hungry for it.
François de Chateaubriand

Justice is the ligament which holds civilized beings and civilized nations together.   *Daniel Webster*

The love of justice in most men is only the fear of themselves suffering by injustice.   *François de La Rochefoucauld*

Justice is the insurance which we have on our lives and property. Obedience is the premium which we pay for it.   *William Penn*

Justice is the crowning glory of the virtues.   *Cicero*

There is no such thing as justice—in or out of court.   *Clarence Darrow*

Justice is a commodity which in a more or less adulterated condition the State sells to the citizen as a reward for his allegiance, taxes and personal service.   *Ambrose Bierce*

Whenever a separation is made between liberty and justice, neither, in my opinion, is safe.   *Edmund Burke*

Though force can protect in emergency, only justice, fairness, consideration and cooperation can finally lead men to the dawn of eternal peace.
Dwight D. Eisenhower

The sentiment of justice is so natural, and so universally acquired by all mankind, that it seems to be independent of all law, all party, all religion.
Voltaire

Justice is justice though it's always delayed and finally done only by mistake.   *George Bernard Shaw*

Justice is the firm and continuous desire to render to everyone that which is his due.   *Justinian*

Children are innocent and love justice, while most adults are wicked and prefer mercy.   *Gilbert K. Chesterton*

Rather suffer an injustice than commit one.   *Anonymous*

An honest man nearly always thinks justly.   *Jean Jacques Rousseau*

Justice and power must be brought together, so that whatever is just may be powerful, and whatever is powerful may be just.   *Blaise Pascal*

One man's word is no man's word; we should quietly hear both sides.
Johann Wolfgang von Goethe

Justice is the first virtue of those who command, and stops the complaints of those who obey.   *Denis Diderot*

K

KILLING . . . See ASSASSINATION

KINDNESS *Also see:* CHARITY, HELP.

Human kindness has never weakened the stamina or softened the fiber of a free people. A nation does not have to be cruel in order to be tough.
Franklin Delano Roosevelt

He that has done you a kindness will be more ready to do you another, than he whom you yourself have obliged. *Benjamin Franklin*

The best portion of a good man's life is his little, nameless, unremembered acts of kindness and of love. *William Wordsworth*

We hate the kindness which we understand. *Henry David Thoreau*

Kindness goes a long ways lots of times when it ought to stay at home.
Kin Hubbard

A kind heart is a fountain of gladness, making everything in its vicinity freshen into smiles. *Washington Irving*

Kindness is a language the dumb can speak and the deaf can hear and understand. *Christian Nestell Bovee*

You cannot do a kindness too soon, for you never know how soon it will be too late. *Ralph Waldo Emerson*

Kindness is loving people more than they deserve. *Joseph Joubert*

KING *Also see:* ARISTOCRACY, BLINDNESS.

A king is one who has "few things to desire and many things to fear."
Francis Bacon

Wise kings generally have wise counsellors; and he must be a wise man himself who is capable of distinguishing one. *Diogenes*

The modern king has become a vermiform appendix: useless when quiet; when obtrusive, in danger of removal. *Austin O'Malley*

Kings is mostly rapscallions. *Mark Twain*

Royalty consists not in vain pomp, but in great virtues. *Agesilaus II*

Every king springs from a race of slaves, and every slave had kings among his ancestors. *Plato*

The right kind of monarchy is one where everybody goes about with the permanent conviction that the king can do no wrong. *Gilbert K. Chesterton*

One of the strongest natural proofs of the folly of hereditary right in kings is, that nature disapproves it; otherwise she would not so frequently turn it into ridicule by giving mankind an ass in place of a lion. *Thomas Paine*

KISS *Also see:* AFFECTION, PAIN.

A kiss is a lovely trick designed by nature to stop speech when words become superfluous. *Ingrid Bergman*

A kiss can be a comma, a question mark or an exclamation point. *Mistinguette*

It is the passion that is in a kiss that gives to it its sweetness; it is the affection in a kiss that sanctifies it. *Christian Nestell Bovee*

A man snatches the first kiss, pleads for the second, demands the third, takes the fourth, accepts the fifth—and endures all the rest. *Helen Rowland*

> A kiss, when all is said, what is it?
> A rosy dot placed on the "i" in loving;
> 'Tis a secret told to the mouth instead of to the ear. *Edmond Rostand*

A peculiar proposition. Of no use to one, yet absolute bliss to two. The small boy gets it for nothing, the young man has to lie for it, and the old man has to buy it. The baby's right, the lover's privilege, and the hypocrite's mask. To a young girl, faith; to a married woman, hope; and to an old maid, charity. *V.P.I. Skipper*

God pardons like a mother who kisses the offense into everlasting forgetfulness. *Henry Ward Beecher*

KNOWLEDGE *Also see:* CIVILIZATION, DANGER, DOUBT, DUTY, EDUCATION, POWER.

I am not young enough to know everything. *James Matthew Barrie*

Knowledge is like money: the more he gets, the more he craves. *Josh Billings*

The essence of knowledge is, having it, to apply it; not having it, to confess your ignorance. *Confucius*

Knowledge is knowing that we cannot know. *Ralph Waldo Emerson*

What a man knows is everywhere at war with what he wants. *Joseph Wood Krutch*

Knowledge is the small part of ignorance that we arrange and classify. *Ambrose Bierce*

Knowledge is the eye of desire and can become the pilot of the soul. *Will Durant*

All wish to possess knowledge, but few, comparatively speaking, are willing to pay the price. *Juvenal*

> I keep six honest serving-men
>   (They taught me all I knew);
> Their names are What and Why and When
>   And How and Where and Who. *Rudyard Kipling*

L

LABOR *Also see:* AUTOMATION, EFFORT, EMPLOYMENT, INDUSTRY, LEISURE, MACHINE, WAGE, WORK.

Labor is man's greatest function. He is nothing, he can do nothing, he can achieve nothing, he can fulfill nothing, without working. *Orville Dewey*

The fruit derived from labor is the sweetest of all pleasures. *Luc de Clapiers*

A man's best friends are his ten fingers. *Robert Collyer*

Excellence in any department can be attained only by the labor of a lifetime; it is not to be purchased at a lesser price. *Samuel Johnson*

Every man is dishonest who lives upon the labor of others, no matter if he occupies a throne. *Robert Green Ingersoll*

There is no real wealth but the labor of man. *Percy Bysshe Shelley*

He that hath a trade hath an estate; he that hath a calling hath an office of profit and honor. *Benjamin Franklin*

It is only through labor and painful effort, by grim energy and resolute courage, that we move on to better things. *Theodore Roosevelt*

Who will not suffer labor in this world, let him not be born. *John Florio*

I pity the man who wants a coat so cheap that the man or woman who produces the cloth will starve in the process. *Benjamin Harrison*

LANGUAGE *Also see:* CONVERSATION, LITERATURE, MUSIC, SPEECH, WORD.

Language is the blood of the soul into which thoughts run and out of which they grow. *Oliver Wendell Holmes*

Language is the dress of thought. *Samuel Johnson*

Language is only the instrument of science, and words are but the signs of ideas. *Samuel Johnson*

Think like a wise man but communicate in the language of the people. *William Butler Yeats*

Spoken language is merely a series of squeaks. *Alfred North Whitehead*

Because everyone uses language to talk, everyone thinks he can talk about language. *Johann Wolfgang von Goethe*

Language is a city to the building of which every human being brought a stone. *Ralph Waldo Emerson*

Language is the armory of the human mind, and at once contains the trophies of its past and the weapons of its future conquests. *Samuel Taylor Coleridge*

LAUGHTER *Also see:* BABY, CHEERFULNESS, HUMOR, SMILE.

Those who bring sunshine to the lives of others cannot keep it from themselves.
James Matthew Barrie

Laughter is the tonic, the relief, the surcease for pain.   *Charlie Chaplin*

Men show their character in nothing more clearly than by what they think laughable.
Johann Wolfgang von Goethe

The young man who has not wept is a savage, and the old man who will not laugh is a fool.
George Santayana

A hearty laugh gives one a dry cleaning, while a good cry is a wet wash.
Puzant Kevork Thomajan

If you don't learn to laugh at trouble, you won't have anything to laugh at when you're old.
Ed Howe

A man isn't poor if he can still laugh.   *Raymond Hitchcock*

Laughter is the sun that drives winter from the human face.   *Victor Hugo*

The most thoroughly wasted of all days is that on which one has not laughed.
Chamfort

He laughs best who laughs last.   *English Proverb*

I can usually judge a fellow by what he laughs at.   *Wilson Mizner*

LAW *Also see:* DISSENT, EQUALITY, GOVERNMENT.

Petty laws breed great crimes.   *Ouida*

A law is valuable not because it is law, but because there is right in it.
Henry Ward Beecher

If we desire respect for the law, we must first make the law respectable.
Louis D. Brandeis

The best way to get a bad law repealed is to enforce it strictly.
Abraham Lincoln

It is the spirit and not the form of law that keeps justice alive.   *Earl Warren*

There is plenty of law at the end of a nightstick.   *Grover A. Whalen*

Laws that do not embody public opinion can never be enforced.
Elbert Hubbard

No law can be sacred to me but that of my nature.   *Ralph Waldo Emerson*

You can't legislate intelligence and common sense into people.   *Will Rogers*

We can not expect to breed respect for law and order among people who do not share the fruits of our freedom.
Hubert H. Humphrey

LEADERSHIP *Also see:* AUTHORITY, COURAGE, HEROISM.

And when we think we lead, we are most led. *Lord Byron*

Leadership is the other side of the coin of loneliness, and he who is a leader must always act alone. And acting alone, accept everything alone.
Ferdinand Edralin Marcos

Leadership: The art of getting someone else to do something you want done because he wants to do it. *Dwight D. Eisenhower*

If the blind lead the blind, both shall fall into the ditch. *Matthew 15:14*

The nation will find it very hard to look up to the leaders who are keeping their ears to the ground. *Winston Churchill*

The final test of a leader is that he leaves behind him in other men the conviction and the will to carry on. *Walter Lippmann*

In the great mass of our people there are plenty individuals of intelligence from among whom leadership can be recruited. *Herbert Hoover*

LEARNING *Also see:* DISCRETION, EDUCATION, KNOWLEDGE, STUDY, TEACHING.

The brighter you are the more you have to learn. *Don Herold*

The secret of education lies in respecting the pupil. *Ralph Waldo Emerson*

I've known countless people who were reservoirs of learning yet never had a thought. *Wilson Mizner*

We should live and learn; but by the time we've learned, it's too late to live. *Carolyn Wells*

Acquire new knowledge whilst thinking over the old, and you may become a teacher of others. *Confucius*

The wisest mind has something yet to learn. *George Santayana*

To be proud of learning is the greatest ignorance. *Jeremy Taylor*

I am always ready to learn, but I do not always like being taught.
Winston Churchill

He who adds not to his learning diminishes it. *The Talmud*

Men learn while they teach. *Seneca*

A man learns to skate by staggering about making a fool of himself; indeed, he progresses in all things by making a fool of himself.
George Bernard Shaw

Wear your learning like your watch, in a private pocket, and do not pull it out and strike it merely to show that you have one. *Lord Chesterfield*

LEISURE *Also see:* IDLENESS, OPPORTUNITY, REST.

Leisure is a beautiful garment, but it will not do for constant wear.
Anonymous

The end of labor is to gain leisure. *Aristotle*

A poor life this if, full of care, we have no time to stand and stare.
William Henry Davies

We give up leisure in order that we may have leisure, just as we go to war in order that we may have peace. *Aristotle*

He does not seem to me to be a free man who does not sometimes do nothing. *Cicero*

They talk of the dignity of work. Bosh. The dignity is in leisure.
Herman Melville

Leisure is the mother of philosophy. *Thomas Hobbes*

Employ thy time well, if thou meanest to gain leisure. *Benjamin Franklin*

In this theater of man's life, it is reserved only for God and angels to be lookers-on. *Pythagoras*

LIBERTY *Also see:* DEMOCRACY, FREEDOM of PRESS, JUSTICE, RIGHTS.

Absolute liberty is absence of restraint; responsibility is restraint; therefore, the ideally free individual is responsible to himself. *Henry Brooks Adams*

Free people, remember this maxim: we may acquire liberty, but it is never recovered if it is once lost. *Jean Jacques Rousseau*

Liberty, not communism, is the most contagious force in the world.
Earl Warren

Liberty is the only thing you can't have unless you give it to others.
William Allen White

Liberty consists in wholesome restraint. *Daniel Webster*

Liberty means responsibility. That is why most men dread it.
George Bernard Shaw

Liberty doesn't work as well in practice as it does in speeches.
Will Rogers

I believe in only one thing: liberty; but I do not believe in liberty enough to want to force it upon anyone. *H. L. Mencken*

What light is to the eyes—what air is to the lungs—what love is to the heart, liberty is to the soul of man. *Robert Green Ingersoll*

Liberty is always dangerous, but it is the safest thing we have.
Harry Emerson Fosdick

LIFE *Also see:* AMUSEMENT, CERTAINTY, CHANGE, CHOICE, EMPLOY-
MENT, ENJOYMENT, IMMORTALITY, MAN, SOUL.

We are here to add what we can to life, not to get what we can from it.
William Osler

Life is the childhood of our immortality. *Johann Wolfgang von Goethe*

Life is not lost by dying; life is lost minute by minute, day by dragging
day, in all the thousand small uncaring ways. *Stephen Vincent Benét*

Life is the continuous adjustment of internal relations to external relations.
Herbert Spencer

The best use of life is to spend it for something that outlasts life.
William James

Life is a dead-end street. *H. L. Mencken*

Life is a series of little deaths out of which life always returns.
Charles Feidelson, Jr.

Life is a tragedy for those who feel, and a comedy for those who think.
Jean de La Bruyére

Let us so live that when we come to die even the undertaker will be sorry.
Mark Twain

Do not take life too seriously; you will never get out of it alive.
Elbert Hubbard

Life is like a cash register, in that every account, every thought, every deed,
like every sale, is registered and recorded. *Fulton J. Sheen*

Were it offered to my choice, I should have no objection to a repetition
of the same life from its beginning, only asking the advantages authors have
in a second edition to correct some faults in the first. *Benjamin Franklin*

LIGHT

There are two kinds of light—the glow that illumines, and the glare that
obscures. *James Thurber*

The thing to do is supply light and not heat. *Woodrow Wilson*

Light is the first of painters. There is no object so foul that intense light
will not make it beautiful. *Ralph Waldo Emerson*

Light is the symbol of truth. *James Russell Lowell*

The pursuit of perfection, then, is the pursuit of sweetness and light.
Matthew Arnold

LITERATURE *Also see:* BOOK, LANGUAGE, PLAGIARISM, READING.

Literature is the immortality of speech. *August Wilhelm von Schlegel*

Great literature is simply language charged with meaning to the utmost possible degree. *Ezra Pound*

Only those things are beautiful which are inspired by madness and written by reason. *André Gide*

A sequel is an admission that you've been reduced to imitating yourself. *Don Marquis*

Writing is the only profession where no one considers you ridiculous if you earn no money. *Jules Renard*

Literature is the art of writing something that will be read twice. *Cyril Connolly*

The decline of literature indicates the decline of a nation. *Johann Wolfgang von Goethe*

Literature is news that stays news. *Ezra Pound*

Our high respect for a well-read man is praise enough of literature. *Ralph Waldo Emerson*

Literature is the orchestration of platitudes. *Thornton Wilder*

LOGIC *Also see:* ARGUMENT, REASON, PHILOSOPHY, SCIENCE.

The mind has its own logic but does not often let others in on it. *Bernard Augustine de Voto*

Logic, like whiskey, loses its beneficial effect when taken in too large quantities. *Lord Dunsany*

Logic is the art of going wrong with confidence. *Joseph Wood Krutch*

Logic: an instrument used for bolstering a prejudice. *Elbert Hubbard*

Logic is the anatomy of thought. *John Locke*

Man is not logical and his intellectual history is a record of mental reserves and compromises. He hangs on to what he can in his old beliefs even when he is compelled to surrender their logical basis. *John Dewey*

Men are apt to mistake the strength of their feeling for the strength of their argument. The heated mind resents the chill touch and relentless scrutiny of logic. *William E. Gladstone*

Logic is neither a science nor an art, but a dodge. *Benjamin Jowett*

LONELINESS *Also see:* ABSENCE, DISTRUST, LEADERSHIP, SOLITUDE.

In cities no one is quiet but many are lonely; in the country, people are quiet but few are lonely.   *Geoffrey Francis Fisher*

People are lonely because they build walls instead of bridges.
Joseph F. Newton

The surest cure for vanity is loneliness.   *Thomas Wolfe*

I was never less alone than when by myself.   *Edward Gibbon*

Language has created the word *loneliness* to express the pain of being alone, and the word *solitude* to express the glory of being alone.
Paul Tillich

The whole conviction of my life now rests upon the belief that loneliness, far from being a rare and curious phenomenon, peculiar to myself and to a few other solitary men, is the central and inevitable fact of human existence.   *Thomas Wolfe*

LOQUACITY *Also see:* BORE, DIPLOMACY, ELOQUENCE.

He who talks much cannot talk well.   *Carlo Goldoni*

Every absurdity has a champion to defend it, for error is always talkative.
Oliver Goldsmith

They always talk who never think, and who have the least to say.
Matthew Prior

Speaking much is a sign of vanity, for he that is lavish with words is a niggard in deed.   *Sir Walter Raleigh*

No fool can be silent at a feast.   *Solon*

Loquacity and lying are cousins.   *German Proverb*

LOSS *Also see:* ADVERSITY, DEFEAT, GAIN, WASTE.

When wealth is lost, nothing is lost; when health is lost, something is lost; when character is lost, all is lost.   *German Motto*

It's the good loser who finally loses out.   *Kin Hubbard*

The cheerful loser is the winner.   *Elbert Hubbard*

Lose an hour in the morning, and you will spend all day looking for it.
Richard Whately

No evil is without its compensation. The less money, the less trouble; the less favor, the less envy. Even in those cases which put us out of wits, it is not the loss itself, but the estimate of the loss that troubles us.   *Seneca*

Wise men never sit and wail their loss, but cheerily seek how to redress their harms.   *William Shakespeare*

LOVE *Also see:* AFFECTION, DEATH, DELUSION, FAITH, MARRIAGE, PASSION.

If there is anything better than to be loved it is loving. *Anonymous*

The way to love anything is to realize that it might be lost.
Gilbert K. Chesterton

Love's like the measles, all the worse when it comes late. *Douglas Jerrold*

Love built on beauty, soon as beauty, dies. *John Donne*

To love is to place our happiness in the happiness of another.
Gottfried Wilhelm von Leibnitz

Love gives itself; it is not bought. *Henry Wadsworth Longfellow*

Love does not consist in gazing at each other but in looking outward together in the same direction. *Antoine de Saint-Exupéry*

It is better to have loved and lost, than not to have loved at all.
Alfred, Lord Tennyson

Love is a canvas furnished by Nature and embroidered by imagination.
Voltaire

He that falls in love with himself will have no rivals. *Benjamin Franklin*

Love: the delusion that one woman differs from another. *H. L. Mencken*

There is only one sort of love, but there are a thousand copies.
François de La Rochefoucauld

I love a hand that meets my own with a grasp that causes some sensation.
Samuel Osgood

Love is the word used to label the sexual excitement of the young, the habituation of the middle-aged, and the mutual dependence of the old.
John Ciardi

I never knew how to worship until I knew how to love.
Henry Ward Beecher

There is a Law that man should love his neighbor as himself. In a few years it should be as natural to mankind as breathing or the upright gait; but if he does not learn it he must perish. *Alfred Adler*

All mankind loves a lover. *Ralph Waldo Emerson*

A coward is incapable of exhibiting love; it is the prerogative of the brave.
Mahatma Gandhi

We are shaped and fashioned by what we love.
Johann Wolfgang von Goethe

LOYALTY *Also see:* COUNTRY, DIPLOMACY, FIDELITY.

Unless you can find some sort of loyalty, you cannot find unity and peace in your active living.
Josiah Royce

Loyalty means nothing unless it has at its heart the absolute principle of self-sacrifice.
Woodrow Wilson

Fidelity purchased with money, money can destroy.
Seneca

Loyalty to petrified opinion never yet broke a chain or freed a human soul.
Mark Twain

We join ourselves to no party that does not carry the American flag, and keep step to the music of the Union.
Rufus Choate

My country right or wrong; when right, to keep her right; when wrong, to put her right.
Carl Schurz

Loyalty . . . is a realization that America was born of revolt, flourished in dissent, became great through experimentation.
Henry S. Commager

LUCK *Also see:* CHANCE, DESTINY, DIGNITY, FORTUNE.

The only sure thing about luck is that it will change.
Wilson Mizner

Shallow men believe in luck. Strong men believe in cause and effect.
Ralph Waldo Emerson

Chance favors the prepared mind.
Louis Pasteur

So unlucky that he runs into accidents which started out to happen to somebody else.
Don Marquis

Depend on the rabbit's foot if you will, but remember it didn't work for the rabbit.
R. E. Shay

Good luck is a lazy man's estimate of a worker's success.
Anonymous

I believe in luck: how else can you explain the success of those you dislike?
Jean Cocteau

It is the mark of an inexperienced man not to believe in luck.
Joseph Conrad

If a man who cannot count finds a four-leaf clover, is he lucky?
Stanislaw J. Lec

As long as we are lucky we attribute it to our smartness; our bad luck we give the gods credit for.
Josh Billings

A pound of pluck is worth a ton of luck.
James A. Garfield

Better an ounce of luck than a pound of gold.
Yiddish Proverb

LUXURY *Also see:* AVARICE, EXTRAVAGANCE, WEALTH.

War destroys men, but luxury destroys mankind; at once corrupts the body and the mind.
John Crowne

Luxury may possibly contribute to give bread to the poor; but if there were no luxury, there would be no poor.
Henry Home

Give us the luxuries of life and we'll dispense with the necessaries.
Oliver Wendell Holmes

We live in an age when unnecessary things are our only necessities.
Oscar Wilde

On the soft bed of luxury most kingdoms have expired. *Edward Young*

Most of the luxuries, and many of the so-called comforts of life, are not only indispensable, but positive hindrances to the elevation of mankind.
Henry David Thoreau

Possessions, outward success, publicity, luxury—to me these have always been contemptible. I believe that a simple and unassuming manner of life is best for every one, best for both the body and the mind.
Albert Einstein

Luxury is the first, second and third cause of the ruin of republics. It is the vampire which soothes us into a fatal slumber while it sucks the life-blood of our veins.
Edward Payson

LYING *Also see:* CREDULITY, DECEIT, DISHONESTY, EXCUSES, HYPOC-RISY, LOQUACITY.

Never chase a lie. Let it alone, and it will run itself to death. I can work out a good character much faster than anyone can lie me out of it.
Lyman Beecher

You can best reward a liar by believing nothing of what he says.
Aristippus

I do not mind lying, but I hate inaccuracy. *Samuel Butler*

One ought to have a good memory when he has told a lie. *Corneille*

The liar's punishment is not in the least that he is not believed, but that he cannot believe anyone else. *George Bernard Shaw*

There is no worse lie than a truth misunderstood by those who hear it.
William James

Sin has many tools, but a lie is the handle that fits them all.
Oliver Wendell Holmes

The truth that survives is simply the lie that is pleasantest to believe.
H. L. Mencken

Any fool can tell the truth, but it requires a man of some sense to know how to lie well. *Samuel Butler*

M

MACHINE *Also see:* AUTOMATION, TECHNOLOGY.

One machine can do the work of fifty ordinary men. No machine can do the work of one extraordinary man. *Elbert Hubbard*

To curb the machine and limit art to handicraft is a denial of opportunity. *Lewis Mumford*

A tool is but the extension of a man's hand, and a machine is but a complex tool. He that invents a machine augments the power of man and the well-being of mankind. *Henry Ward Beecher*

Men have become tools of their tools. *Henry David Thoreau*

On mechanical slavery, on the slavery of the machine, the future of the world depends. *Oscar Wilde*

To me, there is something superbly symbolic in the fact that an astronaut, sent up as assistant to a series of computers, found that he worked more accurately and more intelligently than they. Inside the capsule, *man* is still in charge. *Adlai E. Stevenson*

As machines get to be more and more like men, men will come to be more like machines. *Joseph Wood Krutch*

The machine unmakes the man. Now that the machine is so perfect, the engineer is nobody. *Ralph Waldo Emerson*

MAJORITY *Also see:* DEMOCRACY, MINORITY.

It never troubles the wolf how many the sheep may be. *Vergil*

We go by the major vote, and if the majority are insane, the sane must go to the hospital. *Horace Mann*

There is one body that knows more than anybody, and that is everybody. *Alexandre de Talleyrand-Périgord*

Whenever you find that you are on the side of the majority, it is time to reform. *Mark Twain*

Any man more right than his neighbors, constitutes a majority of one. *Henry David Thoreau*

The voice of the majority is no proof of justice. *Johann Von Schiller*

One, with God, is always a majority, but many a martyr has been burned at the stake while the votes were being counted. *Thomas B. Reed*

When you get too big a majority, you're immediately in trouble. *Sam Rayburn*

It is my principle that the will of the majority should always prevail. *Thomas Jefferson*

MAN

Also see: AVERAGE, BELIEF, BOOK, BOYS, CAUSE, CITIZENSHIP, CLASS, FAILURE, FATHER, FOOL, GOD, HUMAN NATURE, MACHINE, WOMAN.

Man is a reasoning rather than a reasonable animal. *Alexander Hamilton*

Man is a piece of the universe made alive. *Ralph Waldo Emerson*

The ablest man I ever met is the man you think you are.
Franklin Delano Roosevelt

All that I care to know is that a man is a human being—that is enough for me; he can't be any worse. *Mark Twain*

Man is the only creature that refuses to be what he is. *Albert Camus*

Man is a special being, and if left to himself, in an isolated condition, would be one of the weakest creatures; but associated with his kind, works wonders. *Daniel Webster*

Man is a political animal by nature; he is a scientist by chance or choice; he is a moralist because he is a man. *Hans J. Morgenthau*

I am the inferior of any man whose rights I trample under foot. Men are not superior by reason of the accidents of race or color. They are superior who have the best heart—the best brain. The superior man . . . stands erect by bending above the fallen. He rises by lifting others.
Robert Green Ingersoll

No man is an island entire of itself; every man is part of the main . . . Any man's death diminishes me because I am involved in mankind, and therefore never send to know for whom the bell tolls; it tolls for thee. *John Donne*

MANNERS

Also see: BEHAVIOR, COURTESY, GENTLEMAN, HASTE.

To succeed in the world it is not enough to be stupid, you must also be well-mannered. *Voltaire*

Nothing so much prevents our being natural as the desire of appearing so.
François de La Rochefoucauld

It is a mistake that there is no bath that will cure people's manners, but drowning would help. *Mark Twain*

A man's own good breeding is the best security against other people's ill manners. *Lord Chesterfield*

A man's own manner and character is what most becomes him. *Cicero*

Nowadays, manners are easy and life is hard. *Benjamin Disraeli*

Savages we call them because their manners differ from ours.
Benjamin Franklin

Manners easily and rapidly mature into morals. *Horace Mann*

MARRIAGE *Also see:* ANCESTRY, BACHELOR, HUSBAND, SEX, WIFE.

The difficulty with marriage is that we fall in love with a personality, but must live with a character.   *Peter DeVries*

Marriage is that relation between man and woman in which the independence is equal, the dependence mutual, and the obligation reciprocal.
Louis K. Anspacher

Marriage is our last, best chance to grow up.   *Joseph Barth*

Men marry to make an end; women to make a beginning.   *Alexis Dupuy*

Where there's marriage without love, there will be love without marriage.
Benjamin Franklin

It takes two to make a marriage a success and only one to make it a failure.
Herbert Samuel

I guess the only way to stop divorce is to stop marriage.   *Will Rogers*

Well-married, a man is winged: ill-matched, he is shackled.
Henry Ward Beecher

Marriage is the torment of one, the felicity of two, the strife and enmity of three.   *Washington Irving*

The bonds of matrimony are like any other bonds—they mature slowly.
Peter DeVries

A successful marriage is an edifice that must be rebuilt every day.
André Maurois

God help the man who won't marry until he finds a perfect woman, and God help him still more if he finds her.   *Benjamin Tillett*

Marriage resembles a pair of shears, so joined that they cannot be separated; often moving in opposite directions, yet always punishing any one who comes between them.   *Sydney Smith*

MARTYR *Also see:* HEROISM, SACRIFICE.

The way of the world is, to praise dead saints, and persecute living ones.
Nathaniel Howe

It is more difficult, and it calls for higher energies of soul, to live a martyr than to die one.   *Horace Mann*

It is the cause and not merely the death that makes the martyr.
Napoleon Bonaparte

A thing is not necessarily true because a man dies for it.   *Oscar Wilde*

I think the most uncomfortable thing about martyrs is that they look down on people who aren't.   *Samuel N. Behrman*

MATURITY *Also see:* AGE.

Maturity is often more absurd than youth and very frequently is most unjust to youth.
Thomas A. Edison

The immature man wants to die nobly for a cause, while the mature man wants to live humanely for one.
Wilhelm Stekel

Maturity is the time of life when, if you had the time, you'd have the time of your life.
Anonymous

Only the middle-aged have all their five senses in the keeping of their wits.
Hervey Allen

By the age of twenty, any young man should know whether or not he is to be a specialist and just where his tastes lie. By postponing the question we have\set on immaturity a premium which controls most American personality to its deathbed.
Robert S. Hillyer

MAXIM

A man of maxims only, is like a cyclops with one eye, and that in the back of his head.
Samuel Taylor Coleridge

Pithy sentences are like sharp nails which force truth upon our memory.
Denis Diderot

Maxims are the condensed good sense of nations.
James Mackintosh

Maxims are like lawyers who must need to see but one side of the case.
Frank Gelett Burgess

They are like the clue in the labyrinth, or the compass in the night.
Joseph Joubert

All maxims have their antagonist maxims; proverbs should be sold in pairs, a single one being but a half truth.
William Mathews

MEANS . . . See END and MEANS

MEDICINE *Also see:* DISEASE, DRUGS, HEALTH, PROFESSION.

The only profession that labors incessantly to destroy the reason for its own existence.
James Bryce

God heals and the doctor takes the fee.
Benjamin Franklin

He is the best physician who is the most ingenious inspirer of hope.
Samuel Taylor Coleridge

I firmly believe that if the whole *materia medica* could be sunk to the bottom of the sea, it would be all the better for mankind, and all the worse for the fishes.
Oliver Wendell Holmes

MEDITATION ... See THOUGHT

MEMORY *Also see:* LYING, MONUMENT.

Many a man fails to become a thinker only because his memory is too good.   *Nietzsche*

Memory is the cabinet of imagination, the treasury of reason, the registry of conscience, and the council chamber of thought.   *St. Basil*

Unless we remember we cannot understand.   *Edward M. Forster*

Experience teaches that a strong memory is generally joined to a weak judgment.   *Michel de Montaigne*

Those who cannot remember the past are condemned to repeat it.
George Santayana

Recollection is the only paradise from which we cannot be turned out.
Jean Paul Richter

If you have to keep reminding yourself of a thing, perhaps it isn't so.
Christopher Morley

A retentive memory is a good thing, but the ability to forget is the true token of greatness.   *Elbert Hubbard*

> The leaves of memory seemed to make
> A mournful rustling in the dark.   *Henry Wadsworth Longfellow*

A man of great memory without learning hath a rock and a spindle and no staff to spin.   *George Herbert*

Every man's memory is his private literature.   *Aldous Huxley*

MERCY *Also see:* COMPASSION, FIRMNESS, FORGIVENESS, PITY.

> Teach me to feel another's woe,
>   To hide the fault I see:
> That mercy I to others show,
>   That mercy show to me.   *Alexander Pope*

Sweet mercy is nobility's true badge.   *William Shakespeare*

Mercy among the virtues is like the moon among the stars . . . It is the light that hovers above the judgment seat.   *Edwin Hubbel Chapin*

> The quality of mercy is not strain'd;
> It droppeth as the gentle rain from heaven
> Upon the place beneath. It is twice blest:
> It blesseth him that gives and him that takes.   *William Shakespeare*

Hate shuts her soul when dove-eyed mercy pleads.   *Charles Sprague*

179

MERIT *Also see:* CREDIT, WORTH.

If you wish your merit to be known, acknowledge that of other people.
Oriental Proverb

Nature makes merit, and fortune puts it to work.
François de La Rochefoucauld

Contemporaries appreciate the man rather than his merit; posterity will regard the merit rather than the man.
Charles Caleb Colton

The world rewards the appearance of merit oftener than merit itself.
François de La Rochefoucauld

It never occurs to fools that merit and good fortune are closely united.
Johann Wolfgang von Goethe

There's a proud modesty in merit; averse from asking, and resolved to pay ten times the gifts it asks.
John Dryden

MIND *Also see:* DISEASE, INTELLIGENCE, NATION, REASON, SELF-KNOWLEDGE, UNDERSTANDING.

Few minds wear out; more rust out.
Christian Nestell Bovee

Commonplace minds usually condemn what is beyond the reach of their understanding.
François de La Rochefoucauld

The mind is like the stomach. It is not how much you put into it that counts, but how much it digests.
Albert Jay Nock

I not only use all the brains I have, but all that I can borrow.
Woodrow Wilson

I have a prodigious quantity of mind; it takes me as much as a week sometimes to make it up.
Mark Twain

The defects of the mind, like those of the face, grow worse as we grow old.
François de La Rochefoucauld

Old minds are like old horses; you must exercise them if you wish to keep them in working order.
John Quincy Adams

The mind does not create what it perceives, any more than the eye creates the rose.
Ralph Waldo Emerson

Some men are like pyramids, which are very broad where they touch the ground, but grow narrow as they reach the sky.
Henry Ward Beecher

Life is not a static thing. The only people who do not change their minds are incompetents in asylums, who can't, and those in cemeteries.
Everett M. Dirksen

MINORITY *Also see:* MAJORITY.

Minorities are the stars of the firmament; majorities, the darkness in which they float. *Martin H. Fischer*

Every new opinion, at its starting, is precisely in a minority of one. *Thomas Carlyle*

That cause is strong which has not a multitude, but one strong man behind it. *James Russell Lowell*

All history is a record of the power of minorities, and of minorities of one. *Ralph Waldo Emerson*

The only tyrannies from which men, women and children are suffering in real life are the tyrannies of minorities. *Theodore Roosevelt*

The smallest number, with God and truth on their side, are weightier than thousands. *Charles Simmons*

If a man is in a minority of one, we lock him up. *Oliver Wendell Holmes*

The minority of a country is never known to agree, except in its efforts to reduce and oppress the majority. *James Fenimore Cooper*

The political machine works because it is a united minority acting against a divided majority. *Will Durant*

MIRTH . . . See JOY

MISER *Also see:* AVARICE, GOLD, GREED, MONEY, SELFISHNESS.

The miser is as much in want of that which he has, as of that which he has not. *Publilius Syrus*

The miser, poor fool, not only starves his body, but also his own soul. *Theodore Parker*

The happiest miser on earth is the man who saves up every friend he can make. *Robert Emmet Sherwood*

Through life's dark road his sordid way he wends; an incarnation of fat dividends. *Charles Sprague*

The devil lies brooding in the miser's chest. *Thomas Fuller*

Misers mistake gold for good, whereas it is only a means of obtaining it. *François de La Rochefoucauld*

The miser, starving his brother's body, starves also his own soul, and at death shall creep out of his great estate of injustice, poor and naked and miserable. *Theodore Parker*

A miser grows rich by seeming poor; an extravagant man grows poor by seeming rich. *William Shenstone*

MISERY *Also see:* ADVERSITY, GRIEF, PAIN, SORROW.

Misery loves company, but company does not reciprocate.

Addison Mizner

He that is down need fear no fall.

John Bunyan

If misery loves company, misery has company enough.

Henry David Thoreau

There is no greater grief than to remember days of joy when misery is at hand.

Dante

Man is only miserable so far as he thinks himself so.　　*Jacopo Sannazaro*

Threescore years and ten is enough; if a man can't suffer all the misery he wants in that time, he must be numb.

Josh Billings

There are a good many real miseries in life that we cannot help smiling at, but they are the smiles that make wrinkles and not dimples.

Oliver Wendell Holmes

A misery is not to be measured from the nature of the evil, but from the temper of the sufferer.

Joseph Addison

MOB *Also see:* RIOT, VIOLENCE.

A mob is a group of persons with heads but no brains.　　*Thomas Fuller*

The nose of a mob is its imagination. By this, at any time, it can be quietly led.

Edgar Allan Poe

The mob is man voluntarily descending to the nature of the beast.

Ralph Waldo Emerson

A crowd always thinks with its sympathy, never with its reason.

William Rounseville Alger

Get together a hundred or two men, however sensible they may be, and you are very likely to have a mob.

Samuel Johnson

The mob is the mother of tyrants.

Diogenes

Every man has a mob self and an individual self, in varying proportions.

D. H. Lawrence

It is proof of a bad cause when it is applauded by the mob.　　*Seneca*

A mob is the scum that rises upmost when the nation boils.　　*John Dryden*

Every numerous assembly is a mob; everything there depends on instantaneous turns.

Cardinal de Retz

A crowd is not company, and faces are but a gallery of pictures.

Francis Bacon

MODERATION *Also see:* ABSTINENCE, BARGAIN, SELF-CONTROL.

In everything the middle road is the best; all things in excess bring trouble to men.
Plautus

It is better to rise from life as from a banquet—neither thirsty nor drunken.
Aristotle

Moderation in temper is always a virtue; but moderation in principle is always a vice.
Thomas Paine

Moderation is the inseparable companion of wisdom, but with it genius has not even a nodding acquaintance.
Charles Caleb Colton

Moderation is a fatal thing: nothing succeeds like excess.
Oscar Wilde

Temperate temperance is best; intemperate temperance injures the cause of temperance.
Mark Twain

To go beyond the bounds of moderation is to outrage humanity.
Blaise Pascal

The pursuit, even of the best things, ought to be calm and tranquil.
Cicero

He will always be a slave who does not know how to live upon a little.
Horace

MODESTY *Also see:* BLUSH, HUMILITY, MERIT.

Modesty is not only an ornament, but also a guard to virtue.
Joseph Addison

There's a lot to be said for the fellow who doesn't say it himself.
Maurice Switzer

Modesty may make a fool seem a man of sense.
Jonathan Swift

False modesty is the refinement of vanity. It is a lie.
Jean de La Bruyère

Modesty antedates clothes and will be resumed when clothes are no more. Modesty died when clothes were born. Modesty died when false modesty was born.
Mark Twain

It is easy for a somebody to be modest, but it is difficult to be modest when one is a nobody.
Jules Renard

Modesty is the conscience of the body.
Honoré de Balzac

Modesty is the only sure bait when you angle for praise.
Lord Chesterfield

With people of only moderate ability modesty is mere honesty; but with those who possess great talent it is hypocrisy.
Arthur Schopenhauer

MONEY *Also see:* BORROWING, CREDIT, DEBT, DIPLOMACY, ECONO-
MY, FINANCE, GOLD, KNOWLEDGE, WEALTH.

The chief value of money lies in the fact that one lives in a world in which
it is overestimated. *H. L. Mencken*

He that is of the opinion money will do everything may well be suspected
of doing everything for money. *Benjamin Franklin*

The safest way to double your money is to fold it over once and put it in
your pocket. *Kin Hubbard*

The use of money is all the advantage there is in having it.
Benjamin Franklin

Money often costs too much. *Ralph Waldo Emerson*

> Never ask of money spent
> Where the spender thinks it went.
> Nobody was ever meant
> To remember or invent
> What he did with every cent. *Robert Frost*

Money is not required to buy one necessity of the soul.
Henry David Thoreau

Money is like a sixth sense, and you can't make use of the other five without it. *W. Somerset Maugham*

I'm tired of love, I'm still more tired of rhyme, but money gives me pleasure all the time. *Hilaire Belloc*

Money does all things for reward. Some are pious and honest as long as
they thrive upon it, but if the devil himself gives better wages, they soon
change their party. *Seneca*

Put not your trust in money, but put your money in trust.
Oliver Wendell Holmes

MONUMENT *Also see:* ACHIEVEMENT, GRAVE.

Those only deserve a monument who do not need one. *William Hazlitt*

Deeds, not stones, are the true monuments of the great. *John L. Motley*

The marble keeps merely a cold and sad memory of a man who would else
be forgotten. No man who needs a monument ever ought to have one.
Nathaniel Hawthorne

Monuments are the grappling-irons that bind one generation to another.
Joseph Joubert

Tombs are the clothes of the dead; a grave is but a plain suit; a rich monument is an embroidered one. *Thomas Fuller*

If I have done any deed worthy of remembrance, that deed will be my
monument. If not, no monument can preserve my memory. *Agesilaus II*

MORALITY *Also see:* ART, BOREDOM, MANNERS, VIRTUE.

Moralizing and morals are two entirely different things and are always found in entirely different people. *Don Herold*

Turning the other cheek is a kind of moral jiu-jitsu. *Gerald S. Lee*

So far, about morals, I know only that what is moral is what you feel good after and what is immoral is what you feel bad after. *Ernest Hemingway*

To denounce moralizing out of hand is to pronounce a moral judgment. *H. L. Mencken*

Morality is the best of all devices for leading mankind by the nose. *Nietzsche*

All sects are different, because they come from men; morality is everywhere the same, because it comes from God. *Voltaire*

Morality is simply the attitude we adopt toward people whom we personally dislike. *Oscar Wilde*

MORTALITY . . . See DEATH

MOTHER *Also see:* BIRTH, BIRTH CONTROL, CHILDREN, CLEVERNESS, DESTINY, EARTH, FATHER, PARENT, WIFE, WOMAN.

Men are what their mothers made them. *Ralph Waldo Emerson*

A mother is not a person to lean on but a person to make leaning unnecessary. *Dorothy Canfield Fisher*

The hand that rocks the cradle is the hand that rules the world. *W. S. Ross*

God could not be everywhere, and therefore he made mothers. *Jewish Proverb*

All that I am, or hope to be, I owe to my angel mother. *Abraham Lincoln*

The mother's heart is the child's schoolroom. *Henry Ward Beecher*

MURDER *Also see:* ASSASSINATION, BIRTH CONTROL.

Every unpunished murder takes away something from the security of every man's life. *Daniel Webster*

Criminals do not die by the hands of the law; they die by the hands of other men. *George Bernard Shaw*

It is forbidden to kill; therefore all murderers are punished unless they kill in large numbers and to the sound of trumpets. *Voltaire*

The very emphasis of the commandment: Thou shalt not kill, makes it certain that we are descended from an endlessly long chain of generations of murderers, whose love of murder was in their blood as it is perhaps also in ours. *Sigmund Freud*

MUSIC *Also see:* JAZZ.

Music is well said to be the speech of angels. *Thomas Carlyle*

After silence that which comes nearest to expressing the inexpressible is music. *Aldous Huxley*

Music is the only language in which you cannot say a mean or sarcastic thing. *Lord Erskine*

Music is the universal language of mankind. *Henry Wadsworth Longfellow*

Classical music is the kind that we keep hoping will turn into a tune. *Kin Hubbard*

Music is harmony, harmony is perfection, perfection is our dream, and our dream is heaven. *Amiel*

> I listened, motionless and still;
> And, as I mounted up the hill,
> The music in my heart I bore,
> Long after it was heard no more. *William Wordsworth*

Composers should write tunes that chauffeurs and errand boys can whistle. *Thomas Beecham*

The musician who always plays on the same string is laughed at. *Horace*

MYSTERY *Also see:* SECRECY.

All is mystery; but he is a slave who will not struggle to penetrate the dark veil. *Benjamin Disraeli*

It is hard to say whether the doctors of law or divinity have made the greater advances in the lucrative business of mystery. *Edmund Burke*

The most beautiful experience we can have is the mysterious. It is the fundamental emotion which stands at the cradle of true art and true science. *Albert Einstein*

It is the dim haze of mystery that adds enchantment to pursuit. *Antoine Rivarol*

Mystery is the wisdom of blockheads. *Horace Walpole*

Mystery and innocence are not akin. *Hosea Ballou*

Mystery is another name for our ignorance; if we were omniscient, all would be perfectly plain. *Tryon Edwards*

What has puzzled us before seems less mysterious, and the crooked paths look straighter as we approach the end. *Jean Paul Richter*

N

NAME *Also see:* REPUTATION.

A person with a bad name is already half-hanged.   *Proverb*

To live in mankind is far more than to live in a name.   *Vachel Lindsay*

The beginning of wisdom is to call things by their right names.
Chinese Proverb

A good name, like good will, is got by many actions and lost by one.
Lord Jeffery

The invisible thing called a Good Name is made up of the breath of numbers that speak well of you.   *Lord Halifax*

Sticks and stones will break my bones, but names will never hurt me.
English Proverb

What's in a name? That which we call a rose by any other name would smell as sweet.   *William Shakespeare*

Nicknames stick to people, and the most ridiculous are the most adhesive.
Thomas C. Haliburton

Some men do as much begrudge others a good name, as they want one themselves: and perhaps that is the reason of it.   *William Penn*

NATION *Also see:* AMERICA, UNITED NATIONS, UNITY.

A nation is a totality of men united through community of fate into a community of character.   *Otto Bauer*

Territory is but the body of a nation. The people who inhabit its hills and valleys are its soul, its spirit, its life.   *James A. Garfield*

A nation never falls but by suicide.   *Ralph Waldo Emerson*

A nation is a thing that lives and acts like a man, and men are the particulars of which it is composed.   *Josiah Gilbert Holland*

There was never a nation great until it came to the knowledge that it had nowhere in the world to go for help.   *Charles Dudley Warner*

The nation's honor is dearer than the nation's comfort; yes, than the nation's life itself.   *Woodrow Wilson*

A nation, like a person, has a mind—a mind that must be kept informed and alert, that must know itself, that understands the hopes and needs of its neighbors—all the other nations that live within the narrowing circle of the world.   *Franklin Delano Roosevelt*

No nation is fit to sit in judgment upon any other nation.
Woodrow Wilson

NATIONALISM   *Also see:* CITIZENSHIP, PATRIOTISM.

Nationalism is an infantile disease. It is the measles of mankind.

Albert Einstein

We are in the midst of a great transition from narrow nationalism to international partnership.   *Lyndon Baines Johnson*

There is a higher form of patriotism than nationalism, and that higher form is not limited by the boundaries of one's country; but by a duty to mankind to safeguard the trust of civilization.   *Oscar S. Strauss*

Born in iniquity and conceived in sin, the spirit of nationalism has never ceased to bend human institutions to the service of dissension and distress.   *Thorstein Veblen*

The root of the problem is very simply stated: if there were no sovereign independent states, if the states of the civilized world were organized in some sort of federalism, as the states of the American Union, for instance, are organized, there would be no international war as we know it . . . The main obstacle is nationalism.   *Norman Angell*

NATURE   *Also see:* ART, BEAUTY, CRUELTY, EARTH, FAMILY, FORTUNE, KISS.

The ignorant man marvels at the exceptional; the wise man marvels at the common; the greatest wonder of all is the regularity of nature.

George Dana Boardman

Nature does not complete things. She is chaotic. Man must finish, and he does so by making a garden and building a wall.   *Robert Frost*

Nature knows no pause in progress and development, and attaches her curse on all inaction.   *Johann Wolfgang von Goethe*

Nature encourages no looseness, pardons no errors.

Ralph Waldo Emerson

Nature creates ability; luck provides it with opportunity.

François de La Rochefoucauld

Nature is an infinite sphere whose center is everywhere and whose circumference is nowhere.   *Blaise Pascal*

Whether man is disposed to yield to nature or to oppose her, he cannot do without a correct understanding of her language.   *Jean Rostand*

A life in harmony with nature, the love of truth and virtue, will purge the eyes to understanding her text.   *Ralph Waldo Emerson*

I love to think of nature as an unlimited broadcasting station, through which God speaks to us every hour, if we only will tune in.

George Washington Carver

Man must go back to nature for information.   *Thomas Paine*

NECESSITY
Also see: CIVILIZATION, ENDURANCE, HABIT, LUXURY, WANT.

Make yourself necessary to somebody.   *Ralph Waldo Emerson*

Necessity is the mother of invention.   *Jonathan Swift*

Our necessities are few but our wants are endless.   *Josh Billings*

Without death and decay, how could life go on?   *John Burroughs*

Necessity knows no law except to conquer.   *Publilius Syrus*

Necessity has no law.   *Benjamin Franklin*

Necessity is the plea for every infringement of human freedom. It is the argument of tyrants; it is the creed of slaves.   *William Pitt*

We do what we must, and call it by the best names. *Ralph Waldo Emerson*

It is surprising what a man can do when he has to, and how little most men will do when they don't have to.   *Walter Linn*

Whatever necessity lays upon thee, endure; whatever she commands, do.
                    Johann Wolfgang von Goethe

Necessity is blind until it becomes conscious. Freedom is the consciousness of necessity.   *Karl Marx*

NEGLECT
Also see: IDLENESS, PROCRASTINATION.

Negligence is the rust of the soul, that corrodes through all her best resolves.   *Owen Felltham*

He that thinks he can afford to be negligent is not far from being poor.
                    Samuel Johnson

It is the neglect of timely repair that makes rebuilding necessary.
                    Richard Whately

A little neglect may breed great mischief.   *Benjamin Franklin*

It will generally be found that men who are constantly lamenting their ill luck are only reaping the consequences of their own neglect, mismanagement, and improvidence, or want of application.   *Samuel Smiles*

NEUTRALITY
Also see: TOLERANCE.

Neutral men are the devil's allies.   *Edwin Hubbel Chapin*

Neutrality, as a lasting principle, is an evidence of weakness. *Lajos Kossuth*

People who demand neutrality in any situation are usually not neutral but in favor of the status quo.   *Max Eastman*

A wise neuter joins with neither, but uses both as his honest interest leads him.   *William Penn*

NEWSPAPER *Also see:* FREEDOM of the PRESS, JOURNALISM.

A newspaper is a circulating library with high blood pressure.
Arthur "Bugs" Baer

From the American newspapers you'd think America was populated solely by naked women and cinema stars. *Lady Astor*

Newspapers are the schoolmasters of the common people.
Henry Ward Beecher

A newspaper should be the maximum of information, and the minimum of comment. *Richard Cobden*

Newspapers are the world's mirrors. *James Ellis*

If words were invented to conceal thought, newspapers are a great improvement of a bad invention. *Henry David Thoreau*

We live under a government of men and morning newspapers.
Wendell Phillips

The man who reads nothing at all is better educated than the man who reads nothing but newspapers. *Thomas Jefferson*

Were it left to me to decide whether we should have a government without newspapers or newspapers without government, I should not hesitate a moment to prefer the latter. *Thomas Jefferson*

All I know is what I see in the papers. *Will Rogers*

The morning paper is just as necessary for an American as dew is to the grass. *Josh Billings*

NOVELTY *Also see:* ORIGINALITY, VARIETY.

There is nothing new under the sun. *George M. Cohan*

It is not only old and early impressions that deceive us; the charms of novelty have the same power. *Blaise Pascal*

Novelty is the great parent of pleasure. *Robert South*

Some degree of novelty must be one of the materials in almost every instrument which works upon the mind; and curiosity blends itself, more or less, with all our pleasures. *Edmund Burke*

Novelty has charms that our minds can hardly withstand.
William Makepeace Thackeray

In science, as in common life, we frequently see that a novelty in system, or in practice, cannot be duly appreciated till time has sobered the enthusiasm of its advocates. *Maud*

The earth was made so various, that the mind of desultory man, studious of change, and pleased with novelty, might be indulged. *William Cowper*

NUCLEAR WARFARE *Also see:* TECHNOLOGY, WAR.

We've opened a door—maybe a treasure house, maybe only the realization of a maniac's dream of destruction.   *John Anderson*

People who talk of outlawing the atomic bomb are mistaken—what needs to be outlawed is war.   *Leslie Richard Groves*

Idealists maintain that all nations should share the atomic bomb. Pessimists maintain that they will.   *Punch*

The hydrogen bomb is history's exclamation point. It ends an age-long sentence of manifest violence.   *Marshall McLuhan*

We develop weapons, not to wage war, but to prevent war. Only in the clear light of this greater truth can we properly examine the lesser matter of the testing of our nuclear weapons.   *Dwight D. Eisenhower*

O

OBEDIENCE *Also see:* CHILDREN, DUTY, JUSTICE.
Wicked men obey from fear; good men, from love.   *Aristotle*

The only safe ruler is he who has learned to obey willingly.
                                                                Thomas á Kempis

There are two kinds of men who never amount to much: those who cannot do what they are told, and those who can do nothing else.   *Cyrus H. Curtis*

Obedience alone gives the right to command.   *Ralph Waldo Emerson*

OBLIGATION . . . See DUTY

OBSCURITY . . . See AMBIGUITY

OBSERVATION *Also see:* PERCEPTION, SCIENCE.
Each one sees what he carries in his heart.   *Johann Wolfgang von Goethe*

Observation—activity of both eyes and ears.   *Horace Mann*

He alone is an acute observer, who can observe minutely without being observed.   *Johann Kaspar Lavater*

If I were to prescribe one process in the training of men which is fundamental to success in any direction, it would be thoroughgoing training in the habit of accurate observation. It is a habit which every one of us should be seeking ever more to perfect.   *Eugene G. Grace*

Every man who observes vigilantly and resolves steadfastly grows unconsciously into genius.   *Edward G. Bulwer-Lytton*

We are very much what others think of us. The reception our observations meet with gives us courage to proceed, or damps our efforts.
                                                                William Hazlitt

OPINION *Also see:* BELIEF, FORCE, FREEDOM, IDEA, JUDGMENT, MINORITY, OPPRESSION, PREJUDICE.

Don't judge a man by his opinions, but by what his opinions have made him. *G. C. Lichtenberg*

The foolish and the dead alone never change their opinions. *James Russell Lowell*

People do not seem to realize that their opinion of the world is also a confession of character. *Ralph Waldo Emerson*

It is the difference of opinion that makes horse races. *Mark Twain*

Those who never retract their opinions love themselves more than they love truth. *Joseph Joubert*

He that never changes his opinions, never corrects his mistakes, and will never be wiser on the morrow than he is today. *Tryon Edwards*

With effervescing opinions, the quickest way to let them get flat is to let them get exposed to the air. *Oliver Wendell Holmes*

Opinions cannot survive if one has no chance to fight for them. *Thomas Mann*

Public opinion is a weak tyrant, compared with our private opinion—what a man thinks of himself, that is which determines, or rather indicates his fate. *Henry David Thoreau*

OPPORTUNITY *Also see:* ABILITY, ACHIEVEMENT, CHANCE, CIVILIZATION, FORTUNE, LUCK.

A wise man will make more opportunities than he finds. *Francis Bacon*

You will never "find" time for anything. If you want time you must make it. *Charles Buxton*

Do not wait for extraordinary circumstances to do good; try to use ordinary situations. *Jean Paul Richter*

The commonest form, one of the most often neglected, and the safest opportunity for the average man to seize, is hard work. *Arthur Brisbane*

Occasions are rare; and those who know how to seize upon them are rarer. *Josh Billings*

It is less important to redistribute wealth than it is to redistribute opportunity. *Arthur H. Vandenberg*

The world does not owe men a living, but business, if it is to fulfill its ideal, owes men an opportunity to earn a living. *Owen D. Young*

Plough deep while sluggards sleep. *Benjamin Franklin*

You cannot make your opportunities concur with the opportunities of people whose incomes are ten times greater than yours. *Edward S. Martin*

OPPRESSION *Also see:* ABUSE, CRUELTY, TYRANNY.

You can't hold a man down without staying down with him.
Booker T. Washington

A desire to resist oppression is implanted in the nature of man. *Tacitus*

He that would make his own liberty secure must guard even his enemy from oppression; for if he violates this duty, he establishes a precedent that will reach to himself. *Thomas Paine*

No other offense has ever been visited with such severe penalties as seeking to help the oppressed. *Clarence Darrow*

The oppression of any people for opinion's sake has rarely had any other effect than to fix those opinions deeper and render them more important.
Hosea Ballou

OPTIMISM *Also see:* CHEERFULNESS, PESSIMISM, TRADITION.

In these times you have to be an optimist to open your eyes in the morning. *Carl Sandburg*

Do not expect the world to look bright, if you habitually wear gray-brown glasses. *Charles Eliot*

The only limit to our realization of tomorrow will be our doubts of today.
Franklin Delano Roosevelt

There is no sadder sight than a young pessimist, except an old optimist.
Mark Twain

Optimist: a proponent of the doctrine that black is white. *Ambrose Bierce*

So of cheerfulness, or a good temper, the more it is spent, the more of it remains. *Ralph Waldo Emerson*

The optimist proclaims that we live in the best of all possible worlds; and the pessimist fears this is true. *James Branch Cabell*

An optimist is a man who has never had much experience. *Don Marquis*

The habit of looking on the bright side of every event is worth more than a thousand pounds a year. *Samuel Johnson*

ORDER *Also see:* CIVILIZATION, DISCOVERY, EFFICIENCY.

A place for everything, everything in its place. *Benjamin Franklin*

The art of progress is to preserve order amid change, and to preserve change amid order. Life refuses to be embalmed alive.
Alfred North Whitehead

He who has no taste for order, will be often wrong in his judgment, and seldom considerate or conscientious in his actions. *Johann Kaspar Lavater*

ORIGINALITY
Also see: CREATIVITY, FASHION, INVENTION, PLAGIARISM.

What a good thing Adam had—when he said a good thing, he knew nobody had said it before.　　　　*Mark Twain*

Originality is simply a pair of fresh eyes.　　*Thomas Wentworth Higginson*

It is better to create than to be learned; creating is the true essence of life.
Barthold Georg Niebuhr

Many a man fails as an original thinker simply because his memory is too good.　　　　*Nietzsche*

What the world calls originality is only an unaccustomed method of tickling it.　　　　*George Bernard Shaw*

The merit of originality is not novelty, it is sincerity. The believing man is the original man; he believes for himself, not for another.

Thomas Carlyle

> No bird has ever uttered note
> 　That was not in some first bird's throat;
> Since Eden's freshness and man's fall
> 　No rose has been original.　　*Thomas Bailey Aldrich*

Originality is nothing but judicious imitation.　　　　*Voltaire*

OSTENTATION
Also see: PRETENSION, PRIDE.

Do what good thou canst unknown, and be not vain of what ought rather to be felt than seen.　　　　*William Penn*

Ostentation is the signal flag of hypocrisy.　　*Edwin Hubbel Chapin*

I know that a man who shows me his wealth is like the beggar who shows me his poverty; they are both looking for alms from me, the rich man for the alms of my envy, the poor man for the alms of my guilt.　*Ben Hecht*

An ostentatious man will rather relate a blunder or an absurdity he has committed, than be debarred from talking of his own dear person.
Joseph Addison

Whatever is done without ostentation, and without the people being witnesses of it, is, in my opinion, most praiseworthy: not that the public eye should be entirely avoided, for good actions desire to be placed in the light; but notwithstanding this, the greatest theater for virtue is conscience.
Cicero

Pride is the master sin of the devil, and the devil is the father of lies.
Edwin Hubbel Chapin

That which is given with pride and ostentation is rather an ambition than a bounty.　　　　*Seneca*

The charity that hastens to proclaim its good deeds, ceases to be charity, and is only pride and ostentation.　　　　*William Hutton*

P

PAIN   *Also see:* SUFFERING.

Pain adds rest unto pleasure, and teaches the luxury of health.
Martin F. Tupper

The pain of the mind is worse than the pain of the body.
Publilius Syrus

> Never a lip is curved with pain
> That can't be kissed into smiles again.   *Bret Harte*

Pain dies quickly, and lets her weary prisoners go; the fiercest agonies have shortest reign.   *William Cullen Bryant*

Pain and pleasure, like light and darkness, succeed each other.
Laurence Sterne

Pain is life—the sharper, the more evidence of life.   *Charles Lamb*

> Nothing begins, and nothing ends,
>   That is not paid with moan;
> For we are born in others' pain,
>   And perish in our own.
>
> *Francis Thompson*

Man endures pain as an undeserved punishment; woman accepts it as a natural heritage.   *Anonymous*

PARDON . . . See FORGIVENESS

PARENTS

The joys of parents are secret, and so are their griefs and fears.
Francis Bacon

There are times when parenthood seems nothing more than feeding the hand that bites you.   *Peter De Vries*

The first half of our lives is ruined by our parents and the second half by our children.   *Clarence Darrow*

> Children aren't happy with nothing to ignore,
> And that's what parents were created for.   *Ogden Nash*

We never know the love of the parent till we become parents ourselves.
Henry Ward Beecher

The most important thing a father can do for his children is to love their mother.   *Theodore M. Hesburgh*

How many hopes and fears, how many ardent wishes and anxious apprehensions are twisted together in the threads that connect the parent with the child!   *Samuel Griswold Goodrich*

PARTY *Also see:* GOVERNMENT, POLITICS.

Party is the madness of many, for the gains of a few.   *Alexander Pope*

He serves his party best who serves the country best.   *Rutherford B. Hayes*

Any party which takes credit for the rain must not be surprised if its opponents blame it for the drought.   *Dwight W. Morrow*

All parties without exception, when they seek for power, are varieties of absolutism.   *Pierre Joseph Proudhon*

I am not a member of any organized party—I am a Democrat.   *Will Rogers*

I know my Republican friends were glad to see my wife feeding an elephant in India. She gave him sugar and nuts. But of course the elephant wasn't satisfied.   *John Fitzgerald Kennedy*

The best system is to have one party govern and the other party watch.
        Thomas B. Reed

Party honesty is party expediency.   *Grover Cleveland*

PASSION *Also see:* ANGER, DESIRE, EMOTION, ENTHUSIASM, PATIENCE, POETRY.

Passion is the mob of the man, that commits a riot upon his reason.
        William Penn

Act nothing in furious passion. It's putting to sea in a storm.
        Thomas Fuller

Passion is universal humanity. Without it religion, history, romance and art would be useless.   *Honoré de Balzac*

If we resist our passions, it is more through their weakness than from our strength.   *François de La Rochefoucauld*

The passions are like fire, useful in a thousand ways and dangerous only in one, through their excess.   *Christian Nestell Bovee*

Passion, though a bad regulator, is a powerful spring.
        Ralph Waldo Emerson

He only employs his passion who can make no use of his reason.   *Cicero*

Passion makes idiots of the cleverest men, and makes the biggest idiots clever.   *François de La Rochefoucauld*

Our passions are like convulsion fits, which, though they make us stronger for the time, leave us the weaker ever after.   *Jonathan Swift*

He submits to be seen through a microscope, who suffers himself to be caught in a fit of passion.   *Johann Kaspar Lavater*

PAST   *Also see:* FUTURE, HISTORY, PRESENT.

I tell you the past is a bucket of ashes.   *Carl Sandburg*

Those who cannot remember the past are condemned to repeat it.
George Santayana

The past always looks better than it was; it's only pleasant because it isn't here.   *Finley Peter Dunne*

Some are so very studious of learning what was done by the ancients that they know not how to live with the moderns.   *William Penn*

The free world must now prove itself worthy of its own past.
Dwight D. Eisenhower

Study the past if you would divine the future.   *Confucius*

Many are always praising the by-gone time, for it is natural that the old should extol the days of their youth; the weak, the time of their strength; the sick, the season of their vigor; and the disappointed, the spring-tide of their hopes.   *Caleb Bingham*

To look back to antiquity is one thing, to go back to it is another.
Charles Caleb Colton

The present contains nothing more than the past, and what is found in the effect was already in the cause.   *Henri Bergson*

PATIENCE   *Also see:* ANGER, ENDURANCE.

Adopt the pace of nature: her secret is patience.   *Ralph Waldo Emerson*

He that can have patience can have what he will.   *Benjamin Franklin*

They also serve who only stand and wait.   *John Milton*

Beware the fury of a patient man.   *John Dryden*

Our patience will achieve more than our force.   *Edmund Burke*

Patience is power; with time and patience the mulberry leaf becomes silk.
Chinese Proverb

Everything comes to him who hustles while he waits.   *Thomas A. Edison*

Patience is a minor form of despair, disguised as a virtue.   *Ambrose Bierce*

Patience is bitter, but its fruit is sweet.   *Jean Jacques Rousseau*

Patience and time do more than strength or passion.   *Jean de La Fontaine*

If we could have a little patience, we should escape much mortification; time takes away as much as it gives.   *Marquise de Sévigné*

PATRIOTISM *Also see:* CITIZENSHIP, COUNTRY, NATIONALISM.

Patriotism is easy to understand in America; it means looking out for yourself by looking out for your country. *Calvin Coolidge*

I only regret that I have but one life to give for my country.

Nathan Hale

Ask not what your country can do for you: Ask what you can do for your country. *John Fitzgerald Kennedy*

Patriotism is the last refuge of a scoundrel. *Samuel Johnson*

Love of country is like love of woman—he loves her best who seeks to bestow on her the highest good. *Felix Adler*

This heroism at command, this senseless violence, this accursed bombast of patriotism—how intensely I despise them! *Albert Einstein*

A man's country is not a certain area of land, of mountains, rivers, and woods, but it is a principle; and patriotism is loyalty to that principle.

George William Curtis

> Breathes there the man with soul so dead,
> Who never to himself hath said,
> This is my own, my native land! *Walter Scott*

You'll never have a quiet world till you knock the patriotism out of the human race. *George Bernard Shaw*

A man's feet must be planted in his country, but his eyes should survey the world. *George Santayana*

PEACE *Also see:* BLOOD, DISARMAMENT, HOME, LEISURE, LOYALTY, WAR.

Peace, in international affairs, is a period of cheating between two periods of fighting. *Ambrose Bierce*

Peace has its victories no less than war, but it doesn't have as many monuments to unveil. *Kin Hubbard*

If they want peace, nations should avoid the pin-pricks that precede cannon-shots. *Napoleon Bonaparte*

Peace is rarely denied to the peaceful. *Johann von Schiller*

Peace is the one condition of survival in this nuclear age.

Adlai E. Stevenson

We seek peace, knowing that peace is the climate of freedom.

Dwight D. Eisenhower

If we are to live together in peace, we must come to know each other better. *Lyndon Baines Johnson*

PERCEPTION *Also see:* SCIENCE, UNDERSTANDING.

Only in quiet waters things mirror themselves undistorted. Only in a quiet mind is adequate perception of the world. *Hans Margolius*

Simple people . . . are very quick to see the live facts which are going on about them. *Oliver Wendell Holmes*

The heart has eyes which the brain knows nothing of.
Charles H. Parkhurst

To see what is right, and not do it, is want of courage, or of principle.
Confucius

The clearsighted do not rule the world, but they sustain and console it.
Agnes Repplier

Penetration seems a kind of inspiration; it gives me an idea of prophecy.
Fulke Greville

PERFECTION

Trifles make perfection, and perfection is no trifle. *Michelangelo*

Aim at perfection in everything, though in most things it is unattainable. However, they who aim at it, and persevere, will come much nearer to it than those whose laziness and despondency make them give it up as unattainable. *Lord Chesterfield*

If a man should happen to reach perfection in this world, he would have to die immediately to enjoy himself. *Josh Billings*

Perfection is attained by slow degrees; it requires the hand of time.
Voltaire

No good work whatever can be perfect, and the demand for perfection is always a sign of a misunderstanding of the ends of art. *John Ruskin*

This is the very perfection of a man, to find out his own imperfections.
St. Augustine

Faultily faultless, icily regular, splendidly null, dead perfection; no more.
Alfred, Lord Tennyson

The artist who aims at perfection in everything achieves it in nothing.
Delacroix

It is reasonable to have perfection in our eye that we may always advance toward it, though we know it can never be reached. *Samuel Johnson*

One that desires to excel should endeavor in those things that are in themselves most excellent. *Epictetus*

All things excellent are as difficult as they are rare. *Benedict Spinoza*

PERSEVERANCE *Also see:* DIGNITY, DILIGENCE, ENDURANCE, PATIENCE, PURPOSE.

The difference between perseverance and obstinacy is, that one often comes from a strong will, and the other from a strong won't.

Henry Ward Beecher

By gnawing through a dike, even a rat may drown a nation. *Edmund Burke*

Consider the postage stamp, my son. It secures success through its ability to stick to one thing till it gets there. *Josh Billings*

Big shots are only little shots who keep shooting. *Christopher Morley*

Perseverance is the most overrated of traits, if it is unaccompanied by talent; beating your head against a wall is more likely to produce a concussion in the head than a hole in the wall. *Sydney Harris*

No rock so hard but that a little wave may beat admission in a thousand years. *Alfred, Lord Tennyson*

We make way for the man who boldly pushes past us.

Christian Nestell Bovee

There is no failure except in no longer trying. There is no defeat except from within, no really insurmountable barrier save our own inherent weakness of purpose. *Kin Hubbard*

Perseverance is more prevailing than violence; and many things which cannot be overcome when they are together yield themselves up when taken little by little. *Plutarch*

PERSONALITY *Also see:* CHARACTER, INDIVIDUALITY, MATURITY.

Everyone is a moon, and has a dark side which he never shows to anybody.

Mark Twain

Some persons are likeable in spite of their unswerving integrity. *Don Marquis*

If you have anything really valuable to contribute to the world it will come through the expression of your own personality, that single spark of divinity that sets you off and makes you different from every other living creature.

Bruce Barton

Personality is to a man what perfume is to a flower. *Charles M. Schwab*

PESSIMISM *Also see:* CYNIC, OPTIMISM, SKEPTICISM, TRADITION.

A pessimist is one who feels bad when he feels good for fear he'll feel worse when he feels better. *Anonymous*

Cheer up, the worst is yet to come. *Philander Johnson*

Pessimism is only the name that men of weak nerves give to wisdom.

Bernard De Voto

My pessimism goes to the point of suspecting the sincerity of the pessimists.

Edmond Rostand

PHILOSOPHY *Also see:* DISCRETION, GOD, REASON, RELIGION, SCIENCE, THEORY.

Philosophy: unintelligible answers to insoluble problems.
Henry Brooks Adams

The philosophy of one century is the common sense of the next.
Henry Ward Beecher

It is easy to build a philosophy—it doesn't have to run.
Charles F. Kettering

All philosophy lies in two words, sustain and abstain.   *Epictetus*

Philosophy is an unusually ingenious attempt to think fallaciously.
Bertrand Russell

Philosophy triumphs easily over past and over future evils, but present evils triumph over philosophy.   *François de La Rochefoucauld*

Philosophy is the science which considers truth.   *Aristotle*

Philosophy, when superficially studied, excites doubt; when thoroughly explored, it dispels it.   *Francis Bacon*

Philosophy goes no further than probabilities, and in every assertion keeps a doubt in reserve.   *James A. Froude*

No stream rises higher than its source. What ever man might build could never express or reflect more than he was. It was no more than what he felt. He could record neither more nor less than he had learned of life when the buildings were built . . . His philosophy, true or false, is there.
Frank Lloyd Wright

PITY *Also see:* COMPASSION, SYMPATHY.

Pity is best taught by fellowship in woe.   *Samuel Taylor Coleridge*

Pity costs nothing, and it ain't worth nothing.   *Josh Billings*

Compassion is the only one of the human emotions the Lord permitted Himself and it has carried the divine flavor ever since.   *Dagobert D. Runes*

She knows as well as anyone that pity, having played, soon tires.
Edwin Arlington Robinson

We pity in others only those evils which we have ourselves experienced.
Jean Jacques Rousseau

Pity is not natural to man. Children and savages are always cruel. Pity is acquired and improved by the cultivation of reason. We may have uneasy sensations from seeing a creature in distress, without pity; but we have not pity unless we wish to relieve him.   *Samuel Johnson*

Pity the meek, for they shall inherit the earth.   *Don Marquis*

PLAGIARISM *Also see:* ORIGINALITY, WRITER.

When you take stuff from one writer, it's plagiarism; but when you take it from many writers, it's research. *Wilson Mizner*

Plagiarists have, at least, the merit of preservation. *Benjamin Disraeli*

About the most originality that any writer can hope to achieve honestly is to steal with good judgment. *Josh Billings*

Borrowed thoughts, like borrowed money, only show the poverty of the borrower. *Marguerite Gardiner*

Literature is full of coincidences, which some love to believe are plagiarisms. There are thoughts always abroad in the air which it takes more wit to avoid than to hit upon. *Oliver Wendell Holmes*

A certain awkwardness marks the use of borrowed thoughts; but as soon as we have learned what to do with them, they become our own. *Ralph Waldo Emerson*

Plagiarists are always suspicious of being stolen from. *Samuel Taylor Coleridge*

Every man is a borrower and a mimic, life is theatrical and literature a quotation. *Ralph Waldo Emerson*

Though old the thought and oft exprest,
'Tis his at last who says it best. *James Russell Lowell*

PLEASURE *Also see:* ANXIETY, CHEERFULNESS, COURTESY, JOY.

That man is the richest whose pleasures are the cheapest. *Henry David Thoreau*

In diving to the bottom of pleasure we bring up more gravel than pearls. *Honoré de Balzac*

Pleasure's couch is virtue's grave. *Augustine J. Duganne*

We tire of those pleasures we take, but never of those we give. *John Petit-Senn*

The average man does not get pleasure out of an idea because he thinks it is true; he thinks it is true because he gets pleasure out of it. *H. L. Mencken*

Whenever you are sincerely pleased you are nourished. *Ralph Waldo Emerson*

To make pleasures pleasant shorten them. *Charles Buxton*

There is no sterner moralist than pleasure. *Lord Byron*

POETRY   *Also see:* ARTIST.

With me poetry has not been a purpose, but a passion.   *Edgar Allan Poe*

Poetry is the art of substantiating shadows, and of lending existence to nothing.   *Edmund Burke*

The job of the poet is to render the world—to see it and report it without loss, without perversion. No poet ever talks about feelings. Only sentimental people do.   *Mark Van Doren*

Writing free verse is like playing tennis with the net down.   *Robert Frost*

When power leads man toward arrogance, poetry reminds him of his limitations. When power narrows the areas of man's concern, poetry reminds him of the richness and diversity of his existence. When power corrupts, poetry cleanses.   *John Fitzgerald Kennedy*

Poetry comes nearer to vital truth than history.   *Plato*

Poetry is boned with ideas, nerved and blooded with emotions, all held together by the delicate, tough skin of words.   *Paul Engle*

You will not find poetry anywhere unless you bring some of it with you.   *Joseph Joubert*

Poetry is the utterance of deep and heart-felt truth—the true poet is very near the oracle.   *Edwin Hubbel Chapin*

POLITICS   *Also see:* DEFEAT, GOVERNMENT, INDEPENDENCE, PARTY, POWER, PROFESSION, PROSPERITY, REVOLUTION.

Politics is not a game. It is an earnest business.   *Winston Churchill*

Politics is a profession; a serious, complicated and, in its true sense, a noble one.   *Dwight D. Eisenhower*

Politics is too serious a matter to be left to the politicians.   *Charles de Gaulle*

Politics is the conduct of public affairs for private advantage.   *Ambrose Bierce*

The world of politics is always twenty years behind the world of thought.   *John Jay Chapman*

A politician thinks of the next election; a statesman, of the next generation.   *J. F. Clarke*

Politicians are the same all over. They promise to build a bridge even where there is no river.   *Nikita Khrushchev*

The political world is stimulating. It's the most interesting thing you can do. It beats following the dollar.   *John Fitzgerald Kennedy*

POLLUTION *Also see:* CONSERVATION.

Among these treasures of our land is water—fast becoming our most valuable, most prized, most critical resource. A blessing where properly used—but it can bring devastation and ruin when left uncontrolled.
Dwight D. Eisenhower

We in Government have begun to recognize the critical work which must be done at all levels—local, State and Federal—in ending the pollution of our waters.
Robert F. Kennedy

The economic and technological triumphs of the past few years have not solved as many problems as we thought they would, and, in fact, have brought us new problems we did not foresee.
Henry Ford II

The American people have a right to air that they and their children can breathe without fear.
Lyndon Baines Johnson

The automobile has not merely taken over the street, it has dissolved the living tissue of the city . . . Gas-filled, nosiy and hazardous, our streets have become the most inhumane landscape in the world.
James M. Fitch

As soils are depleted, human health, vitality and intelligence go with them.
Louis Bromfield

POPULARITY *Also see:* FAME, REPUTATION.

Avoid popularity if you would have peace.
Abraham Lincoln

Seek not the favor of the multitude; it is seldom got by honest and lawful means. But seek the testimony of the few; and number not voices, but weigh them.
Immanuel Kant

Popular opinion is the greatest lie in the world.
Thomas Carlyle

Applause waits on success.
Benjamin Franklin

Popularity is exhausting. The life of the party almost always winds up in a corner with an overcoat over him.
Wilson Mizner

True popularity is not the popularity which is followed after, but the popularity which follows after.
Lord Mansfield

Popularity is glory's small change.
Victor Hugo

To his dog, every man is Napoleon; hence the constant popularity of dogs.
Aldous Huxley

Whatever is popular deserves attention.
James Mackintosh

Avoid popularity; it has many snares, and no real benefit.
William Penn

POPULATION *Also see:* BIRTH, BIRTH CONTROL.

We have been God-like in our planned breeding of our domesticated plants and animals, but we have been rabbit-like in our unplanned breeding of ourselves. *Arnold Joseph Toynbee*

The world is populated in the main by people who should not exist. *George Bernard Shaw*

Population, when unchecked, increases in a geometrical ratio. *Thomas Robert Malthus*

The hungry world cannot be fed until and unless the growth of its resources and the growth of its population come into balance. Each man and woman —and each nation—must make decisions of conscience and policy in the face of this great problem. *Lyndon Baines Johnson*

POVERTY *Also see:* AVARICE, LUXURY, PRIDE, TAX, WANT.

Poverty is the step-mother of genius. *Josh Billings*

Poverty often deprives a man of all spirit and virtue; it is hard for an empty bag to stand upright. *Benjamin Franklin*

I wasn't born in a log cabin, but my family moved into one as soon as they could afford it. *Melville D. Landon*

The greatest man in history was the poorest. *Ralph Waldo Emerson*

I thank fate for having made me born poor. Poverty taught me the true value of the gifts useful to life. *Anatole France*

For every talent that poverty has stimulated it has blighted a hundred. *John W. Gardner*

As society advances the standard of poverty rises. *Theodore Parker*

In a country well governed poverty is something to be ashamed of. In a country badly governed wealth is something to be ashamed of. *Confucius*

Hard as it may appear in individual cases, dependent poverty ought to be held disgraceful. *Thomas Robert Malthus*

The child was diseased at birth, stricken with a hereditary ill that only the most vital men are able to shake off. I mean poverty—the most deadly and prevalent of all diseases. *Eugene O'Neill*

He who knows how to be poor knows everything. *Jules Michelet*

Poverty is the openmouthed relentless hell which yawns beneath civilized society. And it is hell enough. *Henry George*

Poverty . . . It is life near the bone, where it is sweetest. *Henry David Thoreau*

POWER *Also see:* ABUSE, AUTHORITY, BEAUTY, DESIRE, FORCE, PARTY, PATIENCE, POETRY, VIOLENCE.

Most powerful is he who has himself in his own power. *Seneca*

Nothing destroys authority so much as the unequal and untimely interchange of power, pressed too far and relaxed too much. *Francis Bacon*

We cannot live by power, and a culture that seeks to live by it becomes brutal and sterile. But we can die without it. *Max Lerner*

A few great minds are enough to endow humanity with monstrous power, but a few great hearts are not enough to make us worthy of using it. *Jean Rostand*

Man is born to seek power, yet his actual condition makes him a slave to the power of others. *Hans J. Morgenthau*

I know of nothing sublime which is not some modification of power. *Edmund Burke*

There is no knowledge that is not power. *Ralph Waldo Emerson*

We often say how impressive power is. But I do not find it impressive at all. The guns and the bombs, the rockets and the warships, are all symbols of human failure. They are necessary symbols. They protect what we cherish. But they are witness to human folly. *Lyndon Baines Johnson*

In the past, those who foolishly sought power by riding on the back of the tiger ended up inside. *John Fitzgerald Kennedy*

Power will intoxicate the best hearts, as wine the strongest heads. No man is wise enough, nor good enough to be trusted with unlimited power. *Charles Caleb Colton*

The imbecility of men is always inviting the impudence of power. *Ralph Waldo Emerson*

Power does not corrupt man; fools, however, if they get into a position of power, corrupt power. *George Bernard Shaw*

———

PRAISE *Also see:* FLATTERY, MODESTY.

When we disclaim praise, it is only showing our desire to be praised a second time. *François de La Rochefoucauld*

Get someone else to blow your horn and the sound will carry twice as far. *Will Rogers*

He who praises everybody, praises nobody. *Samuel Johnson*

I can live for two months on a good compliment. *Mark Twain*

> Sweet is the scene where genial friendship plays
> The pleasing game of interchanging praise. *Oliver Wendell Holmes*

PRAYER

I don't know of a single foreign product that enters this country untaxed, except the answer to prayer.
Mark Twain

What men usually ask for when they pray to God is, that two and two may not make four.
Russian Proverb

Practical prayer is harder on the soles of your shoes than on the knees of your trousers.
Austin O'Malley

Certain thoughts are prayers. There are moments when, whatever be the attitude of the body, the soul is on its knees.
Victor Hugo

Prayer is the key of the morning and the bolt of the evening.
Mahatma Gandhi

No man ever prayed heartily without learning something.
Ralph Waldo Emerson

God hears no more than the heart speaks; and if the heart be dumb, God will certainly be deaf.
Thomas Brooks

The fewer words the better prayer.
Martin Luther

Pray as if everything depended on God, and work as if everything depended upon man.
Francis Cardinal Spellman

Prayer is a confession of one's own unworthiness and weakness.
Mahatma Gandhi

PREACHING *Also see:* SIN.

I won't take my religion from any man who never works except with his mouth and never cherishes any memory except the face of the woman on the American silver dollar.
Carl Sandburg

Only the sinner has a right to preach.
Christopher Morley

The world is dying for want, not of good preaching, but of good hearing.
George Dana Boardman

One of the proofs of the divinity of our gospel is the preaching it has survived.
Woodrow Wilson

Sermons are like pie-crust, the shorter the better.
Austin O'Malley

The minister's brain is often the "poor-box" of the church.
Edwin Percy Whipple

The test of a preacher is that his congregation goes away saying, not "What a lovely sermon" but, "I will do something!"
St. Francis de Sales

None preaches better than the ant, and she says nothing.
Benjamin Franklin

The best of all the preachers are the men who live their creeds.
Edgar A. Guest

PREJUDICE *Also see:* BIGOTRY, INTOLERANCE, QUESTION, RACE.

Prejudice is being down on something you're not up on. *Anonymous*

A great many people think they are thinking when they are merely rearranging their prejudices. *William James*

To lay aside all prejudices, is to lay aside all principles. He who is destitute of principles is governed by whims. *Friedrich H. Jacobi*

Prejudice, which sees what it pleases, cannot see what is plain.
Aubrey T. de Vere

A prejudice is a vagrant opinion without visible means of support.
Ambrose Bierce

When dealing with people, remember you are not dealing with creatures of logic, but with creatures of emotion, creatures bristling with prejudice and motivated by pride and vanity. *Dale Carnegie*

The time is past when Christians in America can take a long spoon and hand the gospel to the black man out the back door.
Mordecai W. Johnson

Ignorance is stubborn and prejudice is hard. *Adlai E. Stevenson*

Beware prejudices. They are like rats, and men's minds are like traps; prejudices get in easily, but it is doubtful if they ever get out. *Lord Jeffrey*

Prejudice is a raft onto which the shipwrecked mind clambers and paddles to safety. *Ben Hecht*

He that is possessed with a prejudice is possessed with a devil, and one of the worst kinds of devils, for it shuts out the truth, and often leads to ruinous error. *Tryon Edwards*

A fox should not be of the jury at a goose's trial. *Thomas Fuller*

PRESENT *Also see:* PAST, TIME.

He to whom the present is the only thing that is present, knows nothing of the age in which he lives. *Oscar Wilde*

The future is purchased by the present. *Samuel Johnson*

Those who live to the future must always appear selfish to those who live to the present. *Ralph Waldo Emerson*

Since Time is not a person we can overtake when he is gone, let us honor him with mirth and cheerfulness of heart while he is passing.
Johann Wolfgang von Goethe

Man, living, feeling man, is the easy sport of the over-mastering present.
Johann von Schiller

PRESIDENT

No man will ever bring out of the Presidency the reputation which carries him into it.
Thomas Jefferson

The White House is the finest prison in the world.
Harry S. Truman

I seek the Presidency not because it offers me a chance to be somebody but because it offers a chance to do something.
Richard M. Nixon

The American presidency will demand more than ringing manifestos issued from the rear of the battle. It will demand that the President place himself in the very thick of the fight; that he care passionately about the fate of the people he leads . . .
John Fitzgerald Kennedy

President means chief servant.
Mahatma Gandhi

I think this is the most extraordinary collection of talent, of human knowledge, that has ever been gathered at the White House—with the possible exception of when Thomas Jefferson dined alone.
John Fitzgerald Kennedy

My most fervent prayer is to be a President who can make it possible for every boy in this land to grow to manhood by loving his country—instead of dying for it.
Lyndon Baines Johnson

When I was a boy I was told that anybody could become President; I'm beginning to believe.
Clarence Darrow

PRETENSION *Also see:* OSTENTATION, PRIDE, SCANDAL, SELF-CONFIDENCE.

The only good in pretending is the fun we get out of fooling ourselves that we fool somebody.
Booth Tarkington

The hardest tumble a man can make is to fall over his own bluff.
Ambrose Bierce

Where there is much pretension, much has been borrowed; nature never pretends.
Johann Kaspar Lavater

Pretension almost always overdoes the original, and hence exposes itself.
Hosea Ballou

True glory strikes root, and even extends itself; all false pretensions fall as do flowers, nor can any feigned thing be lasting.
Cicero

We had better appear what we are, than affect to appear what we are not.
François de La Rochefoucauld

Man is a make-believe animal: he is never so truly himself as when he is acting a part.
William Hazlitt

To give up pretensions is as blessed a relief as to get them gratified.
William James

PRIDE *Also see:* OSTENTATION, PRETENSION, RIVALRY, TAX, VANITY.

There is this paradox in pride—it makes some men ridiculous, but prevents others from becoming so.   *Charles Caleb Colton*

Pride is an admission of weakness; it secretly fears all competition and dreads all rivals.   *Fulton J. Sheen*

Pride breakfasted with Plenty, dined with Poverty, supped with Infamy.
                    Benjamin Franklin

One of the best temporary cures for pride and affection is seasickness; a man who wants to vomit never puts on airs.   *Josh Billings*

There was one who thought himself above me, and he was above me until he had that thought.   *Elbert Hubbard*

The infinitely little have a pride infinitely great.   *Voltaire*

To be proud and inaccessible is to be timid and weak.
                    Jean Baptiste Masillon

Pride is seldom delicate; it will please itself with very mean advantages.
                    Samuel Johnson

The passions grafted on wounded pride are the most inveterate; they are green and vigorous in old age.   *George Santayana*

PRIVACY *Also see:* COMMUNICATION, LONELINESS, SOLITUDE.

Privacy is the right to be alone—the most comprehensive of rights, and the right most valued by civilized man.   *Louis D. Brandeis*

Let there be spaces in your togetherness.   *Kahlil Gibran*

Modern Americans are so exposed, peered at, inquired about, and spied upon as to be increasingly without privacy—members of a naked society and denizens of a goldfish bowl.   *Edward V. Long*

Far from the madding crowd's ignoble strife.   *Thomas Gray*

PROCRASTINATION *Also see:* ACTION, IDLENESS, NEGLECT.

In delay there lies no plenty.   *William Shakespeare*

Procrastination is the art of keeping up with yesterday.   *Don Marquis*

Even if you're on the right track—you'll get run over if you just sit there.
                    Arthur Godfrey

Never leave that till tomorrow which you can do today.
                    Benjamin Franklin

Putting off an easy thing makes it hard, and putting off a hard one makes it impossible.   *George H. Lorimer*

PRODUCTION *Also see:* ECONOMY, EFFICIENCY, INDUSTRY, LABOR.

Mass production is for the masses. *E. A. Filene*

Production is the only answer to inflation. *Chester Bowles*

The goose lays the golden egg. Payrolls make consumers.
George Humphrey

It is one of the greatest economic errors to put any limitation upon production. . . . We have not the power to produce more than there is a potential to consume. *Louis D. Brandeis*

Unless each man produces more than he receives, increases his output, there will be less for him than all the others. *Bernard M. Baruch*

We seem to want mass production, but we must remember that men are individuals not to be satisfactorily dealt with in masses, and the making of men is more important than the production of things. *Ralph W. Sockman*

PROFANITY *Also see:* WICKEDNESS.

Nothing is greater, or more fearful sacrilege than to prostitute the great name of God to the petulancy of an idle tongue. *Jeremy Taylor*

The foolish and wicked practice of profane cursing and swearing is a vice so mean and low that every person of sense and character detests and despises it. *George Washington*

Profaneness is a brutal vice. He who indulges in it is no gentleman.
Edwin Hubbel Chapin

It chills my blood to hear the blest Supreme
Rudely appealed to on each trifling theme.
Maintain your rank, vulgarity despise.
To swear is neither brave, polite, nor wise. *William Cowper*

PROFESSION *Also see:* MEDICINE, POLITICS.

I hold every man a debtor to his profession. *Francis Bacon*

Medicine is my lawful wife and literature my mistress; when I get tired of one, I spend the night with the other. *Anton Chekhov*

Professional men, they have no cares; whatever happens, they get theirs.
Ogden Nash

In all professions each affects a look and an exterior to appear what he wishes the world to believe that he is. Thus we may say that the whole world is made up of appearances. *François de La Rochefoucauld*

We forget that the most successful statesmen have been professionals. Lincoln was a professional politician. *Felix Frankfurter*

PROFIT . . . See GAIN

PROGRESS *Also see:* AMERICA, BEHAVIOR, DIFFERENCE, DIFFICULTY, DISCONTENT, EDUCATION, IMPROVEMENT, ORDER, SELF-IMPROVEMENT.

He that is good, will infallibly become better, and he that is bad, will as certainly become worse; for vice, virtue and time are three things that never stand still. *Charles Caleb Colton*

Progress is the process whereby the human race is getting rid of whiskers, the veriform appendix and God. *H. L. Mencken*

All that is human must retrograde if it does not advance. *Edward Gibbon*

The reasonable man adapts himself to the world, but the unreasonable man tries to adapt the world to him—therefore, all progress depends upon the unreasonable man. *Samuel Butler*

There is no advancement to him who stands trembling because he cannot see the end from the beginning. *E. J. Klemme*

I have found some of the best reasons I ever had for remaining at the bottom simply by looking at the men at the top. *Frank Moore Colby*

Social advance depends as much upon the process through which it is secured as upon the result itself. *Jane Addams*

Not to go back is somewhat to advance, and men must walk, at least, before they dance. *Alexander Pope*

Speak softly, and carry a big stick; you will go far. *Theodore Roosevelt*

Those who work most for the world's advancement are the ones who demand least. *Henry Doherty*

PROMISE . . . See VOW

PROPAGANDA *Also see:* ART, DECEIT, RELIGION, TRUTH, WORD.

Propaganda must not serve the truth, especially insofar as it might bring out something favorable for the opponent. *Adolf Hitler*

Some of mankind's most terrible misdeeds have been committed under the spell of certain magic words or phrases. *James Bryant Conant*

Propaganda replaces moral philosophy. *Hans J. Morgenthau*

A propagandist is a specialist in selling attitudes and opinions. *Hans Speier*

We have made the Reich by propaganda. *Joseph Paul Goebbels*

Today the world is the victim of propaganda because people are not intellectually competent. More than anything the United States needs effective citizens competent to do their own thinking. *William Mather Lewis*

PROPERTY *Also see:* WEALTH.

Material blessings, when they pay beyond the category of need, are weirdly fruitful of headache.   *Philip Wylie*

No man acquires property without acquiring with it a little arithmetic also.
                                                          Ralph Waldo Emerson

Mine is better than ours.   *Benjamin Franklin*

Private property began the instant somebody had a mind of his own.
                                                               E. E. Cummings

Property is the fruit of labor; property is desirable; it is a positive good in the world.   *Abraham Lincoln*

Ultimately property rights and personal rights are the same thing.
                                                             Calvin Coolidge

If a man owns land, the land owns him.   *Ralph Waldo Emerson*

What we call real estate—the solid ground to build a house on—is the broad foundation on which nearly all the guilt of this world rests.
                                                          Nathaniel Hawthorne

The highest law gives a thing to him who can use it.
                                                          Henry David Thoreau

It is preoccupation with possession, more than anything else, that prevents men from living freely and nobly.   *Bertrand Russell*

PROSPERITY *Also see:* ADVERSITY, ADVICE, WEALTH.

Prosperity doth best discover vice, but adversity doth best discover virtue.
                                                              Francis Bacon

Prosperity makes friends, adversity tries them.   *Publilius Syrus*

Prosperity is something the businessmen created for politicians to take credit for.   *Brunswick (Ga.) Pilot*

The prosperous man is never sure that he is loved for himself.   *Lucan*

Prosperity is only an instrument to be used, not a deity to be worshipped.
                                                             Calvin Coolidge

Prosperity is the surest breeder of insolence I know.   *Mark Twain*

Everything in the world may be endured except continual prosperity.
                                                     Johann Wolfgang von Goethe

When prosperity comes, do not use all of it.   *Confucius*

PROVIDENCE *Also see:* GOD, FATE.

There are many scapegoats for our sins, but the most popular is providence.
Mark Twain

Friends, I agree with you in Providence; but I believe in the Providence of the most men, the largest purse, and the longest cannon.
Abraham Lincoln

God hangs the greatest weights upon the smallest wires.   *Francis Bacon*

God's providence is on the side of clear heads.   *Henry Ward Beecher*

The superior man is the providence of the inferior. He is eyes for the blind, strength for the weak, and a shield for the defenseless.
Robert Green Ingersoll

The longer I live, the more convincing proofs I see of this truth, that God governs in the affairs of man; and if a sparrow cannot fall to the ground without his notice, is it probable that an empire can rise without his aid?
Benjamin Franklin

PRUDENCE *Also see:* MODERATION, QUESTION, WISDOM.

The prudence of the best heads is ofen defeated by the tenderness of the best of hearts.   *Henry Fielding*

It is by the goodness of God that in our country we have those three unspeakably precious things: freedom of speech, freedom of conscience, and the prudence never to practice either.   *Mark Twain*

He that fights and runs away will live to fight another day.
Old English Rhyme

Men are born with two eyes, but with one tongue, in order that they should see twice as much as they say.   *Charles Caleb Colton*

Prudence is an attitude that keeps life safe, but does not often make it happy.   *Samuel Johnson*

There is nothing more imprudent than excessive prudence.
Charles Caleb Colton

PSYCHOLOGY *Also see:* MIND.

Anybody who is 25 or 30 years old has physical scars from all sorts of things, from tuberculosis to polio. It's the same with the mind.
Moses R. Kaufman

A wonderful discovery—psychoanalysis. Makes quite simple people feel they're complex.   *Samuel N. Behrman*

Psychoanalysis has changed American psychology from a diagnostic to a therapeutic science, not because so many patients are cured by the psychoanalytic technique, but because of the new understanding of phychiatric patients it has given us, and the new and different concept of illness and health.   *Karl A. Menninger*

PUBLIC *Also see:* PUBLICITY, TASTE.

The public wishes itself to be managed like a woman; one must say nothing to it except what it likes to hear. *Johann Wolfgang von Goethe*

If there's anything a public servant hates to do it's something for the public. *Kin Hubbard*

The public is wiser than the wisest critic. *George Bancroft*

In a free and republican government, you cannot restrain the voice of the multitude. *George Washington*

That miscellaneous collection of a few wise and many foolish individuals, called the public. *John Stuart Mill*

The people are to be taken in very small doses. *Ralph Waldo Emerson*

The public have neither shame nor gratitude. *William Hazlitt*

The trouble with the public is that there is too much of it; what we need in public is less quantity and more quality. *Don Marquis*

The public is a ferocious beast: one must either chain it up or flee from it. *Voltaire*

PUBLICITY *Also see:* ADVERTISING, NEWSPAPER.

Without publicity there can be no public support, and without public support every nation must decay. *Benjamin Disraeli*

I don't care what they call me as long as they mention my name. *George M. Cohan*

Publicity, publicity, PUBLICITY is the greatest moral factor and force in our public life. *Joseph Pulitzer*

Modern business and persons and organizations that seek publicity must recognize their obligations to the public and to the press. *Henry F. Woods, Jr.*

The effect of power and publicity on all men is the aggravation of self, a sort of tumor that ends by killing the victim's sympathies. *Henry Brooks Adams*

PUNCTUALITY

I could never think well of a man's intellectual or moral character, if he was habitually unfaithful to his appointments. *Nathaniel Emmons*

Unfaithfulness in the keeping of an appointment is an act of clear dishonesty. You may as well borrow a person's money as his time. *Horace Mann*

If you're there before it's over, you're on time. *James J. Walker*

Punctuality is one of the cardinal business virtues: always insist on it in your subordinates. *Don Marquis*

PUNISHMENT *Also see:* CRIME, DISCONTENT, LYING, PAIN, SIN.

One man meets an infamous punishment for that crime which confers a diadem on others. *Juvenal*

The best of us being unfit to die, what an unexpressible absurdity to put the worst to death. *Nathaniel Hawthorne*

Punishment is justice for the unjust. *St. Augustine*

We are not punished for our sins, but by them. *Elbert Hubbard*

Many a man spanks his children for the things his own father should have spanked out of him. *Don Marquis*

If punishment makes not the will supple it hardens the offender. *John Locke*

It is as expedient that a wicked man be punished as that a sick man be cured by a physician; for all chastisement is a kind of medicine. *Plato*

Crime and punishment grow out of one stem. *Ralph Waldo Emerson*

PURPOSE *Also see:* AIM, FIRMNESS, IDEAL, INSTINCT, SUCCESS.

The secret of success is constancy to purpose. *Benjamin Disraeli*

Great minds have purposes, others have wishes. *Washington Irving*

Lack of something to feel important about is almost the greatest tragedy a man may have. *Arthur E. Morgan*

Only the consciousness of a purpose that is mightier than any man and worthy of all men can fortify and inspirit and compose the souls of men. *Walter Lippmann*

The good man is the man who, no matter how morally unworthy he has been, is moving to become better. *John Dewey*

PURSUIT *Also see:* ADVENTURE, ENTHUSIASM, MYSTERY.

The rapture of pursuing is the prize the vanquished gain. *Henry Wadsworth Longfellow*

The crowning fortune of a man is to be born to some pursuit which finds him employment and happiness, whether it be to make baskets, or broadswords, or canals, or statues, or songs. *Ralph Waldo Emerson*

Men tire themselves in pursuit of rest. *Laurence Sterne*

> Like one that on a lonesome road
>   Doth walk in fear and dread,
> And having once turned round walks on,
>   And turns no more his head;
> Because he knows a frightful fiend
>   Doth close behind him tread.

Samuel Taylor Coleridge

Q

QUALITY *Also see:* PUBLIC, VALUE, WORTH.

We are never so ridiculous by the qualities we have, as by those we affect to have. *François de La Rochefoucauld*

Everything runs to excess; every good quality is noxious if unmixed.
Ralph Waldo Emerson

It is the quality of our work which will please God and not the quantity.
Mahatma Gandhi

Nothing endures but personal qualities. *Walt Whitman*

I think there is only one quality worse than hardness of heart, and that is softness of head. *Theodore Roosevelt*

The best is the cheapest. *Benjamin Franklin*

Many individuals have, like uncut diamonds, shining qualities beneath a rough exterior. *Juvenal*

There is hardly anything in the world that some man cannot make a little worse and sell a little cheaper. *John Ruskin*

QUARREL *Also see:* ANGER, ARGUMENT, CHEERFULNESS, COWARDICE.

When chickens quit quarrelling over their food they often find that there is enough for all of them. I wonder if it might not be the same with the human race. *Don Marquis*

People generally quarrel because they cannot argue.
Gilbert K. Chesterton

Every quarrel begins in nothing and ends in a struggle for supremacy.
Elbert Hubbard

He that blows the coals in quarrels he has nothing to do with has no right to complain if the sparks fly in his face. *Benjamin Franklin*

Two cannot fall out if one does not choose. *Spanish Proverb*

A long dispute means that both parties are wrong. *Voltaire*

Cut quarrels out of literature, and you will have very little history or drama or fiction or epic poetry left. *Robert Lynd*

I never take my own side in a quarrel. *Robert Frost*

Those who in quarrels interpose,
    Must often wipe a bloody nose. *John Gay*

In quarrelling the truth is always lost. *Publilius Syrus*

When we quarrel, how we wish we had been blameless!
Ralph Waldo Emerson

QUESTION *Also see:* CONVERSATION, CURIOSITY, DOUBT.

No man really becomes a fool until he stops asking questions.

Charles Steinmetz

A fool may ask more questions in an hour than a wise man can answer in seven years.

English Proverb

No question is so difficult to answer as that to which the answer is obvious.

George Bernard Shaw

Man will not live without answers to his questions.

Hans Morgenthau

By nature's kindly disposition most questions which it is beyond a man's power to answer do not occur to him at all.

George Santayana

Judge a man by his questions rather than his answers.

Voltaire

He must be very ignorant for he answers every question he is asked.

Voltaire

I am prejudiced in favor of him who, without impudence, can ask boldly. He has faith in humanity, and faith in himself. No one who is not accustomed to giving grandly can ask nobly and with boldness.

Johann Kaspar Lavater

A prudent question is one-half of wisdom.

Francis Bacon

QUIET *Also see:* REST, SILENCE.

The good and the wise lead quiet lives.

Euripides

To have a quiet mind is to possess one's mind wholly; to have a calm spirit is to possess one's self.

Hamilton Mable

An inability to stay quiet is one of the conspicuous failings of mankind.

Walter Bagehot

Very often the quiet fellow has said all he knows.

Kin Hubbard

Quiet minds cannot be perplexed or frightened but go on in fortune or misfortune at their own private pace, like a clock during a thunderstorm.

Robert Louis Stevenson

If we have not quiet in our minds, outward comfort will do no more for us than a golden slipper on a gouty foot.

John Bunyan

God gives quietness at last.

John Greenleaf Whittier

Quiet is what home would be without children.

Anonymous

Stillness of person and steadiness of features are signal marks of good breeding.

Oliver Wendell Holmes

QUOTATION *Also see:* MAXIM, PLAGIARISM, WRITER.

You could compile the worst book in the world entirely out of selected passages from the best writers in the world.   *Gilbert K. Chesterton*

The profoundest thought or passion sleeps as in a mine, until an equal mind and heart finds and publishes it.   *Ralph Waldo Emerson*

Now we sit through Shakespeare in order to recognize the quotations.
Orson Welles

He presents me with what is always an acceptable gift who brings me news of a great thought before unknown. He enriches me without impoverishing himself.   *Ralph Waldo Emerson*

Certain brief sentences are peerless in their ability to give one the feeling that nothing remains to be said.   *Jean Rostand*

Next to the originator of a good sentence is the first quoter of it.
Ralph Waldo Emerson

R

RACE *Also see:* DIGNITY, PREJUDICE.

Mere connection with what is known as a superior race will not permanently carry an individual forward unless the individual has worth.
Booker T. Washington

The difference of race is one of the reasons why I fear war may always exist; because race implies difference, difference implies superiority, and superiority leads to predominance.   *Benjamin Disraeli*

The existence of any pure race with special endowments is a myth, as is the belief that there are races all of whose members are foredoomed to eternal inferiority.   *Franz Boas*

A heavy guilt rests upon us for what the whites of all nations have done to the colored peoples. When we do good to them, it is not benevolence— it is atonement.   *Albert Schweitzer*

I have one criticism about the Negro troops who fought under my command in the Korean War. They didn't send me enough of them.
Douglas MacArthur

At the heart of racism is the religious assertion that God made a creative mistake when He brought some people into being.   *Friedrich Otto Hertz*

In the gain or loss of one race all the rest have equal claim.
James Russell Lowell

When white and black and brown and every other color decide they're going to live together as Christians, then and only then are we going to see an end to these troubles.   *Barry M. Goldwater*

RADICAL *Also see:* EXTREMES, REBELLION, REVOLUTION, VIOLENCE.

A radical is one who speaks the truth. *Charles A. Lindbergh*

If a man is right, he can't be too radical; if he is wrong, he can't be too conservative. *Josh Billings*

A radical is a man with both feet firmly planted in the air. *Franklin Delano Roosevelt*

I am trying to do two things: dare to be a radical and not a fool, which is a matter of no small difficulty. *James A. Garfield*

RANK *Also see:* ANCESTRY, CLASS.

It is an interesting question how far men would retain their relative rank if they were divested of their clothes. *Henry David Thoreau*

Rank and riches are chains of gold, but still chains. *Giovanni Ruffini*

To be vain of one's rank or place, is to show that one is below it. *Stanislas I*

I weigh the man, not his title; 'tis not the king's stamp can make the metal better. *William Wycherley*

What men prize most is a privilege, even if it be that of chief mourner at a funeral. *James Russell Lowell*

READING *Also see:* BOOK, LITERATURE, NEWSPAPER.

I divide all readers into two classes: those who read to remember and those who read to forget. *William Lyon Phelps*

A classic is something that everybody wants to have read and nobody wants to read. *Mark Twain*

Reading is to the mind what exercise is to the body. *Joseph Addison*

When I am dead, I hope it may be said: "His sins were scarlet, but his books were read." *Hilaire Belloc*

We should be as careful of the books we read, as of the company we keep. The dead very often have more power than the living. *Tryon Edwards*

No entertainment is so cheap as reading, nor any pleasure so lasting. *Mary Wortley Montagu*

Reading is a basic tool in the living of a good life. *Mortimer J. Adler*

Read the best books first, or you may not have a chance to read them all. *Henry David Thoreau*

Reading is like permitting a man to talk a long time, and refusing you the right to answer. *Ed Howe*

I would sooner read a timetable or a catalog than nothing at all. *W. Somerset Maugham*

REALITY *Also see:* APPEARANCE, DREAM, ILLUSION, TRUTH.

Facts are facts and will not disappear on account of your likes.
Jawaharlal Nehru

My greatest enemy is reality. I have fought it successfully for thirty years.
Margaret Anderson

A theory must be tempered with reality.
Jawaharlal Nehru

I accept reality and dare not question it.
Walt Whitman

The realist is the man, who having weighed all the visible factors in a given situation and having found that the odds are against him, decides that fighting is useless.
Raoul de Sales

REASON *Also see:* ANGER, ARGUMENT, COMMON SENSE, FORCE, HEART, LOGIC, MIND, TEMPER, UNDERSTANDING.

He that will not reason is a bigot; he that cannot reason is a fool; and he that dares not reason is a slave.
William Drummond

Most of our so-called reasoning consists in finding arguments for going on believing as we already do.
James Robinson

Hear reason, or she'll make you feel her.
Benjamin Franklin

If you follow reason far enough it always leads to conclusions that are contrary to reason.
Samuel Butler

Reason has never failed men. Only force and repression have made the wrecks in the world.
William Allen White

Man has received direct from God only one instrument wherewith to know himself and to know his relation to the universe—he has no other—and that instrument is reason.
Leo Tolstoi

A man always has two reasons for doing anything—a good reason and the real reason.
J. P. Morgan

Man is a reasoning rather than a reasonable animal.
Alexander Hamilton

An appeal to the reason of the people has never been known to fail in the long run.
James Russell Lowell

Error of opinion may be tolerated where reason is left free to admit it.
Thomas Jefferson

Reason can in general do more than blind force.
Gallus

Reason is the wise man's guide, example the fool's.
Welsh Proverb

Many are destined to reason wrongly; others, not to reason at all; and others, to persecute those who do reason.
Voltaire

221

REBELLION   *Also see:* DISSENT, OPPRESSION, REVOLUTION, RIOT, TREASON.

Rebellion against tyrants is obedience to God.   *Benjamin Franklin*

As long as the world shall last there will be wrongs, and if no man objected and no man rebelled, those wrongs would last forever.
Clarence Darrow

A little rebellion now and then . . . is a medicine necessary for the sound health of government.   *Thomas Jefferson*

An oppressed people are authorized whenever they can to rise and break their fetters.   *Henry Clay*

Men seldom, or rather never for a length of time and deliberately, rebel against anything that does not deserve rebelling against.   *Thomas Carlyle*

As long as our social order regards the good of institutions rather than the good of men, so long will there be a vocation for the rebel.
Richard Roberts

It doesn't take a majority to make a rebellion; it takes only a few determined leaders and a sound cause.   *H. L. Mencken*

REFLECTION . . . See THOUGHT

REFORM   *Also see:* IMPROVEMENT, PROGRESS.

Nothing so needs reforming as other people's habits.   *Mark Twain*

Reform must come from within, not from without. You cannot legislate for virtue.   *James Cardinal Gibbons*

What is a man born for but to be a reformer, a remaker of what has been made, a denouncer of lies, a restorer of truth and good?
Ralph Waldo Emerson

To reform a man, you must begin with his grandmother.   *Victor Hugo*

The church is always trying to get other people to reform; it might not be a bad idea to reform itself.   *Mark Twain*

A reformer is a man who rides through a sewer in a glass-bottomed boat.
James J. Walker

The race could save one-half its wasted labor
   Would each reform himself and spare his neighbor.

Frank Putnam

The hole and the patch should be commensurate.   *Thomas Jefferson*

I think I am better than the people who are trying to reform me.

Ed Howe

REGRET *Also see:* REMORSE.

Regret is an appalling waste of energy; you can't build on it; it's only good for wallowing in.   *Katherine Mansfield*

I only regret that I have but one life to give for my country.
Nathan Hale

For of all sad words of tongue or pen, the saddest are these: "It might have been!"   *John Greenleaf Whittier*

Regret for time wasted can become a power for good in the time that remains, if we will only stop the waste and the idle, useless regretting.
Arthur Brisbane

RELIGION *Also see:* CHRISTIANITY, CHURCH and STATE, CONSCIENCE, HEAVEN, HYPOCRISY, JUDAISM, PREACHING.

All religions must be tolerated, for every man must get to heaven in his own way.   *Frederick the Great*

The true meaning of religion is thus not simply morality, but morality touched by emotion.   *Matthew Arnold*

Many have quarreled about religion that never practiced it.
Benjamin Franklin

It is the test of a good religion whether you can joke about it.
Gilbert K. Chesterton

Religion is the sum of the expansive impulses of a being.   *Henry H. Ellis*

Every man, either to his terror or consolation, has some sense of religion.
James Harrington

Science without religion is lame; religion without science is blind.
Albert Einstein

Measure not men by Sundays, without regarding what they do all the week after.   *Thomas Fuller*

To swallow and follow, whether old doctrine or new propaganda, is a weakness still dominating the human mind.   *Charlotte P. Gilbert*

A religious life is a struggle and not a hymn.   *Madame de Staël*

Our hope of immortality does not come from any religions, but nearly all religions come from that hope.   *Robert Green Ingersoll*

Religion is a candle inside a multicolored lantern. Everyone looks through a particular color, but the candle is always there.   *Mohammed Neguib*

You can change your faith without changing gods, and vice versa.
Stanislaw J. Lec

Religion has not civilized man, man has civilized religion.
Robert Green Ingersoll

REMORSE *Also see:* GRIEF, GUILT, REGRET.

Remorse is the pain of sin.
Theodore Parker

To be left alone, and face to face with my own crime, had been just retribution.
Henry Wadsworth Longfellow

Remorse is the echo of a lost virtue.
Edward G. Bulwer-Lytton

Remorse: beholding heaven and feeling hell.
George Moore

Remorse is virtue's root; its fair increase are fruits of innocence and blessedness.
William Cullen Bryant

Remorse is regret that one waited so long to do it.
H. L. Mencken

REPENTANCE *Also see:* CONFESSION, GUILT, SIN.

It is much easier to repent of sins that we have committed than to repent of those that we intend to commit.
Josh Billings

Of all acts of man repentance is the most divine. The greatest of all faults is to be conscious of none.
Thomas Carlyle

It is foolish to lay out money for the purchase of repentance.
Benjamin Franklin

True repentance is to cease from sinning.
Ambrose of Milan

Most people repent their sins by thanking God they ain't so wicked as their neighbors.
Josh Billings

Bad men are full of repentance.
Aristotle

Great is the difference betwixt a man's being frightened at, and humbled for his sins.
Thomas Fuller

Repentance is another name for aspiration.
Henry Ward Beecher

REPETITION *Also see:* LOQUACITY.

Like warmed-up cabbage served at each repast,
The repetition kills the wretch at last.
Juvenal

Iteration, like friction, is likely to generate heat instead of progress.
George Eliot

Men get opinions as boys learn to spell,
By reiteration chiefly.
Elizabeth Barrett Browning

There is no absurdity so palpable but that it may be firmly planted in the human head if you only begin to inculcate it before the age of five, by constantly repeating it with an air of great solemnity. *Arthur Schopenhauer*

REPUTATION   *Also see:* CHARACTER, FAME, NAME, PERSONALITY, SLANDER.

A reputation once broken may possibly be repaired, but the world will always keep their eyes on the spot where the crack was.   *Joseph Hall*

Good will, like a good name, is got by many actions, and lost by one.
Lord Jeffrey

Many a man's reputation would not know his character if they met on the street.   *Elbert Hubbard*

Associate with men of good quality if you esteem your own reputation; for it is better to be alone than in bad company.   *George Washington*

The reputation of a man is like his shadow, gigantic when it precedes him, and pigmy in its proportions when it follows.
Alexandre de Talleyrand-Périgord

Kindly words do not enter so deeply into men as a reputation for kindness.
Mencius

A doctor's reputation is made by the number of eminent men who die under his care.   *George Bernard Shaw*

The two most precious things this side of the grave are our reputation and our life. But it is to be lamented that the most contemptible whisper may deprive us of the one, and the weakest weapon of the other.
Charles Caleb Colton

What people say behind your back is your standing in the community.
Ed Howe

RESENTMENT . . . See DISCONTENT

RESIGNATION   *Also see:* ENDURANCE, RETIREMENT.
It seems that nothing ever gets to going good till there's a few resignations.
Kin Hubbard

Resignation is the courage of Christian sorrow.   *Alexandre Vinet*

Welcome death, quoth the rat, when the trap fell.   *Thomas Fuller*

A wise man cares not for what he cannot have.   *Jack Herbert*

For after all, the best thing one can do when it's raining is to let it rain.
Henry Wadsworth Longfellow

What is called resignation is confirmed desperation.   *Henry David Thoreau*

We cannot conquer fate and necessity, yet we can yield to them in such a manner as to be greater than if we could.   *Walter S. Landor*

Resignation is putting God between ourselves and our troubles.
Anne Sophie Swetchine

RESOLUTION *Also see:* AIM, FIRMNESS, PURPOSE, SECURITY, VOW.

Good resolutions are simply checks that men draw on a bank where they have no account. *Oscar Wilde*

Clothe with life the weak intent, let me be the thing I meant.
John Greenleaf Whittier

The block of granite which is an obstacle in the pathway of the weak, becomes a stepping-stone in the pathway of the strong. *Thomas Carlyle*

Either I will find a way, or I will make one. *Philip Sidney*

It is always during a passing state of mind that we make lasting resolutions. *Marcel Proust*

Resolve to perform what you ought; perform without fail what you resolve. *Benjamin Franklin*

Resolve and thou art free. *Henry Wadsworth Longfellow*

RESPECT *Also see:* ADMIRATION, TYRANNY.

One of the surprising things in this world is the respect a worthless man has for himself. *Ed Howe*

I must respect the opinions of others even if I disagree with them.
Herbert Henry Lehman

There was no respect for youth when I was young, and now that I am old, there is no respect for age—I missed it coming and going. *J. B. Priestly*

I don't know what a scoundrel is like, but I know what a respectable man is like, and it's enough to make one's flesh creep. *J. M. De Maistre*

Men are respectable only as they respect. *Ralph Waldo Emerson*

RESPONSIBILITY *Also see:* DISCIPLINE, DUTY, RIGHTS.

Responsibility is the thing people dread most of all. Yet it is the one thing in the world that develops us, gives us manhood or womanhood fibre.
Frank Crane

Responsibility educates. *Wendell Phillips*

Every human being has a work to carry on within, duties to perform abroad, influence to exert, which are peculiarly his, and which no conscience but his own can teach. *William Ellery Channing*

The only way to get rid of responsibilities is to discharge them.
Walter S. Robertson

Responsibility is the price of greatness. *Winston Churchill*

You will find men who want to be carried on the shoulders of others, who think that the world owes them a living. They don't seem to see that we must all lift together and pull together. *Henry Ford II*

REST   *Also see:* SLEEP.

Eternal rest sounds comforting in the pulpit; well, you try it once, and see how heavy time will hang on your hands.   *Mark Twain*

> Absence of occupation is not rest;
> A mind quite vacant is a mind distressed.   *William Cowper*

Who remembers when we used to rest on Sunday instead of Monday?
Kin Hubbard

He that can take rest is greater than he that can take cities.
Benjamin Franklin

I shall need to sleep three weeks on end to get rested from the rest I've had.   *Thomas Mann*

Rest is a good thing, but boredom is its brother.   *Voltaire*

Rest: the sweet sauce of labor.   *Plutarch*

Put off thy cares with thy clothes; so shall thy rest strengthen thy labor, and so thy labor sweeten thy rest.   *Francis Quarles*

RESULT   *Also see:* ABILITY, CAUSE, END and MEANS.

Results! Why, man, I have gotten a lot of results. I know several thousand things that won't work.   *Thomas A. Edison*

They have sown the wind, and they shall reap the whirlwind.   *Hosea: 8:7*

It has been my observation and experience, and that of my family, that nothing human works out well.   *Don Marquis*

The man who gets the most satisfactory results is not always the man with the most brilliant single mind, but rather the man who can best coordinate the brains and talents of his associates.   *W. Alton Jones*

RETIREMENT   *Also see:* LABOR, RESIGNATION, REST, WORK.

Love prefers twilight to daylight.   *Oliver Wendell Holmes*

The worst of work nowadays is what happens to people when they cease to work.   *Gilbert K. Chesterton*

Don't think of retiring from the world until the world will be sorry that you retire. I hate a fellow whom pride or cowardice or laziness drive into a corner, and who does nothing when he is there but sit and growl. Let him come out as I do, and bark.   *Samuel Johnson*

The best time to start thinking about your retirement is before the boss does.   *Anonymous*

A man is known by the company that keeps him on after retirement age.
Anonymous

227

REVENGE . . . See VENGEANCE

REVERIE *Also see:* DREAM, ILLUSION.

In that sweet mood when pleasant thoughts bring sad thoughts to the mind. *William Wordsworth*

Both mind and heart when given up to reveries and dreaminess, have a thousand avenues open for the entrance of evil. *Charles Simmons*

Sit in reverie and watch the changing color of the waves that break upon the idle seashore of the mind. *Henry Wadsworth Longfellow*

To lose one's self in reverie, one must be either very happy, or very unhappy. Reverie is the child of extremes. *Antoine Rivarol*

Reverie is when ideas float in our mind without reflection or regard of the understanding. *John Locke*

Do anything rather than give yourself to reverie. *William Ellery Channing*

There is no self-delusion more fatal than that which makes the conscience dreamy with the anodyne of lofty sentiments, while the life is groveling and sensual. *James Russell Lowell*

REVOLUTION *Also see:* CHANGE, GOVERNMENT, TYRANNY, VIOLENCE.

Revolution: in politics, an abrupt change in the form of misgovernment. *Ambrose Bierce*

Revolutions are not trifles, but spring from trifles. *Aristotle*

Make revolution a parent of settlement, and not a nursery of future revolutions. *Edmund Burke*

Those who make peaceful revolution impossible will make violent revolution inevitable. *John Fitzgerald Kennedy*

Revolutionary movements attract those who are not good enough for established institutions as well as those who are too good for them. *George Bernard Shaw*

We have a lot of people revolutionizing the world because they've never had to present a working model. *Charles F. Kettering*

Any people anywhere being inclined and having the power have the right to rise up and shake off the existing government, and force a new one that suits them better. *Abraham Lincoln*

Revolutions have never lightened the burden of tyranny: they have only shifted it to another shoulder. *George Bernard Shaw*

Revolutions are not made by men in spectacles. *Oliver Wendell Holmes*

It is impossible to predict the time and progress of revolution. It is governed by its own more or less mysterious laws. *Lenin*

REWARD *Also see:* ACHIEVEMENT, AMBITION, SUCCESS.

Blessings ever wait on virtuous deeds, and though a late, a sure reward succeeds.
William Congreve

The reward of a thing well done is to have done it.   *Ralph Waldo Emerson*

No man, who continues to add something to the material, intellectual and moral well-being of the place in which he lives, is left long without proper reward.
Booker T. Washington

He that does good for good's sake seeks neither paradise nor reward, but he is sure of both in the end.
William Penn

Perhaps the reward of the spirit who tries is not the goal but the exercise.
E. V. Cooke

It is the amends of a short and troublesome life, that doing good and suffering ill entitles man to a longer and better.
William Penn

Not in rewards, but in the strength to strive, the blessing lies.
J. T. Towbridge

He who wishes to secure the good of others has already secured his own.
Confucius

The effects of our actions may be postponed but they are never lost. There is an inevitable reward for good deeds and an inescapable punishment for bad. Meditate upon this truth, and seek always to earn good wages from Destiny.
Wu Ming Fu

No person was ever honored for what he received. Honor has been the reward for what he gave.
Calvin Coolidge

Let the motive be in the deed and not in the event. Be not one whose motive for action is the hope of reward.
Kreeshna

RIDICULE *Also see:* ABSURDITY, IRONY, JESTING, SARCASM.

Scoff not at the natural defects of any which are not in their power to amend. It is cruel to beat a cripple with his own crutches!   *Thomas Fuller*

Mockery is the weapon of those who have no other.   *Hubert Pierlot*

Ridicule is the first and last argument of fools.   *Charles Simmons*

Resort is had to ridicule only when reason is against us.   *Thomas Jefferson*

Ridicule is the language of the devil.   *Thomas Carlyle*

Man learns more readily and remembers more willingly what excites his ridicule than what deserves esteem and respect.   *Horace*

RIGHTS *Also see:* CUSTOM, DIGNITY, EQUALITY, FREEDOM of the PRESS, PRIVACY, PROPERTY, WAGE.

Many a person seems to think it isn't enough for the government to guarantee him the pursuit of happiness. He insists it also run interference for him.
Anonymous

Always do right; this will gratify some people and astonish the rest.
Mark Twain

No man was ever endowed with a right without being at the same time saddled with a responsibility.
Gerald W. Johnson

It is in the American tradition to stand up for one's rights—even if the new way to stand up for one's rights is to sit down.
John Fitzgerald Kennedy

We hold these truths to be self-evident, that all men are created equal, that they are endowed by their Creator with certain unalienable rights, that among these are life, liberty, and the pursuit of happiness.
Thomas Jefferson

No man has a right to do what he pleases, except when he pleases to do right.
Charles Simmons

In giving rights to others which belong to them, we give rights to ourselves and to our country.
John Fitzgerald Kennedy

From the equality of rights springs identity of our highest interests; you cannot subvert your neighbor's rights without striking a dangerous blow at your own.
Carl Schurz

I am the inferior of any man whose rights I trample under foot.
Robert Green Ingersoll

RIOT *Also see:* MOB, REBELLION, REVOLUTION, VIOLENCE.

No nation, no matter how enlightened, can endure criminal violence. If we cannot control it, we are admitting to the world and to ourselves that our laws are no more than a façade that crumbles when the winds of crisis rise.
Alan Bible

The poor suffer twice at the rioter's hands. First, his destructive fury scars their neighborhood; second, the atmosphere of accommodation and consent is changed to one of hostility and resentment.
Lyndon Baines Johnson

If we resort to lawlessness, the only thing we can hope for is civil war, untold bloodshed, and the end of our dreams.
Archie Lee Moore

The Commission believes there is a grave danger that some communities may resort to the indiscriminate and excessive use of force. The harmful effects of overreaction are incalculable.
Commission on Civil Disorder, 1968

RISK *Also see:* DANGER.

The policy of being too cautious is the greatest risk of all.

Jawaharlal Nehru

The willingness to take risks is our grasp of faith.   *George E. Woodberry*

A man sits as many risks as he runs.   *Henry David Thoreau*

Don't be afraid to take a big step if one is indicated; you can't cross a chasm in two small jumps.   *William Lloyd George*

Every noble acquisition is attended with its risks; he who fears to encounter the one must not expect to obtain the other.   *Metastasio*

Everything is sweetened by risk.   *Alexander Smith*

Risk is a part of God's game, alike for men and nations.

George E. Woodberry

I've run less risk driving my way across country than eating my way across it.   *Duncan Hines*

Who bravely dares must sometimes risk a fall.   *Tobias G. Smollett*

It is impossible to win the great prizes of life without running risks, and the greatest of all prizes are those connected with the home.

Theodore Roosevelt

RIVALRY *Also see:* AMBITION, JEALOUSY, SUCCESS.

Nothing is ever done beautifully which is done in rivalship; or nobly, which is done in pride.   *John Ruskin*

In ambition, as in love, the successful can afford to be indulgent toward their rivals. The prize our own, it is graceful to recognize the merit that vainly aspired to it.   *Christian Nestell Bovee*

If we devote our time disparaging the products of our business rivals, we hurt business generally, reduce confidence, and increase discontent.

Edward N. Hurley

It is the privilege of posterity to set matters right between those antagonists who, by their rivalry for greatness, divided a whole age.   *Joseph Addison*

Competition is the keen cutting edge of business, always shaving away at costs.   *Henry Ford II*

Anybody can win unless there happens to be a second entry.   *George Ade*

Rivalry is the life of trade, and the death of the trader.   *Elbert Hubbard*

RUMOR . . . See GOSSIP

S

SACRIFICE   Also see: COMPROMISE, HEROISM, MARTYR.

The mice which helplessly find themselves between the cats' teeth acquire no merit from their enforced sacrifice.   *Mahatma Gandhi*

Good manners are made up of petty sacrifices.   *Ralph Waldo Emerson*

In this world it is not what we take up, but what we give up, that makes us rich.   *Henry Ward Beecher*

One-half of knowing what you want is knowing what you must give up before you get it.   *Sidney Howard*

We can offer up much in the large, but to make sacrifices in little things is what we are seldom equal to.   *Johann Wolfgang von Goethe*

They never fail who die in a great cause.   *Lord Byron*

No sacrifice short of individual liberty, individual self-respect, and individual enterprise is too great a price to pay for permanent peace.

Clark H. Minor

SADNESS . . . See SORROW

SAFETY   Also see: SECURITY, SELF-RESPECT, VIGILANCE.

It is better to be safe than sorry.   *American Proverb*

In skating over thin ice our safety is in our speed.   *Ralph Waldo Emerson*

A ship in harbor is safe, but that is not what ships are built for.

John A. Shedd

The trodden path is the safest.   *Legal Maxim*

He that's secure is not safe.   *Benjamin Franklin*

Let the people know the truth and the country is safe.   *Abraham Lincoln*

SARCASM   Also see: CRITICISM, HUMOR, IRONY, RIDICULE.

Sarcasm is the language of the devil, for which reason I have long since as good as renounced it.   *Thomas Carlyle*

Blows are sarcasms turned stupid.   *George Eliot*

A sneer is the weapon of the weak.   *James Russell Lowell*

Edged tools are dangerous things to handle, and not infrequently do much hurt.   *Agnes Repplier*

It is as hard to satirize well a man of distinguished vices, as to praise well a man of distinguished virtues.   *Jonathan Swift*

To "leave a sting within a brother's heart."   *Edward Young*

SCANDAL   *Also see:* GOSSIP, REPUTATION, SLANDER.

Scandal is what one half of the world takes pleasure inventing, and the other half in believing.   *Paul Chatfield*

There is so much good in the worst of us, and so much bad in the best of us, that it hardly becomes any one of us to talk about the rest of us.
Anonymous

Everybody says it, and what everybody says must be true.
James Fenimore Cooper

How awful to reflect that what people say of us is true.   *Logan P. Smith*

The objection of the scandalmonger is not that she tells of racy doings, but that she pretends to be indignant about them.   *H. L. Mencken*

Think how many blameless lives are brightened by the blazing indiscretions of other people.   *Saki*

Scandal: gossip made tedious by morality.   *Oscar Wilde*

Her mouth is a honey-blossom,
   No doubt, as the poet sings;
But within her lips, the petals,
   Lurks a cruel bee that stings.   *William D. Howells*

Old maids sweeten their tea with scandal.   *Josh Billings*

Scandal dies sooner of itself, than we could kill it.   *Benjamin Rush*

SCHOOL . . . See EDUCATION

SCIENCE   *Also see:* ART, ARTIST, FASHION, IMAGINATION, NOVELTY, RELIGION.

The science of today is the technology of tomorrow.   *Edward Teller*

Science is nothing but perception.   *Plato*

Science is what you know, philosophy is what you don't know.
Bertrand Russell

Every great advance in science has issued from a new audacity of imagination.   *John Dewey*

It stands to the everlasting credit of science that by acting on the human mind it has overcome man's insecurity before himself and before nature.
Albert Einstein

Science is simply common sense at its best—that is, rigidly accurate in observation, and merciless to fallacy in logic.   *Thomas Huxley*

It will free man from his remaining chains, the chains of gravity which still tie him to this planet. It will open to him the gates of heaven.
Wernher Von Braun

SECRECY *Also see:* TRUST.

Three may keep a secret if two of them are dead. *Benjamin Franklin*

To keep your secret is wisdom; but to expect others to keep it is folly.
Samuel Johnson

Never tell a secret to a bride or a groom; wait until they have been married longer. *Ed Howe*

I usually get my stuff from people who promised somebody else that they would keep it a secret. *Walter Winchell*

Secrets are things we give to others to keep for us. *Elbert Hubbard*

Where secrecy or mystery begins, vice or roguery is not far off.
Samuel Johnson

He who trusts secrets to a servant makes him his master. *John Dryden*

Trust him not with your secrets, who, when left alone in your room, turns over your papers. *Johann Kaspar Lavater*

SECURITY *Also see:* COUNTRY, MURDER, REWARD, WAGE.

Too many people are thinking of security instead of opportunity. They seem more afraid of life than death. *James F. Byrnes*

It's an old adage that the way to be safe is never to be secure . . . Each one of us requires the spur of insecurity to force us to do our best.
Harold W. Dodds

Happiness has many roots, but none more important than security.
E. R. Stettinius, Jr.

Security is the priceless product of freedom. Only the strong can be secure, and only in freedom can men produce those material resources which can secure them from want at home and against aggression from abroad.
B. E. Hutchinson

Security is mostly a superstition. It does not exist in nature, nor do the children of men as a whole experience it. Avoiding danger is no safer in the long run than outright exposure. Life is either a daring adventure, or nothing. *Helen Keller*

In no direction that we turn do we find ease or comfort. If we are honest and if we have the will to win we find only danger, hard work and iron resolution. *Wendell K. Willkie*

Uncertainty and expectation are the joys of life. Security is an insipid thing, though the overtaking and possessing of a wish discovers the folly of the chase. *William Congreve*

SELF-CONFIDENCE *Also see:* BEHAVIOR, CONFIDENCE, RESOLUTION.

Do not attempt to do a thing unless you are sure of yourself; but do not relinquish it simply because someone else is not sure of you.
Stewart E. White

Calm self-confidence is as far from conceit as the desire to earn a decent living is remote from greed. *Channing Pollock*

The history of the world is full of men who rose to leadership, by sheer force of self-confidence, bravery and tenacity. *Mahatma Gandhi*

No man is such a conqueror as the man who has defeated himself.
Henry Ward Beecher

They can conquer who believe they can. *Vergil*

SELF-CONTROL *Also see:* BEHAVIOR, CHARACTER, QUIET.

Not to have control over the senses is like sailing in a rudderless ship, bound to break to pieces on coming in contact with the very first rock.
Mahatma Gandhi

It is by presence of mind in untried emergencies that the native metal of man is tested. *James Russell Lowell*

The best time for you to hold your tongue is the time you feel you must say something or bust. *Josh Billings*

Such power there is in clear-eyed self-restraint. *James Russell Lowell*

Prudent, cautious self-control
Is wisdom's root. *Robert Burns*

SELF-IMPROVEMENT *Also see:* CHANGE, HABIT, PURPOSE, REFORM.

The improvement of our way of life is more important than the spreading of it. If we make it satisfactory enough, it will spread automatically. If we do not, no strength of arms can permanently oppose it.
Charles A. Lindbergh

There is no use whatever trying to help people who do not help themselves. You cannot push anyone up a ladder unless he be willing to climb himself. *Andrew Carnegie*

I tell you that as long as I can conceive something better than myself I cannot be easy unless I am striving to bring it into existence or clearing the way for it. *George Bernard Shaw*

People seldom improve when they have no other model but themselves to copy after. *Oliver Goldsmith*

All of us, who are worth anything, spend our manhood in unlearning the follies, or expiating the mistakes of our youth. *Percy Bysshe Shelley*

SELFISHNESS *Also see:* AVARICE, GALLANTRY.

The man who lives by himself and for himself is likely to be corrupted by the company he keeps. *Charles H. Parkhurst*

He who lives only to benefit himself confers on the world a benefit when he dies. *Tertullian*

Selfishness is the greatest curse of the human race *William E. Gladstone*

Next to the very young, the very old are the most selfish.
William Makepeace Thackeray

> That man who lives for self alone,
> Lives for the meanest mortal known. *Joaquin Miller*

SELF-KNOWLEDGE *Also see:* HEROISM, QUIET, REASON, REVERIE.

To understand one's self is the classic form of consolation; to delude one's self is the romantic. *George Santayana*

It's not only the most difficult thing to know one's self, but the most inconvenient. *Josh Billings*

> Trust not yourself, but your defects to know,
> Make use of every friend and every foe. *Alexander Pope*

We know what we are, but know not what we may be.
William Shakespeare

He that knows himself, knows others; and he that is ignorant of himself, could not write a very profound lecture on other men's heads.
Charles Caleb Colton

Other men's sins are before our eyes; our own are behind our backs.
Seneca

> Resolve to be thyself: and know, that he
> Who finds himself, loses his misery. *Matthew Arnold*

SELF-RESPECT *Also see:* LOYALTY, PRIDE, SACRIFICE.

It is necessary to the happiness of a man that he be mentally faithful to himself. *Thomas Paine*

Never violate the sacredness of your individual self-respect.
Theodore Parker

He that respects himself is safe from others; He wears a coat of mail that none can pierce. *Henry Wadsworth Longfellow*

No more duty can be urged upon those who are entering the great theater of life than simple loyalty to their best convictions. *Edwin Hubbel Chapin*

SELF-SACRIFICE *Also see:* GENEROSITY, HEROISM, LOYALTY, REWARD, SACRIFICE.

Self-sacrifice is the real miracle out of which all the reported miracles grow.
Ralph Waldo Emerson

Many men have been capable of doing a wise thing, more a cunning thing, but very few a generous thing. *Alexander Pope*

Behold I do not give lectures or a little charity,
When I give I give myself. *Walt Whitman*

Self-sacrifice is never entirely unselfish, for the giver never fails to receive.
Dolores E. McGuire

Self-sacrifice which denies common sense is not a virtue. It's a spiritual dissipation. *Margaret Deland*

Self-sacrifice enables us to sacrifice other people without blushing.
George Bernard Shaw

For anything worth having one must pay the price; and the price is always work, patience, love, self-sacrifice—no paper currency, no promises to pay, but the gold of real service. *John Burroughs*

The men and women who have the right ideals . . . are those who have the courage to strive for the happiness which comes only with labor and effort and self-sacrifice, and those whose joy in life springs in part from power of work and sense of duty. *Theodore Roosevelt*

SENSUALITY *Also see:* GLUTTON, REVERIE, SEX, SOUL, VICE.

The body of a sensualist is the coffin of a dead soul.
Christian Nestell Bovee

Sensual pleasures are like soap bubbles, sparkling, effervescent. The pleasures of intellect are calm, beautiful, sublime, ever enduring and climbing upward to the borders of the unseen world. *John H. Aughey*

If sensuality were happiness, beasts were happier than men; but human felicity is lodged in the soul, not in the flesh. *Seneca*

I have never known a man who was sensual in his youth, who was high-minded when old. *Charles Sumner*

All sensuality is one, though it takes many forms, as all purity is one. It is the same whether a man eat, or drink, or cohabit, or sleep sensually. They are but one appetite, and we only need to see a person do any one of these things to know how great a sensualist he is. *Henry David Thoreau*

Human brutes, like other beasts, find snares and poison in the provision of life, and are allured by their appetites to their destruction. *Jonathan Swift*

SENTIMENT *Also see:* EMOTION, PASSION, REVERIE.

A sentimentalist is simply one who desires to have the luxury of an emotion without paying for it.
Oscar Wilde

Sentimentality is the only sentiment that rubs you the wrong way.
W. Somerset Maugham

He who molds the public sentiment . . . makes statues and decisions possible or impossible to make.
Abraham Lincoln

Society is infested by persons who, seeing that the sentiments please, counterfeit the expression of them. These we call sentimentalists—talkers who mistake the description for the thing, saying for having.
Ralph Waldo Emerson

Sentiment is intellectualized emotion; emotion precipitated, as it were, in pretty crystals by the fancy.
James Russell Lowell

The world makes up for all its follies and injustices by being damnably sentimental.
Thomas Huxley

Sentimentality—that's what we call the sentiment we don't share.
Graham Greene

The barrenest of all mortals is the sentimentalist.
Thomas Carlyle

Sentiment is the poetry of the imagination.
Alphonse de Lamartine

SEX *Also see:* BIRTH, SENSUALITY.

Sex has become one of the most discussed subjects of modern times. The Victorians pretended it did not exist; the moderns pretend that nothing else exists.
Fulton J. Sheen

Sex is a flame which uncontrolled may scorch; properly guided, it will light the torch of eternity.
Joseph Fetterman

Some things are better than sex, and some are worse, but there's nothing exactly like it.
W. C. Fields

Sex lies at the root of life, and we can never learn to reverence life until we know how to understand sex.
Havelock Ellis

Oh, what a tangled web we weave when first we practice to conceive.
Don Herold

The sexes were made for each other, and only in the wise and loving union of the two is the fullness of health and duty and happiness to be expected.
William Hall

Man is always looking for someone to boast to; woman is always looking for a shoulder to put her head on.
H. L. Mencken

SILENCE *Also see:* CONVERSATION, LOQUACITY, UNDERSTANDING.

Silence is the ultimate weapon of power.   *Charles De Gaulle*

He had occasional flashes of silence that made his conversation perfectly delightful.   *Sydney Smith*

Silence is one of the hardest arguments to refute.   *Josh Billings*

Silence is foolish if we are wise, but wise if we are foolish.
Charles Caleb Colton

Still waters run deep.   *English Proverb*

Blessed is the man who, having nothing to say, abstains from giving wordy evidence of the fact.   *George Eliot*

If you keep your mouth shut you will never put your foot in it.
Austin O'Malley

> A wise old owl sat on an oak,
> The more he saw the less he spoke;
> The less he spoke the more he heard;
> Why aren't we like that wise old bird?   *Edward H. Richards*

If you don't say anything, you won't be called on to repeat it.
Calvin Coolidge

Sometimes silence is not golden—just yellow.   *Anonymous*

SIMPLICITY *Also see:* BREVITY, TASTE, TRUTH.

Simplicity is making the journey of this life with just baggage enough.
Charles Dudley Warner

Our life is frittered away by detail. Simplicity, simplicity, simplicity!
Henry David Thoreau

When thought is too weak to be simply expressed, it's clear proof that it should be rejected.   *Luc de Clapiers*

Nothing is more simple than greatness; indeed, to be simple is to be great.
Ralph Waldo Emerson

Everything should be made as simple as possible, but not simpler.
Albert Einstein

The whole is simpler than the sum of its parts.   *Willard Gibbs*

Simplicity is the glory of expression.   *Walt Whitman*

SIN *Also see:* DEATH, EVIL, GUILT, HUMANITY, PREACHING, PROVIDENCE, PUNISHMENT, REMORSE, REPENTANCE, WICKEDNESS.

He that falls into sin is a man; that grieves at it, is a saint; that boasteth of it, is a devil.
Thomas Fuller

He that is without sin among you, let him cast the first stone.   *John 8:7*

Confess your sins to the Lord, and you will be forgiven; confess them to men, and you will be laughed at.
Josh Billings

Men are not punished for their sins, but by them.   *Elbert Hubbard*

Adam ate the apple, and our teeth still ache.   *Hungarian Proverb*

The wages of sin are sables.   *Anonymous*

Sin is not harmful because it is forbidden, but it is forbidden because it is hurtful.
Benjamin Franklin

Every sin is the result of a collaboration.   *Stephen Crane*

Man-like it is to fall into sin; fiendlike it is to dwell therein.
Henry Wadsworth Longfellow

Only the sinner has a right to preach.   *Christopher Morley*

There is no sin except stupidity.   *Oscar Wilde*

SINCERITY . . . See HONESTY

SKEPTICISM *Also see:* CREDULITY, CYNIC, DOUBT, PESSIMISM.

Skeptics are never deceived.   *French Proverb*

Believe nothing and be on your guard against everything.   *Latin Proverb*

Skepticism, riddling the faith of yesterday, prepared the way for the faith of tomorrow.
Romain Rolland

The path of sound credence is through the thick forest of skepticism.
George Jean Nathan

Skepticism is the chastity of the intellect.   *George Santayana*

Skepticism: the mark and even the pose of the educated mind.
John Dewey

Great intellects are skeptical.   *Nietzsche*

Skepticism is slow suicide.   *Ralph Waldo Emerson*

SLANDER *Also see:* GOSSIP, INJURY, REPUTATION, SCANDAL.

To murder character is as truly a crime as to murder the body: the tongue of the slanderer is brother to the dagger of the assassin. *Tryon Edwards*

Slanders are like flies, that pass all over a man's good parts to light on his sores. *Anonymous*

I hate the man who builds his name on the ruins of another's fame.
John Gay

A slander is like a hornet; if you can't kill it dead the first time, better not strike at it. *Josh Billings*

Never throw mud. You may miss your mark, but you will have dirty hands.
Joseph Parker

Slander is the revenge of a coward, and dissimulation of his defense.
Samuel Johnson

Character assassination is at once easier and surer than physical assault; and it involves far less risk for the assassin. It leaves him free to commit the same deed over and over again, and may, indeed, win him the honors of a hero even in the country of his victims. *Alan Barth*

The worthiest people are the most injured by slander, as is the best fruit which the birds have been pecking at. *Jonathan Swift*

Have patience awhile; slanders are not long-lived. Truth is the child of time; ere long she shall appear to vindicate thee. *Immanuel Kant*

SLEEP *Also see:* REST, SUCCESS.

Fatigue is the best pillow. *Benjamin Franklin*

Sleep she as sound as careless infancy. *William Shakespeare*

Sleep lingers all our lifetime about our eyes, as night hovers all day in the boughs of the fir-tree. *Ralph Waldo Emerson*

It is a delicious moment, certainly, that of being well-nestled in bed and feeling that you shall drop gently to sleep. The good is to come, not past; the limbs are tired enough to render the remaining in one posture delightful; the labor of the day is gone. *Leigh Hunt*

Living is a disease from which sleep gives us relief eight hours a day.
Chamfort

Sleep, Silence's child, sweet father of soft rest,
  Prince whose approach peace to all mortals brings,
Indifferent host to shepherds and kings,
  Sole comforter to minds with grief opprest. *William Drummond*

Sleep is the twin of death. *Homer*

SMILE *Also see:* BEAUTY, CHEERFULNESS, KINDNESS.

Smiles form the channels of a future tear.   *Lord Byron*

Wrinkles should merely indicate where smiles have been.   *Mark Twain*

A stale article, if you dip it in a good, warm, sunny smile, will go off better than a fresh one that you've scowled upon.   *Nathaniel Hawthorne*

If you haven't seen your wife smile at a traffic cop, you haven't seen her smile her prettiest.   *Kin Hubbard*

Wear a smile and have friends; wear a scowl and have wrinkles. What do we live for if not to make the world less difficult for each other?

George Eliot

A lot of men think that if they smile for a second, somebody will take advantage of them, and they are right.   *Don Herold*

There are many kinds of smiles, each having a distinct character. Some announce goodness and sweetness, others betray sarcasm, bitterness and pride; some soften the countenance by their languishing tenderness, others brighten by their spiritual vivacity.   *Johann Kaspar Lavater*

SMOKING *Also see:* HABIT.

To cease smoking is the easiest thing I ever did; I ought to know because I've done it a thousand times.   *Mark Twain*

Pipe-smokers spend so much time cleaning, filling and fooling with their pipes, they don't have time to get into mischief.   *Bill Vaughan*

Much smoking kills live men and cures dead swine.   *George D. Prentice*

I tried to stop smoking cigarettes by telling myself I just didn't want to smoke, but I didn't believe myself.   *Barbara Kelly*

The best way to stop smoking is to carry wet matches.   *Anonymous*

SOCIETY *Also see:* CLASS, HUMANITY, HUMOR, MAN, POVERTY, SENTIMENT.

Society is like a lawn where every roughness is smoothed, every bramble eradicated, and where the eye is delighted by the smiling verdure of a velvet surface.   *Washington Irving*

To get into the best society nowadays, one has either to feed people, amuse people, or shock people.   *Oscar Wilde*

Society is like air; very high up, it is sublimated—too low down, a perfect choke-damp.   *Anonymous*

One great society alone on earth: the noble living and the noble dead.

William Wordsworth

SOCIETY (continued)

Society is a madhouse whose wardens are the officials and the police.
August Strindburg

The pillars of truth and the pillars of freedom—they are the pillars of society.
Henrik Ibsen

SOLDIER *Also see:* CITIZENSHIP, COURAGE, DRAFT, DUTY, WAR.

A good soldier, like a good horse, cannot be of a bad color.
Oliver Wendell Holmes

I want to see you shoot the way you shout.
Theodore Roosevelt

I could have become a soldier if I had waited; I knew more about retreating than the man who invented retreating.
Mark Twain

Every citizen should be a soldier. This was the case with the Greeks and Romans, and must be that of every free state.
Thomas Jefferson

I rose by sheer military ability to the rank of corporal.
Thornton Wilder

> Theirs is not to make reply,
> Theirs is not to reason why,
> Theirs is but to do and die.
Alfred, Lord Tennyson

But in a larger sense we cannot dedicate, we cannot consecrate, we cannot hallow this ground. The brave men, living and dead, who struggled here, have consecrated it far above our poor power to add or detract.
Abraham Lincoln

SOLITUDE *Also see:* LONELINESS.

I would rather sit on a pumpkin, and have it all to myself, than be crowded on a velvet cushion.
Henry David Thoreau

I live in that solitude which is painful in youth, but delicious in the years of maturity.
Albert Einstein

Solitude, though it may be silent as light, is like light, the mightiest of agencies; for solitude is essential to man. All men come into this world *alone* and leave it *alone*.
Thomas De Quincey

I never found a companion that was so companionable as solitude.
Henry David Thoreau

It is easy in the world to live after the world's opinions; it is easy in solitude to live after your own; but the great man is he who in the midst of the crowd keeps with perfect sweetness the independence of solitude.
Ralph Waldo Emerson

I have a great deal of company in the house, especially in the morning when nobody calls.
Henry David Thoreau

The right to be alone—the most comprehensive of rights, and the right most valued by civilized man.
Louis D. Brandeis

243

SORROW *Also see:* AFFLICTION, GRIEF, GUILT, HUMOR, RESIGNATION.

Into each life some rain must fall. *Henry Wadsworth Longfellow*

There can be no rainbow without a cloud and a storm. *J. H. Vincent*

It is foolish to tear one's hair in grief, as if grief could be lessened by baldness. *Cicero*

Sorrow makes men sincere. *Henry Ward Beecher*

The world is so full of care and sorrow that it is a gracious debt we owe to one another to discover the bright crystals of delight hidden in somber circumstances and irksome tasks. *Helen Keller*

Out of suffering have emerged the strongest souls. *Edwin Hubbel Chapin*

Sorrow: a kind of rust of the soul, which every new idea contributes in its passage to scour away. *Samuel Johnson*

Earth hath no sorrow that heaven cannot heal. *Thomas Moore*

Where there is sorrow, there is holy ground. *Oscar Wilde*

SOUL *Also see:* BODY, CONFESSION, CONSCIENCE, CRIME, DRESS, HEAVEN, INFLUENCE, MISER, NEGLECT, PRAYER, PURPOSE, SENSUALITY.

The one thing in the world, of value, is the active soul. *Ralph Waldo Emerson*

It matters not how straight the gait,
  How charged with punishments the scroll;
I am the master of my fate:
  I am the captain of my soul. *W. E. Henley*

The man who is always worrying whether or not his soul would be damned generally has a soul that isn't worth a damn. *Oliver Wendell Holmes*

The soul, like the body, lives by what it feeds on. *Josiah Gilbert Holland*

One of the proofs of the immortality of the soul is that myriads have believed it—they also believed the world was flat. *Mark Twain*

Most people sell their souls and live with a good conscience on the proceeds. *Logan P. Smith*

My mind is inescapable of conceiving such a thing as a soul. I may be in error, and man may have a soul; but I simply do not believe it. *Thomas A. Edison*

The wealth of a soul is measured by how much it can feel; its poverty by how little. *William Rounseville Alger*

SPACE   *Also see:* SCIENCE, TECHNOLOGY.

Here's one small step for a man . . . one giant leap for mankind.
Neil Armstrong

There is beauty in space, and it is orderly. There is no weather, and there is regularity. It is predictable . . . Everything in space obeys the laws of physics. If you know these laws and obey them, space will treat you kindly. And don't tell me man doesn't belong out there. Man belongs wherever he wants to go.
Wernher von Braun

The moon and other celestial bodies should be free for exploration and use by all countries. No country should be permitted to advance a claim of sovereignty.
Lyndon Baines Johnson

The question is not so much whether there is life on Mars as whether it will continue to be possible to live on Earth.
Anonymous

The sky is no longer the limit.
Richard M. Nixon

It's only during an eclipse that the Man in the Moon has a place in the sun.
Anonymous

The universe, as far as we can observe it, is a wonderful and immense engine.
George Santayana

God has no intention of setting a limit to the efforts of man to conquer space.
Pius XII

SPECULATION   *Also see:* BUSINESS, FINANCE.

There are two times in a man's life when he should not speculate: when he can't afford it and when he can.
Mark Twain

Speculation is only a word covering the making of money out of the manipulation of prices, instead of supplying goods and services.
Henry Ford

A speculator is a man who observes the future, and acts before it occurs.
Bernard M. Baruch

If there were no bad speculations there could be no good investments; if there were no wild ventures there would be no brilliantly successful enterprises.
F. W. Hirst

The narrower the mind, the broader the statement.
Ted Cook

The way to stop financial "joy-riding" is to arrest the chauffeur, not the automobile.
Woodrow Wilson

When speculation has done its worst, two and two still make four.
Samuel Johnson

There will always be speculation of some kind. If you throw it out of an organized exchange, you throw it out into the street.
H. C. Emery

SPEECH *Also see:* ELOQUENCE, LANGUAGE, LOQUACITY, MUSIC.

Speak softly, and carry a big stick.   *Theodore Roosevelt*

It usually takes more than three weeks to prepare a good impromptu speech.   *Mark Twain*

Speak clearly, if you speak at all; carve every word before you let it fall.
Oliver Wendell Holmes

Half the world is composed of people who have something to say and can't, and the other half who have nothing to say and keep on saying it.
Robert Frost

The true use of speech is not so much to express our wants as to conceal them.   *Oliver Goldsmith*

Speech is power: speech is to persuade, to convert, to compel.
Ralph Waldo Emerson

Better pointed bullets than pointed speeches.   *Otto von Bismarck*

We speak little if not egged on by vanity.   *François de La Rochefoucauld*

Speech is human nature itself, with none of the artificiality of written language.   *Alfred North Whitehead*

When you have spoken the word, it reigns over you. When it is unspoken you reign over it.   *Arabian Proverb*

SPIRIT *Also see:* COWARDICE, CULTURE, ENERGY, ENTHUSIASM, ZEAL.

One truth stands firm. All that happens in world history rests on something spiritual. If the spiritual is strong, it creates world history. If it is weak, it suffers world history.   *Albert Schweitzer*

It must be of the spirit if we are to save the flesh.   *Douglas MacArthur*

Of my own spirit let me be in sole though feeble mastery.   *Sara Teasdale*

Great men are they who see that the spiritual is stronger than any material force.   *Ralph Waldo Emerson*

There are only two forces in the world, the sword and the spirit. In the long run the sword will always be conquered by the spirit.
Napoleon Bonaparte

He that loseth wealth, loseth much; he that loseth friends, loseth more; but he that loseth his spirit loseth all.   *Spanish Maxim*

Every spirit makes its house, but as afterwards the house confines the spirit, you had better build well.   *Elbert Hubbard*

STRENGTH *Also see:* CHEERFULNESS, RESOLUTION, REWARD, WILL.

A threefold cord is not quickly broken.
Ecclesiastes 4:12

O, it is excellent to have a giant's strength, but it is tyrannous to use it like a giant.
William Shakespeare

Don't hit at all if it is honorably possible to avoid hitting, but never hit soft.
Theodore Roosevelt

We acquire the strength we have overcome.
Ralph Waldo Emerson

Concentration is the secret of strength.
Ralph Waldo Emerson

The weakest link in a chain is the strongest because it can break it.
Stanislaw J. Lec

I wish to preach not the doctrine of ignoble ease, but the doctrine of strenuous life.
Theodore Roosevelt

Don't expect to build up the weak by pulling down the strong.
Calvin Coolidge

The strength of a man consists in finding out the way God is going, and going that way.
Henry Ward Beecher

Three things give us hardy strength: sleeping on hairy mattresses, breathing cold air, and eating dry food.
Welsh Proverb

STRESS . . . See ANXIETY

STUDY *Also see:* LEARNING, SELF-IMPROVEMENT, THOUGHT.

No student knows his subject: the most he knows is where and how to find out the things he does not know.
Woodrow Wilson

The world's great men have not commonly been great scholars, nor its great scholars great men.
Oliver Wendell Holmes

The noblest exercise of the mind within doors, and most befitting a person of quality, is study.
William Ramesy

The mind of the scholar, if he would leave it large and liberal, should come in contact with other minds.
Henry Wadsworth Longfellow

There are more men ennobled by study than by nature.
Cicero

I would live to study, and not study to live.
Francis Bacon

Our delight in any particular study, art, or science rises and improves in proportion to the application which we bestow upon it. Thus, what was at first an exercise becomes at length an entertainment.
Joseph Addison

The more we study the more we discover our ignorance.
Percy Bysshe Shelley

SUCCESS
Also see: ACHIEVEMENT, AMBITION, CONFIDENCE, DEFEAT, ENEMY, LUCK, POPULARITY, REWARD, VICTORY.

If A equal success, then the formula is A equals X plus Y and Z, with X being work, Y play, and Z keeping your mouth shut.   *Albert Einstein*

All you need in this life is ignorance and confidence, and then Success is sure.   *Mark Twain*

If man has good corn, or wood, or boards, or pigs to sell, or can make better chairs or knives, crucibles, or church organs, than anybody else, you will find a broad, hard-beaten road to his house, tho it be in the woods.
          Ralph Waldo Emerson

There is only one success—to spend your life in your own way.
          Christopher Morley

Try not to become a man of success but rather try to become a man of value.   *Albert Einstein*

The gent who wakes up and finds himself a success hasn't been asleep.
          Wilson Mizner

The penalty of success is to be bored by the attentions of people who formerly snubbed you.   *M. W. Little*

To climb steep hills requires slow pace at first.   *William Shakespeare*

Success has always been a great liar.   *Nietzsche*

SUFFERING
Also see: ABSENCE, AFFLICTION, FEAR, PAIN, REWARD, SORROW.

I have suffered too much in this world not to hope for another.
          Jean Jacques Rousseau

How little it takes to make life unbearable: a pebble in the shoe, a cockroach in the spaghetti, a woman's laugh.   *H. L. Mencken*

It requires more courage to suffer than to die.   *Napoleon Bonaparte*

It is a glorious thing to be indifferent to suffering, but only to one's own suffering.   *Robert Lynd*

The salvation of the world is in man's suffering.   *William Faulkner*

If you suffer, thank God! It is a sure sign that you are alive.
          Elbert Hubbard

Suffering becomes beautiful when anyone bears great calamities with cheerfulness, not through insensibility but through greatness of mind.   *Aristotle*

We are healed of a suffering only by experiencing it in full.   *Marcel Proust*

SUPERSTITION *Also see:* BELIEF, CREDULITY, IDOLATRY, IGNO-
RANCE, SECURITY.

Let me make the superstitions of a nation and I care not who makes its
laws or its songs either.   *Mark Twain*

Superstition is a senseless fear of God.   *Cicero*

Superstition is . . . religion which is incongruous with intelligence.
                                                                 John Tyndall

Superstition is the poison of the mind.   *Joseph Lewis*

Superstition, idolatry, and hypocrisy have ample wages, but truth goes beg-
ging.   *Martin Luther*

We are all tattooed in our cradles with the beliefs of our tribe.
                                                          Oliver Wendell Holmes

Men are probably nearer the central truth in their superstitions than in their
science.   *Henry David Thoreau*

Superstition is the religion of feeble minds.   *Edmund Burke*

Superstitions are, for the most part, but the shadows of great truths.
                                                                 Tryon Edwards

---

SUSPICION *Also see:* DISTRUST, DOUBT, GUILT.

Suspicions which may be unjust need not be stated.   *Abraham Lincoln*

The less we know the more we suspect.   *Josh Billings*

The louder he talked of his honor, the faster we counted our spoons.
                                                           Ralph Waldo Emerson

A woman of honor should not expect of others things she would not do
herself.   *Marguerite De Valois*

We are always paid for our suspicion by finding what we suspect.
                                                         Henry David Thoreau

---

SYMPATHY *Also see:* COMPASSION, KINDNESS, MERCY, PITY.

Sympathy is a virtue unknown in nature.   *Paul Eipper*

When you are in trouble, people who call to sympathize are really looking
for the particulars.   *Ed Howe*

Harmony of aim, not identity of conclusion, is the secret of sympathetic
life.   *Ralph Waldo Emerson*

A sympathetic heart is like a spring of pure water bursting forth from the
mountain side.   *Anonymous*

If there was less sympathy in the world, there would be less trouble in the
world.   *Oscar Wilde*

T

TACT *Also see:* COURTESY, DIPLOMACY, DISCRETION, GALLANTRY.

Tact: the ability to describe others as they see themselves.
Abraham Lincoln

Women and foxes, being weak, are distinguished by superior tact.
Ambrose Bierce

Be kind and considerate to others, depending somewhat upon who they are.
Don Herold

Tact is one of the first mental virtues, the absence of which is often fatal to the best of talents; it supplies the place of many talents.
William Gillmore Simms

Tact consists in knowing how far to go too far.   *Jean Cocteau*

Without tact you can learn nothing.   *Benjamin Disraeli*

Tact: to lie about others as you would have them lie about you.
Oliver Herford

Don't flatter yourself that friendship authorizes you to say disagreeable things to your intimates. The nearer you come into relation with a person, the more necessary do tact and courtesy become.   *Oliver Wendell Holmes*

TALENT . . . See ABILITY

TALKING . . . See LOQUACITY

TASTE *Also see:* DESIRE, TEMPER, VARIETY, VULGARITY.

Taste is the feminine of genius.   *Edward FitzGerald*

I would rather be able to appreciate things I cannot have than to have things I am not able to appreciate.   *Elbert Hubbard*

Good taste is the excuse I've always given for leading such a bad life.
Oscar Wilde

Partial culture runs to the ornate; extreme culture to simplicity.
Christian Nestell Bovee

Taste is, so to speak, the microscope of the judgment.
Jean Jacques Rousseau

Taste: a quality possessed by persons without originality or moral courage.
George Bernard Shaw

Bad taste is a species of bad morals.   *Christian Nestell Bovee*

No one ever went broke underestimating the taste of the American public.
H. L. Mencken

TAX *Also see:* CENSURE, GOVERNMENT.

Death and taxes are inevitable. *Thomas C. Haliburton*

Never before have so many been taken for so much and left with so little. *Van Panopoulos*

I'm proud to pay taxes in the United States; the only thing is, I could be just as proud for half the money. *Arthur Godfrey*

The thing generally raised on city land is taxes. *Charles Dudley Warner*

The income tax has made more liars out of the American people than gold has. *Will Rogers*

The power to tax involves the power to destroy. *John Marshall*

What is the difference between a taxidermist and a tax collector? The taxidermist takes only your skin. *Mark Twain*

For every benefit you receive a tax is levied. *Ralph Waldo Emerson*

The tax collector must love poor people—he's creating so many of them. *Bill Vaughan*

To tax and to please, no more than to love and to be wise, is not given to men. *Edmund Burke*

Taxes are the sinews of the state. *Cicero*

TEACHING *Also see:* EDUCATION, KNOWLEDGE, LEARNING.

You cannot teach a man anything; you can only help him find it within himself. *Galileo*

One good schoolmaster is worth a thousand priests. *Robert Green Ingersoll*

Knowledge exists to be imparted. *Ralph Waldo Emerson*

The teacher is one who makes two ideas grow where only one grew before. *Elbert Hubbard*

What we want is to see the child in pursuit of knowledge, and not knowledge in pursuit of the child. *George Bernard Shaw*

The man who can make hard things easy is the educator. *Ralph Waldo Emerson*

To be good is noble, but to teach others how to be good is nobler—and less trouble. *Mark Twain*

Most subjects at universities are taught for no other purpose than that they may be retaught when the students become teachers. *G. C. Lichtenberg*

A teacher affects eternity; he can never tell where his influence stops. *Henry Brooks Adams*

TECHNOLOGY *Also see:* SCIENCE, SPACE.

Where there is the necessary technical skill to move mountains, there is no need for the faith that moves mountains. *Eric Hoffer*

The economic and technological triumphs of the past few years have not solved as many problems as we thought they would, and, in fact, have brought us new problems we did not foresee. *Henry Ford II*

What is more difficult, to think of an encampment on the moon or of Harlem rebuilt? Both are now within the reach of our resources. Both now depend upon human decision and human will. *Adlai E. Stevenson*

As nuclear and other technological achievements continue to mount, the normal life span will continue to climb. The hourly productivity of the worker will increase. *Dwight D. Eisenhower*

TELEVISION *Also see:* COMMUNICATION.

Television is now so desparately hungry for material that they're scraping the top of the barrel. *Gore Vidal*

Time has convinced me of one thing: Television is for appearing on—not for looking at. *Noel Coward*

I hate television. I hate it as much as peanuts. But I can't stop eating peanuts. *Orson Welles*

Television is a corporate vulgarity. *John Leonard*

TEMPER *Also see:* ANGER, MISERY, MODERATION, SELF-CONTROL.

Good temper is an estate for life. *William Hazlitt*

The worst-tempered people I've ever met were people who knew they were wrong. *Wilson Mizner*

A tart temper never mellows with age; and a sharp tongue is the only edged tool that grows keener with constant use. *Washington Irving*

Man is a rational animal who always loses his temper when called upon to act in accordance with the dictates of reason. *Oscar Wilde*

Men lose their tempers in defending their taste. *Ralph Waldo Emerson*

Nothing does reason more right, than the coolness of those that offer it: For Truth often suffers more by the heat of its defenders, than from the arguments of its opposers. *William Penn*

The happiness and misery of men depend no less on temper than fortune. *François de La Rochefoucauld*

TEMPTATION *Also see:* COWARDICE, DESIRE, PASSION, SELF-CONTROL.

Few men have virtue to withstand the highest bidder. *George Washington*

Temptation is an irresistible force at work on a moveable body.
H. L. Mencken

I can resist anything except temptation. *Oscar Wilde*

There are several good protections against temptation, but the surest is cowardice. *Mark Twain*

He who cannot resist temptation is not a man. *Horace Mann*

The only way to get rid of a temptation is to yield to it. *Oscar Wilde*

Better shun the bait than struggle in the snare. *John Dryden*

As the Sandwich-Islander believes that the strength and valor of the enemy he kills passes into himself, so we gain the strength of the temptations we resist. *Ralph Waldo Emerson*

It is easier to stay out than get out. *Mark Twain*

THEOLOGY *Also see:* ATHEISM, CHRISTIANITY, HELL, JUDAISM, RELIGION.

Theology is the effort to explain the unknowable in terms of the not worth knowing. *H. L. Mencken*

Division has done more to hide Christ from the view of all men than all the infidelity that has ever been spoken. *George MacDonald*

My theology, briefly, is that the universe was dictated but not signed.
Christopher Morley

Theology is a science of mind applied to God. *Henry Ward Beecher*

The best theology is rather a divine life than a divine knowledge.
Jeremy Taylor

Theologians always try to turn the Bible into a book without common sense.
G. C. Lichtenberg

Theology is but our ideas of truth classified and arranged.
Henry Ward Beecher

As the grave grows nearer my theology is growing strangely simple, and it begins and ends with Christ as the only Savior of the lost.
Henry Benjamin Whipple

Let us put theology out of religion. Theology has always sent the worst to heaven, the best to hell. *Robert Green Ingersoll*

THEORY *Also see:* FACTS, PHILOSOPHY, REALITY.

A young boy is a theory, an old man is a fact. *Ed Howe*

Many things difficult to design prove easy to performance. *Samuel Johnson*

Science is organized common sense where many a beautiful theory was killed by an ugly fact. *Thomas Huxley*

A little experience often upsets a lot of theory. *Cadman*

There can be no theory of any account unless it corroborate with the theory of the earth. *Walt Whitman*

Conjecture as to things useful, is good; but conjecture as to what it would be useless to know, is very idle. *Samuel Johnson*

I never once made a discovery . . . I speak without exaggeration that I have constructed *three thousand* different theories in connection with the electric light . . . Yet in only two cases did my experiments prove the truth of my theory. *Thomas A. Edison*

A theory is no more like a fact than a photograph is like a person. *Ed Howe*

In scientific work, those who refuse to go beyond fact rarely get as far as fact. *Thomas Huxley*

THOUGHT *Also see:* ACTION, DISSENT, LANGUAGE, LOGIC, PLAGIARISM, POLITICS, PROPAGANDA, QUOTATION, REVERIE, SELF-KNOWLEDGE, STUDY.

Great thoughts reduced to practice become great acts. *William Hazlitt*

You are today where your thoughts have brought you; you will be tomorrow where your thoughts take you. *James Allen*

The soul of God is poured into the world through the thoughts of men. *Ralph Waldo Emerson*

The busiest of living agents are certain dead men's thoughts. *Christian Nestell Bovee*

I've known countless people who were reservoirs of learning, yet never had a thought. *Wilson Mizner*

Learning without thought is labor lost. *Confucius*

Associate reverently, as much as you can, with your loftiest thoughts. *Henry David Thoreau*

Thought takes man out of servitude, into freedom. *Henry Wadsworth Longfellow*

THRIFT . . . See ECONOMY

TIME *Also see:* BUSY, EFFICIENCY, ETERNITY, HASTE, OPPORTUNITY, PRESENT, PUNCTUALITY, REST, WASTE.

Lost time is never found again. *John H. Aughey*

Dost thou love life? Then do not squander time, for that is the stuff life is made of. *Benjamin Franklin*

As if you could kill time without injuring eternity. *Henry David Thoreau*

Time and tide wait for no man, but time always stands still for a woman of 30. *Robert Frost*

Time is like money; the less we have of it to spare the further we make it go. *Josh Billings*

Time is the wisest of all counselors. *Plutarch*

Lost, yesterday, somewhere between sunrise and sunset, two golden hours, each set with sixty diamond minutes. No reward is offered for they are gone forever. *Horace Mann*

> Time cuts down all,
> Both great and small. *Anonymous*

Time, whose tooth gnaws away at everything else, is powerless against truth. *Thomas Huxley*

TOLERANCE *Also see:* INTOLERANCE, LIBERTY, RIGHTS.

Tolerance is another word for indifference. *W. Somerset Maugham*

No man has a right in America to treat any other man "tolerantly" for tolerance is the assumption of superiority. Our liberties are equal rights of every citizen. *Wendell K. Willkie*

Broad-minded is just another way of saying a fellow's too lazy to form an opinion. *Will Rogers*

It is easy to be tolerant of the principles of other people if you have none of your own. *Herbert Samuel*

Tolerance is the oil which takes the friction out of life. *Wilbert E. Scheer*

People are very open-minded about new things—as long as they're exactly like the old ones. *Charles F. Kettering*

Tolerance comes with age. I see no fault committed that I myself could not have committed at some time or other. *Johann Wolfgang von Goethe*

The responsibility of tolerance lies in those who have the wider vision. *George Eliot*

I have seen gross intolerance shown in support of tolerance. *Samuel Taylor Coleridge*

TRADITION *Also see:* CUSTOM.

Traditionalists are pessimists about the future and optimists about the past.
Lewis Mumford

It takes an endless amount of history to make even a little tradition.
Henry James

Tradition does not mean that the living are dead, but that the dead are living.
Gilbert K. Chesterton

Tradition is an important help to history, but its statements should be carefully scrutinized before we rely on them.
Joseph Addison

What an enormous magnifier is tradition! How a thing grows in the human memory and in the human imagination, when love, worship, and all that lies in the human heart, is there to encourage it.
Thomas Carlyle

TRAGEDY *Also see:* ADVERSITY, DESIRE, LIFE, SORROW.

The tragedy of life is not so much what men suffer, but rather what they miss.
Thomas Carlyle

There are two tragedies in life: one is to lose your heart's desire, the other is to gain it.
George Bernard Shaw

What the American public wants in the theater is a tragedy with a happy ending.
William D. Howells

The world is a comedy to those who think, a tragedy to those who feel.
Horace Walpole

TRANQUILITY . . . See PEACE

TRAVEL *Also see:* ADVENTURE, SPACE, WORLD.

The world is a book, and those who do not travel, read only a page.
St. Augustine

A man travels the world over in search of what he needs, and returns home to find it.
George Moore

In America there are two classes of travel—first class, and with children.
Robert Benchley

The man who goes out alone can start today; but he who travels with another must wait till that other is ready.
Henry David Thoreau

Never a ship sails out of bay but carries my heart as a stowaway.
Roselle Mercier Montgomery

The traveler sees what he sees, the tourist sees what he has come to see.
Gilbert K. Chesterton

TREASON   *Also see:* INGRATITUDE, REBELLION.

We are a rebellious nation. Our whole history is treason; our blood was attained before we were born; our creeds were infidelity to the mother church; our constitution treason to our fatherland.   *Theodore Parker*

Is there not some chosen curse, some hidden thunder in the stores of heaven, red with uncommon wrath, to blast the man who owes his greatness to his country's ruin!   *Joseph Addison*

Treason is like diamonds; there is nothing to be made by the small trader.   *Douglas Jerrold*

There is something peculiarly sinister and insidious in even a charge of disloyalty. Such a charge all too frequently places a strain on the reputation of an individual which is indelible and lasting, regardless of the complete innocence later proved.   *John Lord O'Brian*

Write on my gravestone: "Infidel, Traitor."—infidel to every church that compromises with wrong; traitor to every government that oppresses the people.   *Wendell Phillips*

TRIFLES   *Also see:* AFFECTION, SIMPLICITY.

Little things affect little minds.   *Benjamin Disraeli*

It is the little bits of things that fret and worry us; we can dodge an elephant, but we can't dodge a fly.   *Josh Billings*

Little strokes fell great oaks.   *Benjamin Franklin*

The creation of a thousand forests is in one acorn.   *Ralph Waldo Emerson*

A small leak will sink a great ship.   *Benjamin Franklin*

There is nothing too little for so little a creature as man. It is by studying little things that we attain the great art of having as little misery and as much happiness as possible.   *Samuel Johnson*

> For the want of a nail the shoe was lost,
> For the want of a shoe the horse was lost,
> For the want of a horse the rider was lost,
> For the want of a rider the battle was lost,
> For the want of a battle the kingdom was lost,
> And all for the want of a horse-shoe nail.   *Benjamin Franklin*

Trifles make perfection—and perfection is no trifle.   *Michelangelo*

> Small ills are the fountains of most of our groans.
> Men trip not on mountains, they stumble on stones.
>
> *Chinese Proverb*

TROUBLE . . . See ANXIETY

TRUST *Also see:* CONFIDENCE, CREDIT, DISHONESTY, ILLUSION, MONEY, SECRECY, SYMPATHY, WEALTH.

When a man has no reason to trust himself, he trusts in luck.　　*Ed Howe*

Put your trust in God, but keep your powder dry.　　*Oliver Cromwell*

Trust men and they will be true to you; treat them greatly and they will show themselves great.　　*Ralph Waldo Emerson*

Woe to the man whose heart has not learned while young to hope, to love —and to put its trust in life.　　*Joseph Conrad*

You may be deceived if you trust too much, but you will live in torment if you don't trust enough.　　*Frank Crane*

How calmly may we commit ourselves to the hands of Him who bears up the world.　　*Jean Paul Richter*

I think that we may safely trust a good deal more than we do. We may waive just so much care of ourselves as we honestly bestow elsewhere.　　*Henry David Thoreau*

————————

TRUTH *Also see:* BIBLE, BIGOTRY, CHILDREN, DIPLOMACY, ENEMY, ERROR, GOSSIP, LYING, MAXIM, PHILOSOPHY, PREJUDICE, PROPAGANDA, RADICAL, REFORM, SAFETY, SCANDAL, SUPERSTITION, TIME.

Nobody dies nowadays of fatal truths: there are too many antidotes to them.　　*Nietzsche*

Rather than love, than money, than fame, give me truth.　　*Henry David Thoreau*

A bare assertion is not necessarily the naked truth.　　*George D. Prentice*

Men occasionally stumble over the truth, but most of them pick themselves up and hurry off as if nothing happened.　　*Winston Churchill*

Truth gets well if she is run over by a locomotive, while error dies of lock-jaw if she scratches her finger.　　*William Cullen Bryant*

Never tell the truth to people who are not worthy of it.　　*Mark Twain*

Truth is always served by great minds, even if they fight it.　　*Jean Rostand*

Everyone wishes to have truth on his side, but not everyone wishes to be on the side of truth.　　*Richard Whately*

When you want to fool the world, tell the truth.　　*Otto Von Bismarck*

If you are out to describe the truth, leave elegance to the tailor.　　*Albert Einstein*

The pure and simple truth is rarely pure and never simple.　　*Oscar Wilde*

The truth is more important than the facts.　　*Frank Lloyd Wright*

Truths turn into dogmas the minute they are disputed. *Gilbert K. Chesterton*

Most writers regard truth as their most valuable possession, and therefore are most economical in its use. *Mark Twain*

The greatest homage we can pay to truth, is to use it. *James Russell Lowell*

It is easier to perceive error than to find truth, for the former lies on the surface and is easily seen, while the latter lies in the depth, where few are willing to search for it. *Johann Wolfgang von Goethe*

Truth is the property of no individual but is the treasure of all men. *Ralph Waldo Emerson*

Truth is stranger than fiction, but it is because Fiction is obliged to stick to possibilities; Truth isn't. *Mark Twain*

The greatest friend of truth is Time, her greatest enemy is Prejudice, and her constant companion is Humility. *Charles Caleb Colton*

Craft must have clothes, but truth loves to go naked. *Thomas Fuller*

Ye shall know the truth, and the truth shall make you mad. *Aldous Huxley*

It is man that makes truth great, not truth that makes man great. *Confucius*

As scarce as truth is, the supply has always been in excess of the demand. *Josh Billings*

TYRANNY *Also see:* COMMUNISM, CONSCIENCE, DESTINY, MOB, REBELLION, REVOLUTION, UNITY.

Every tyrant who has lived has believed in freedom—for himself. *Elbert Hubbard*

Tyranny and anarchy are never far asunder. *Jeremy Bentham*

Hateful is the power, and pitiable is the life, of those who wish to be feared rather than loved. *Cornelius Nepos*

Resistance to tyrants is obedience to God. *Thomas Jefferson*

Tyrants are seldom free; the cares and the instruments of their tyranny enslave them. *George Santayana*

The closed door and the sealed lips are prerequisites to tyranny. *Frank L. Stanton*

Tyrants have always some slight shade of virtue; they support the laws before destroying them. *Voltaire*

There is a secret pride in every human heart that revolts at tyranny. You may order and drive an individual, but you cannot make him respect you. *William Hazlitt*

U

UGLINESS *Also see:* BEAUTY.

A point of view: an ulcer is wonderful to a pathologist. *Austin O'Malley*

Better an ugly face than an ugly mind. *James Ellis*

There is a sort of charm in ugliness, if the person has some redeeming qualities and is only ugly enough. *Josh Billings*

Heaven sometimes hedges a rare character about with ungainliness and odium, as the burr that protects the fruit. *Ralph Waldo Emerson*

Ugliness wihout tact is horrible. *Nathaniel Hawthorne*

UNDERSTANDING *Also see:* ANGER, COMMUNICATION, MIND, PERCEPTION, PITY, REVERIE, WORD.

Understanding is a two-way street. *Eleanor Roosevelt*

It is difficult to get a man to understand something when his salary depends upon his not understanding it. *Upton Sinclair*

Whatever you cannot understand, you cannot possess.
Johann Wolfgang Von Goethe

There is a great difference between knowing and understanding: you can know a lot about something and not really understand it.
Charles F. Kettering

He who does not understand your silence will probably not understand your words. *Elbert Hubbard*

The improvement of understanding is for two ends: first, our own increase of knowledge; secondly, to enable us to deliver that knowledge to others.
John Locke

UNHAPPINESS . . . See SORROW

UNION *Also see:* ECONOMICS, LABOR, WORK.

The labor movement's basic purpose is to achieve a better life for its members. A union that fails in this purpose has failed utterly. *New York Times*

We must hang together or assuredly we shall hang separately.
Benjamin Franklin

The trade union movement represents the organized economic power of the workers . . . It is in reality the most potent and the most direct social insurance the workers can establish. *Samuel Gompers*

All for one; one for all. *Alexander Dumas*

UNITED NATIONS

The United Nations is our one great hope for a peaceful and free world.
Ralph Bunche

This organization is created to prevent you from going to hell. It isn't created to take you to heaven.
Henry Cabot Lodge

The whole basis of the United Nations is the right of all nations—great or small—to have weight, to have a vote, to be attended to, to be a part of the twentieth century.
Adlai E. Stevenson

We have actively sought and are actively seeking to make the United Nations an effective instrument of international cooperation.
Dean Acheson

The United Nations is designed to make possible lasting freedom and independence for all its members.
Harry S. Truman

We prefer world law, in the age of self-determination, to world war in the age of mass extermination.
John Fitzgerald Kennedy

The United Nations was not set up to be a reformatory. It was assumed that you would be good before you got in and not that being in would make you good.
John Foster Dulles

UNITY *Also see:* LOYALTY, MARRIAGE, STRENGTH.

Men's hearts ought not to be set against one another, but set with one another, and all against evil only.
Thomas Carlyle

There are no problems we cannot solve together, and very few that we can solve by ourselves.
Lyndon Baines Johnson

We were two and had but one heart between us.
François Villon

Unity to be real must stand the severest strain without breaking.
Mahatma Gandhi

We cannot be separated in interest or divided in purpose. We stand together until the end.
Woodrow Wilson

One country, one constitution, one destiny.
Daniel Webster

We come to reason, not to dominate. We do not seek to have our way, but to find a common way.
Lyndon Baines Johnson

A house divided against itself cannot stand.
Abraham Lincoln

United we stand, divided we fall.
G. P. Morris

The multitude which is not brought to act as a unity, is confusion. That unity which has not its origin in the multitude is tyranny.
Blaise Pascal

UNIVERSE *Also see:* EARTH, MAN, SCIENCE, SPACE, TECHNOLOGY.

The Universe is but one vast symbol of God. *Thomas Carlyle*

A penny will hide the biggest star in the universe if you hold it close enough to your eye. *Samuel Grafton*

The universe is one of God's thoughts. *Johann von Schiller*

The universe is duly in order, everything in its place. *Walt Whitman*

Great is this organism of mud and fire, terrible this vast, painful, glorious experiment. *George Santayana*

An infinite universe is at each moment opened to our view. And this universe is the sign and symbol of Infinite Power, Intelligence, Purity, Bliss, and Love. *William Ellery Channing*

We are all fellow passengers on a dot of earth. And each of us, in the span of time, has really only a moment among our companions. *Lyndon Baines Johnson*

———

UNIVERSITY *Also see:* EDUCATION, TEACHING.

The university is not engaged in making ideas safe for students. It is engaged in making students safe for ideas. *Clark Kerr*

The university most worthy of rational admiration is that one in which your lonely thinker can feel himself lonely, most positively furthered, and most richly fed. *William James*

Universities are full of knowledge; the freshmen bring a little in and the seniors take none away, and knowledge accumulates. *Abbott L. Lowell*

The task of a university is the creation of the future, so far as rational thought and civilized modes of appreciation can affect the issue. *Alfred North Whitehead*

This institution will be based on the illimitable freedom of the human mind. For here we are not afraid to follow truth wherever it may lead, not tolerate error as long as reason is left free to combat it. *Thomas Jefferson*

If I were founding a university I would first found a smoking room; then when I had a little more money in hand I would found a dormitory; then after that, or more probably with it, a decent reading room and a library. After that, if I still had more money that I couldn't use, I would hire a professor and get some text books. *Stephen Butler Leacock*

A university should be a place of light, of liberty, and of learning. *Benjamin Disraeli*

A senior always feels like the university is going to the kids. *Tom Masson*

VACATION *Also see:* REST, VARIETY.

No man needs a vacation so much as the man who has just had one.
Elbert Hubbard

A vacation is over when you begin to yearn for your work.
Morris Fishbein

If some people didn't tell you, you'd never know they'd been away on a vacation. *Kin Hubbard*

The rainy days a man saves for usually seem to arrive during his vacation.
Anonymous

A period of travel and relaxation when you take twice the clothes and half the money you need. *Anonymous*

VALOR . . . See COURAGE

VALUE *Also see:* CIVILIZATION, MERIT, SUCCESS, WORTH.

Some values are . . . like sugar on the doughnut, legitimate, desirable, but insufficient, apart from the doughnut itself. We need substance as well as frosting. *Ralph T. Flewelling*

I conceive that the great part of the miseries of mankind are brought upon them by false estimates they have made of the value of things.
Benjamin Franklin

What we obtain too cheap, we esteem too lightly; it is dearness only that gives everything its value. *Thomas Paine*

Teach us that wealth is not elegance, that profusion is not magnificence, that splendor is not beauty. *Benjamin Disraeli*

Cherish all your happy moments: they make a fine cushion for old age.
Booth Tarkington

The value of a principle is the number of things it will explain; and there is no good theory of disease which does not at once suggest a cure.
Ralph Waldo Emerson

Nothing can have value without being an object of utility. *Karl Marx*

People exaggerate the value of things they haven't got: everybody worships truth and unselfishness because they have no experience with them.
George Bernard Shaw

All that is valuable in human society depends upon the opportunity for development accorded the individual. *Albert Einstein*

Religion is the sole technique for the validating of values. *Allen Tate*

VANITY *Also see:* CURIOSITY, FAME, FAULT, LONELINESS, LOQUACITY, RANK, SPEECH.

Vain-glorious men are the scorn of the wise, the admiration of fools, the idols of paradise, and the slaves of their own vaunts. *Francis Bacon*

A vain man finds it wise to speak good or ill of himself; a modest man does not talk of himself. *Jean de La Bruyère*

It is our own vanity that makes the vanity of others intolerable to us.
François de La Rochefoucauld

Vanity as an impulse has without doubt been of far more benefit to civilization than modesty has ever been. *William E. Woodward*

Virtue would not go far if vanity did not keep it company.
François de La Rochefoucauld

To be a man's own fool is bad enough; but the vain man is everybody's.
William Penn

The highest form of vanity is love of fame. *George Santayana*

A man who is not a fool can rid himself of every folly except vanity.
Jean Jacques Rousseau

The best way to turn a woman's head is to tell her she has a beautiful profile. *Sacha Guitry*

The only cure for vanity is laughter, and the only fault that's laughable is vanity. *Henri Bergson*

VARIETY *Also see:* CHANGE, ORIGINALITY.

With me a change of trouble is as good as a vacation.
William Lloyd George

Variety's the very spice of life, that gives it all its flavor. *William Cowper*

Variety of mere nothings gives more pleasure than uniformity of something.
Jean Paul Richter

I take it to be a principle rule of life, not to be too much addicted to any one thing. *Terence*

It takes all sorts to make a world. *English Proverb*

The most delightful pleasures cloy without variety. *Publilius Syrus*

Sameness is the mother of disgust, variety the cure. *Petrarch*

The best way to keep good acts in memory is to refresh them with new.
Cato

VENGEANCE *Also see:* ANGER, HATE, INJURY, SLANDER.

Vengeance has no foresight. *Napoleon Bonaparte*

Revenge is the abject pleasure of an abject mind. *Juvenal*

The best manner of avenging ourselves is by not resembling him who has injured us. *Jane Porter*

Avenge not yourselves, but rather give place unto wrath: for it is written, Vengeance is mine; I will repay, saith the Lord. *Romans 12:19*

Revenge is an act of passion; vengeance of justice. Injuries are revenged; crimes are avenged. *Joseph Joubert*

VICE *Also see:* CRIME, CRUELTY, EVIL, FANATICISM, PROFANITY, SELF-ISHNESS, SIN, WICKEDNESS.

The willing contemplation of vice is vice. *Arabian Proverb*

This is the essential evil of vice, that it debases man.
Edwin Hubbel Chapin

Many a man's vices have at first been nothing worse than good qualities run wild. *Augustus and Julius Hare*

One big vice in a man is apt to keep out a great many smaller ones.
Bret Harte

When our vices have left us we flatter ourselves that we have left them.
François de La Rochefoucauld

Vices are often habits rather than passions. *Antoine Rivarol*

It has been my experience that folks who have no vices have very few virtues. *Abraham Lincoln*

Men wish to be saved from the mischiefs of their vices, but not from their vices. *Ralph Waldo Emerson*

Wild oats make a bad autumn crop. *Cynics Calendar*

We are double-edged blades, and every time we whet our virtue the return stroke straps our vice. *Henry David Thoreau*

It is but a step from companionship to slavery when one associates with vice. *Hosea Ballou*

Our faith comes in moments; our vice is habitual.
William Ellery Channing

What maintains one vice would bring up two children. *Benjamin Franklin*

There will be vice as long as there are men. *Tacitus*

VICTORY *Also see:* CHARACTER, DEFEAT, SUCCESS, WAR.

Victory and defeat are each of the same price. *Thomas Jefferson*

I do not think that winning is the most important thing. I think winning is the only thing. *Bill Veeck*

One may know how to gain a victory, and know not how to use it. *Barca*

The greatest conquerer is he who overcomes the enemy without a blow. *Chinese Proverb*

We should wage war not to win war, but to win peace. *Paul Hoffman*

Whether in chains or in laurels, liberty knows nothing but victories. *Douglas MacArthur*

Victories that are easy are cheap. Those only are worth having which come as the result of hard fighting. *Henry Ward Beecher*

The smile of God is victory. *John Greenleaf Whittier*

The god of victory is said to be one-handed, but peace gives victory on both sides. *Ralph Waldo Emerson*

It is fatal to enter any war without the will to win it. *Douglas MacArthur*

VIETNAM

If we were not in Vietnam, all that part of the world would be enjoying the obscurity it so richly deserves. *John Kenneth Galbraith*

It (Vietnam) poisons everything. It has disrupted the economy, envenomed our politics, hurt the alliance, divided our people, and now it is interfering with this critical question of the arms race. *James Reston*

This war in Vietnam is, I believe, a war for civilization. Certainly it is not a war of our seeking. It is a war thrust upon us and we cannot yield to tyranny. *Francis Cardinal Spellman*

America is not fighting to win a war. We are fighting to give an application to an old Greek proverb, which is that the purpose of war is not to annihilate an enemy but to get him to mend his ways. And we are confident we can get the enemy to mend his ways. *Arthur J. Goldberg*

I am afraid (if the present trend in Vietnam continues) that direct confrontation, first of all between Washington and Peking, is inevitable. *U Thant*

The Vietnamese people deeply love independence, freedom and peace. But in the face of United States aggression they have risen up, united as one man. *Ho Chi Minh*

VIGILANCE *Also see:* CAUTION, PRUDENCE, WISDOM.

Eternal vigilance is the price of liberty.
Thomas Jefferson

He is most free from danger, who, even when safe, is on his guard.
Publilius Syrus

There is a significant Latin proverb; to wit: Who will guard the guards?
Josh Billings

They that are on their guard and appear ready to receive their adversaries, are in much less danger of being attacked than the supine, secure and negligent.
Benjamin Franklin

There are no permanent changes because change itself is permanent. It behooves the industrialist to research and the investor to be vigilant.
Ralph L. Woods

Experience should teach us to be most on our guard to protect liberty when the government's purposes are beneficent.
Louis D. Brandeis

VIOLENCE *Also see:* HATE, PERSEVERANCE, REVOLUTION, RIOT, TELE-VISION, WAR.

These violent delights have violent ends.
William Shakespeare

The violence done us by others is often less painful than that which we do to ourselves.
François de La Rochefoucauld

Nothing good ever comes of violence.
Martin Luther

Degeneracy follows every autocratic system of violence, for violence inevitably attracts moral inferiors. Time has proven that illustrious tyrants are succeeded by scoundrels.
Albert Einstein

There is a violence that liberates, and a violence that enslaves; there is a violence that is moral and a violence that is immoral.
Benito Mussolini

All violence, all that is dreary and repels, is not power, but the absence of power.
Ralph Waldo Emerson

Violence in the voice is often only the death rattle of reason in the throat.
John F. Boyes

It is organized violence on top which creates individual violence at the bottom. It is the accumulated indignation against organized wrong, organized crime, organized injustice, which drives the political offender to act.
Emma Goldman

Violence cannot build a better society. Disruption and disorder nourish repression, not justice. They strike at the freedom of every citizen. The community cannot—it will not—tolerate coercion and mob rule.
Commission on Civil Disorder, 1968

Violence does even justice unjustly.
Thomas Carlyle

VIRTUE *Also see:* ARISTOCRACY, INNOCENCE, MERCY, MODESTY, WORTH.

Virtue is like a rich stone, best plain set.   *Francis Bacon*

If you can be well without health, you may be happy without virtue.
Edmund Burke

Perfect virtue is to do unwitnessed that which we should be capable of doing before all the world.   *François de La Rochefoucauld*

The person who talks most of his own virtue is often the least virtuous.
Jawaharlal Nehru

Virtue is a state of war, and to live in it we have always to combat with ourselves.   *Jean Jacques Rousseau*

That virtue we appreciate is as much ours as another's. We see so much only as we possess.   *Henry David Thoreau*

Virtue consists, not in abstaining from vice, but in not desiring it.
George Bernard Shaw

Virtue treads paths that end not in the grave.   *James Russell Lowell*

Virtue must be valuable, if men and women of all degrees pretend to have it.   *Ed Howe*

The only reward of virtue is virtue.   *Ralph Waldo Emerson*

VISION *Also see:* BLINDNESS, COURAGE, CYNIC, EYE, IDEAL, IMAGINATION, TOLERANCE, WONDER.

Only eyes washed by tears can see clearly.   *Louis L. Mann*

It is never safe to look into the future with eyes of fear.
Edward H. Harriman

No man that does not see visions will ever realize any high hope or undertake any high enterprise.   *Woodrow Wilson*

The farther back you can look, the farther forward you are likely to see.
Winston Churchill

Where there is no vision a people perish.   *Ralph Waldo Emerson*

You see things and you say "Why?"; but I dream things that never were and I say "Why not?"   *George Bernard Shaw*

I would give all the wealth of the world, and all the deeds of all the heroes, for one true vision.   *Henry David Thoreau*

Vision: the art of seeing things invisible.   *Jonathan Swift*

VOICE *Also see:* DISSENT, PUBLIC, SPEECH, VIOLENCE, WORD.

The sweetest of all sounds is that of the voice of the woman we love.
Jean de La Bruyère

There is no index so sure as the voice. *Tancred*

A man's style is his mind's voice. Wooden minds, wooden voices.
Ralph Waldo Emerson

> Then read from the treasured volume
>   The poem of thy choice,
> And lend to the rhyme of the poet
>   The beauty of thy voice. *Henry Wadsworth Longfellow*

It is the still small voice that the soul heeds; not the deafening blasts of doom. *William D. Howells*

The human voice is the organ of the soul. *Henry Wadsworth Longfellow*

> At some glad moment was it nature's choice
>   To dower a scrap of sunset with a voice? *Edgar Fawcett*

VOTE *Also see:* AMERICA, CITIZENSHIP, DEMOCRACY, POLITICS.

Where annual elections end, there slavery begins. *John Quincy Adams*

A straw vote only shows which way the hot air blows. *O. Henry*

Vote for the man who promises least—he'll be the least disappointing.
Bernard Baruch

Always vote for principle, though you may vote alone, and you may cherish the sweetest reflection that your vote is never lost. *John Quincy Adams*

The future of this republic is in the hands of the American voter.
Dwight D. Eisenhower

You can milk a cow the wrong way once and still be a farmer, but vote the wrong way on a water tower and you can be in trouble.
John Fitzgerald Kennedy

Giving every man a vote has no more made men wise and free than Chistianity has made them good. *H. L. Mencken*

Among free men there can be no successful appeal from the ballot to the bullet. *Abraham Lincoln*

When a fellow tells me he's bipartisan, I know he's going to vote against me. *Harry S. Truman*

There can no longer be anyone too poor to vote. *Lyndon Baines Johnson*

VOID . . . See ABSENCE

VOW *Also see:* MARRIAGE, POLITICS, RESOLUTION.

Your capacity to keep your vow will depend on the purity of your life.
Mahatma Gandhi

Hasty resolutions are of the nature of vows, and to be equally avoided.
William Penn

A vow is a snare for sin. *Samuel Johnson*

A vow is fixed and unalterable determination to do a thing, when such a determination is related to something noble which can only uplift the man who makes the resolve. *Mahatma Gandhi*

Vows made in storms are forgotten in calm. *Thomas Fuller*

Men's vows are women's traitors! *William Shakespeare*

It is the purpose that makes strong the vow; But vows to every purpose must not hold. *William Shakespeare*

Personally, I hold that a man, who deliberately and intelligently takes a pledge and then breaks it, forfeits his manhood. *Mahatma Gandhi*

'Tis not the many oaths that make the truth;
But the plain single vow, that is vow'd true. *William Shakespeare*

VULGARITY *Also see:* ABUSE, AMBITION, HASTE, PROFANITY, TELE-VISION, TASTE.

There are no people who are quite so vulgar as the over-refined. *Mark Twain*

Vulgarity is more obvious in satin than in homespun. *Nathaniel P. Willis*

To endeavor to work upon the vulgar with fine sense is like attempting to hew blocks with a razor. *Alexander Pope*

Vulgarity is the conduct of other people, just as falsehoods are the truths of other people. *Oscar Wilde*

Vulgarity is the garlic in the salad of taste. *Cyril Connolly*

By vulgarity I mean that vice of civilization which makes man ashamed of himself and his next of kin, and pretend to be somebody else.
Solomon Schechter

A thing is not vulgar merely because it is common. *William Hazlitt*

Vulgarity is the rich man's modest contribution to democracy. *Anonymous*

Think with the wise, but talk with the vulgar. *Greek Proverb*

W

WAGE *Also see:* CAPITALISM, EMPLOYMENT, LABOR, REWARD, UNION.

Low wages are not cheap wages.   *Louis D. Brandeis*

It is but a truism that labor is most productive where its wages are largest. Poorly paid labor is inefficient labor, the world over.   *Henry George*

No business which depends for existence on paying less than living wages to its workers has any right to continue in this country.
Franklin Delano Roosevelt

The high wage begins down in the shop. If it is not created there it cannot get into pay envelopes. There will never be a system invented which will do away with the necessity for work.   *Henry Ford*

We declare war with the wages system, which demoralizes alike the hirer and the hired, cheats both, and enslaves the workingman.
Wendell Phillips

"A fair day's wage for a fair day's work": it is as just a demand as governed men ever made of governing. It is the everlasting right of man.
Thomas Carlyle

Men who do things without being told draw the most wages.   *Edwin H. Stuart*

WANT *Also see:* DESIRE, INDEPENDENCE, NECESSITY, POVERTY, SECURITY, SPEECH, WASTE.

Our necessities never equal our wants.   *Benjamin Franklin*

The keener the want the lustier the growth.   *Wendell Phillips*

It is not from nature, but from education and habits, that our wants are chiefly derived.   *Henry Fielding*

He can feel no little wants who is in pursuit of grandeur.
Johann Kaspar Lavater

The stoical scheme of supplying our wants by lopping off our desires, is like cutting off our feet when we want shoes.   *Jonathan Swift*

Want is a growing giant whom the coat of Have was never large enough to cover.   *Ralph Waldo Emerson*

The fewer our wants, the nearer we resemble the gods.   *Socrates*

> The things that I can't have I want,
>   And what I have seems second-rate,
> The things I want to do I can't,
>   And what I have to do I hate.   *Don Marquis*

WAR *Also see:* BLOOD, CAUSE, CIVILIZATION, DIPLOMACY, DISARMA-
MENT, HEROISM, NUCLEAR WARFARE, PEACE, POWER,
RACE, SOLDIER, UNITED NATIONS, VIETNAM, YOUTH.

Soldiers usually win the battles and generals get the credit for them.
Napoleon Bonaparte

The tragedy of war is that it uses man's best to do man's worst.
Harry Emerson Fosdick

I don't know whether war is an interlude during peace, or peace is an interlude during war. *Georges Clemenceau*

War is the science of destruction. *John Abbott*

No one can guarantee success in war, but only deserve it.
Winston Churchill

When people speak to you about a preventive war, you tell them to go and
fight it. After my experience, I have come to hate war. War settles nothing.
Dwight D. Eisenhower

The essence of war is violence. Moderation in war is imbecility.
John A. Fisher

There was never a good war, or a bad peace. *Benjamin Franklin*

Only two great groups of animals, men and ants, indulge in highly organized mass warfare. *Charles H. Maskins*

There is no such thing as an inevitable war. If war comes it will be from
failure of human wisdom. *Andrew B. Law*

The grim fact is that we prepare for war like precocious giants, and for
peace like retarded pygmies. *Lester Bowles Pearson*

War is hell. *William Tecumseh Sherman*

The next World War will be fought with stones. *Albert Einstein*

Diplomats are just as essential in starting a war as soldiers are in finishing
it. *Will Rogers*

How good bad music and bad reasons sound when we march against an
enemy. *Nietzsche*

I have never advocated war except as a means of peace.
Ulysses S. Grant

It is well that war is so terrible—we shouldn't grow too fond of it.
Robert E. Lee

When war is declared, Truth is the first casualty. *Arthur Ponsonby*

The Civil War is not ended: I question whether any serious civil war ever
does end. *T. S. Eliot*

WASTE *Also see:* LOSS, PURSUIT, REFORM, REGRET, WAGE.

Willful waste brings woeful want.   *Thomas Fuller*

Waste neither time nor money, but make the best use of both. Without industry and frugality, nothing will do, and with them everything.
Benjamin Franklin

The waste of life occasioned by trying to do too many things at once is appalling.   *Orison S. Marden*

Short as life is, we make it still shorter by the careless waste of time.
Victor Hugo

A man who dares to waste one hour of life has not discovered the value of life.   *Charles Darwin*

I wish I could stand on a busy street corner, hat in hand, and beg people to throw me all their wasted hours.   *Bernard Berenson*

Everyone should keep a mental wastepaper basket, and the older he grows, the more things will he promptly consign to it.   *Samuel Butler*

Waste is worse than loss. The time is coming when every person who lays claim to ability will keep the question of waste before him constantly. The scope of thrift is limitless.   *Thomas A. Edison*

WEAKNESS *Also see:* COWARDICE, CRUELTY, NEUTRALITY, PRIDE.

There are two kinds of weakness, that which breaks and that which bends.
James Russell Lowell

Better make a weak man your enemy than your friend.   *Josh Billings*

Our strength grows out of our weakness.   *Ralph Waldo Emerson*

We must have a weak spot or two in our character before we can love it much.   *Oliver Wendell Holmes*

The greatest weakness of all is the great fear of appearing weak.
Jacques Bénigne Bossuet

A weak mind is like a microscope, which magnifies trifling things but cannot receive great ones.   *Lord Chesterfield*

You cannot run away from weakness; you must some time fight it out or perish; and if that be so, why not now, and where you stand?
Robert Louis Stevenson

What is bad? All that proceeds from weakness.   *Nietzsche*

The weakest soul, within itself unblest,
    Leans for all pleasure on another's breast.   *Oliver Goldsmith*

WEALTH *Also see:* CAPITALISM, LOSS, MONEY, OPPORTUNITY, PROSPERITY, VALUE.

He does not possess wealth that allows it to possess him.
Benjamin Franklin

Surplus wealth is a sacred trust which its possessor is bound to administer in his lifetime for the good of the community. *Andrew Carnegie*

It is sheer madness to live in want in order to be wealthy when you die.
Juvenal

The gratification of wealth is not found in mere possession or in lavish expenditure, but in its wise application. *Miguel de Cervantes*

Wealth is not his that has it, but his that enjoys it. *Benjamin Franklin*

There's nothing so comfortable as a small bankroll. A big one is always in danger. *Wilson Mizner*

He is richest who is content with the least, for content is the wealth of nature. *Socrates*

Without a rich heart wealth is an ugly beggar. *Ralph Waldo Emerson*

The use of money is all the advantage there is in having money.
Benjamin Franklin

Superfluous wealth can buy superfluities only. *Henry David Thoreau*

WEATHER
Sunshine is delicious, rain is refreshing, wind braces up, snow is exhilarating; there is no such thing as bad weather, only different kinds of good weather. *John Ruskin*

If you don't like the weather in New England, just wait a few minutes.
Mark Twain

Don't knock the weather; nine-tenths of the people couldn't start a conversation if it didn't change once in a while. *Kin Hubbard*

Everybody talks about the weather but nobody does anything about it.
Charles Dudley Warner

Change of weather is the discourse of fools. *Thomas Fuller*

> Oh, what a blamed uncertain thing
>   This pesky weather is;
> It blew and snew and then it thew,
>   And now, by jing, it's friz!
Philander Johnson

The most serious charge which can be brought against New England is not Puritanism but February. *Joseph Wood Krutch*

WICKEDNESS *Also see:* EVIL, PROFANITY, PUNISHMENT, REPENT-
ANCE, SIN.

There is a method in man's wickedness; it grows up by degrees.
Beaumont and Fletcher

To see and listen to the wicked is already the beginning of wickedness.
Confucius

It is a statistical fact that the wicked work harder to reach hell than the righteous do to enter heaven.
Josh Billings

The sun also shines on the wicked.
Seneca

Wickedness is a myth invented by good people to account for the curious attraction of others.
Gideon Wurdz

The world loves a spice of wickedness.
Henry Wadsworth Longfellow

No wickedness proceeds on any grounds of reason.
Livy

God bears with the wicked, but not forever.
Miguel de Cervantes

There is wickedness in the intention of wickedness, even though it be not perpetrated in the act.
Cicero

WIFE *Also see:* ACHIEVEMENT, COMPLIMENT, FIDELITY, HUSBAND,
MARRIAGE, MOTHER.

I chose my wife, as she did her wedding gown, for qualities that would wear well.
Oliver Goldsmith

Wives are young men's mistresses, companions for middle age, and old men's nurses.
Francis Bacon

Of all the home remedies, a good wife is best.
Kin Hubbard

She is but half a wife that is not, nor is capable of being, a friend.
William Penn

Heaven will be no heaven to me if I do not meet my wife there.
Andrew Jackson

All married women are not wives.
Japanese Proverb

A wife is a gift bestowed upon man to reconcile him to the loss of paradise.
Johann Wolfgang von Goethe

He knows little who tells his wife all he knows.
Thomas Fuller

A wife is essential to great longevity; she is the receptacle of half a man's cares, and two-thirds of his ill-humor.
Charles Reade

Teacher, tender comrade, wife,
A fellow-farer true through life.
Robert Louis Stevenson

WILL *Also see:* AIM, DESIRE, PURPOSE, RESOLUTION, TECHNOLOGY, VICTORY.

People do not lack strength; they lack will.   *Victor Hugo*

Great souls have wills; feeble ones have only wishes.   *Chinese Proverb*

To deny the freedom of the will is to make morality impossible.
James A. Froude

Will is character in action.   *William McDougall*

Where there's a will, there's a way.   *English Proverb*

He who is firm in will molds the world to himself.
Johann Wolfgang von Goethe

Strength does not come from physical capacity. It comes from an indomitable will.   *Mahatma Gandhi*

The education of the will is the object of our existence.
Ralph Waldo Emerson

No action will be considered blameless, unless the will was so, for by the will the act was dictated.   *Seneca*

Where there's a will, there's a lawsuit.   *Addison Mizner*

WISDOM *Also see:* COMMON SENSE, JUDGMENT, KNOWLEDGE, LEARNING, QUESTION.

The wisest man is generally he who thinks himself the least so.
Nicolas Boileau-Despréaux

One of the greatest pieces of economic wisdom is to know what you do not know.   *John Kenneth Galbraith*

Among mortals second thoughts are wisest.   *Euripides*

It is unwise to be too sure of one's own wisdom. It is healthy to be reminded that the strongest might weaken and the wisest might err.
Mahatma Gandhi

It is more easy to be wise for others than for ourselves.
François de La Rochefoucauld

The art of being wise is the art of knowing what to overlook.
William James

Nine-tenths of wisdom consists in being wise in time.   *Theodore Roosevelt*

Wisdom is ofttimes nearer when we stoop than when we soar.
William Wordsworth

The older I grow the more I distrust the familiar doctrine that age brings wisdom.   *H. L. Mencken*

The only one who is wiser than anyone is everyone.   *Napoleon Bonaparte*

WIT *Also see:* FOOL, HUMOR, INSANITY, JESTING, MATURITY.

If it were not for the company of fools, a witty man would often be greatly at a loss. *François de La Rochefoucauld*

Wit ought to be a glorious treat, like caviar; never spread it about like marmalade. *Noel Coward*

Wit is the salt of conversation, not the food. *William Hazlitt*

The next best thing to being witty one's self, is to be able to quote another's wit. *Christian Nestell Bovee*

He who has provoked the shaft of wit, cannot complain that he smarts from it. *Samuel Johnson*

To be witty is not enough. One must possess sufficient wit to avoid having too much of it. *André Maurois*

A wise man will live as much within his wit as within his income. *Lord Chesterfield*

Wit makes its own welcome, and levels all distinctions. No dignity, no learning, no force of character, can make any stand against good wit. *Ralph Waldo Emerson*

Less judgment than wit, is more sail than ballast. *William Penn*

WOMAN *Also see:* DRESS, SEX, WIFE.

There is nothing enduring in life for a woman except what she builds in a man's heart. *Judith Anderson*

You see, dear, it is not true that woman was made from man's rib; she was really made from his funny bone. *James Matthew Barrie*

The way to fight a woman is with your hat. Grab it and run. *John Barrymore*

She is not made to be the admiration of all, but the happiness of one. *Edmund Burke*

Being a woman is a terribly difficult task since it consists principally in dealing with men. *Joseph Conrad*

A woman's guess is much more accurate than a man's certainty. *Rudyard Kipling*

Of all the rights of women, the greatest is to be a mother. *Lin Yutang*

A beautiful lady is an accident of nature. A beautiful old lady is a work of art. *Louis Nizer*

On one issue, at least, men and women agree; they both distrust women. *H. L. Mencken*

WONDER   *Also see:*   CURIOSITY, DOUBT, PHILOSOPHY, VISION.

The world will never starve for want of wonders, but for want of wonder.
Gilbert K. Chesterton

It was through the feeling of wonder that men now and at first began to philosophize.
Aristotle

He who can no longer pause to wonder and stand rapt in awe, is as good as dead; his eyes are closed.
Albert Einstein

All wonder is the effect of novelty on ignorance.
Samuel Johnson

As knowledge increases, wonder deepens.
Charles Morgan

> God moves in a mysterious way,
>   His wonders to perform;
> He plants His footsteps in the sea,
>   And rides upon the storm.
William Cowper

Wonder is the basis of worship.
Thomas Carlyle

Men love to wonder and that is the seed of our science.
Ralph Waldo Emerson

WORD   *Also see:*   BREVITY, DIFFERENCE, JOURNALISM, LANGUAGE, LOQUACITY, POETRY, PROPAGANDA, SPEECH.

One great use of words is to hide our thoughts.
Voltaire

Words without actions are the assassins of idealism.
Herbert Hoover

Eating words has never given me indigestion.
Winston Churchill

The finest words in the world are only vain sounds, if you cannot comprehend them.
Anatole France

Words are tools which automatically carve concepts out of experience.
Julian Sorrell Huxley

A thousand words will not leave so deep an impression as one deed.
Henrik Ibsen

The safest words are always those which bring us most directly to facts.
Charles H. Parkhurst

Without knowing the force of words, it is impossible to know men.
Confucius

It is with words as with sunbeams—the more they are condensed, the deeper they burn.
Robert Southey

Suit the action to the word, the word to the action.   *William Shakespeare*

Words are the coins making up the currency of sentences, and there are always too many small coins.
Jules Renard

WORK *Also see:* AUTOMATION, DILIGENCE, EFFORT, INDUSTRY, LABOR, RETIREMENT, WAGE, ZEAL.

Nothing is really work unless you would rather be doing something else.
James Matthew Barrie

A man is a worker. If he is not that he is nothing. *Joseph Conrad*

Work is the meat of life, pleasure the dessert. *Bertie Charles Forbes*

Work is love made visible. *Kahlil Gibran*

I like work; it fascinates me. I can sit and look at it for hours.
Jerome K. Jerome

Work is the greatest thing in the world, so we should always save some of it for tomorrow. *Don Herold*

The world is filled with willing people; some willing to work, the rest willing to let them. *Robert Frost*

I do not like work even when someone else does it. *Mark Twain*

Labor disgraces no man, but occasionally men disgrace labor.
Ulysses S. Grant

I look on that man as happy, who, when there is a question of success, looks into his work for a reply. *Ralph Waldo Emerson*

WORLD *Also see:* CITIZENSHIP, COUNTRY, EARTH, RETIREMENT, UNIVERSE.

One real world is enough. *George Santayana*

In this world nothing is sure but death and taxes. *Benjamin Franklin*

The world gets better every day—then worse again in the evening.
Kin Hubbard

The world always had the same bankrupt look, to foregoing ages as to us.
Ralph Waldo Emerson

This is the way the world ends . . . Not with a bang but with a whimper.
T. S. Eliot

He who imagines he can do without the world deceives himself much; but he who fancies the world cannot do without him is still more mistaken.
François de La Rochefoucauld

The only fence against the world is a thorough knowledge of it.
John Locke

We can only change the world by changing men. *Charles Wells*

The world is not growing worse and it is not growing better—it is just turning around as usual. *Finley Peter Dunne*

WORRY *Also see:* ANXIETY, AUTOMATION, FEAR, TRIFLES.

The freedom now desired by many is not freedom to do and dare but freedom from care and worry. *James Truslow Adams*

Keep cool: it will be all one a hundred years hence.

Ralph Waldo Emerson

It is not work that kills men; it is worry. Worry is rust upon the blade.

Henry Ward Beecher

Worry is interest paid on trouble before it is due. *William Ralph Inge*

I have lost everything, and I am so poor now that I really cannot afford to let anything worry me. *Joseph Jefferson*

It ain't no use putting up your umbrella till it rains. *Alice Caldwell Rice*

Worry gives a small thing a big shadow. *Swedish Proverb*

As a cure for worrying, work is better than whiskey. *Ralph Waldo Emerson*

Worry is the interest paid by those who borrow trouble. *George Lyon*

Don't tell me that worry doesn't do any good. I know better. The things I worry about don't happen. *Anonymous*

There is nothing that wastes the body like worry, and one who has any faith in God should be ashamed to worry about anything whatsoever.

Mahatma Gandhi

The reason why worry kills more people than work is that more people worry than work. *Robert Frost*

WORTH *Also see:* MERIT, QUALITY, RACE, RESPECT.

I believe in the supreme worth of the individual and in his right to life, liberty, and the pursuit of happiness. *John D. Rockefeller*

It's not what you pay a man, but what he costs you that counts.

Will Rogers

All good things are cheap: all bad are very dear. *Henry David Thoreau*

For anything worth having one must pay the price; and the price is always work, patience, love, self-sacrifice. *John Burroughs*

He is rich or poor according to what he *is*, not according to what he *has*.
Henry Ward Beecher

Worth begets in base minds, envy; in great souls, emulation.

Henry Fielding

Where quality is the thing sought after, the thing of supreme quality is cheap, whatever the price one has to pay for it. *William James*

WRITER *Also see:* AMBIGUITY, BOOK, HISTORY, JOURNALISM, LITER-
ATURE, POETRY, QUOTATION, TRUTH, WORD.

A serious writer is not to be confounded with a solemn writer. A serious
writer may be a hawk or a buzzard or even a popinjay, but a solemn writer
is always a bloody owl. *Ernest Hemingway*

Writers seldom write the things they think. They simply write the things
they think other folks think they think. *Elbert Hubbard*

Talent alone cannot make a writer. There must be a man behind the book.
Ralph Waldo Emerson

Nothing gives an author so much pleasure as to find his works respectfully
quoted by other learned authors. *Benjamin Franklin*

Your manuscript is both good and original, but the part that is good is not
original, and the part that is original is not good. *Samuel Johnson*

The most original authors are not so because they advance what is new, but
because they put what they have to say as if it had never been said before.
Johann Wolfgang von Goethe

Neither man nor God is going to tell me what to write. *James T. Farrell*

Every compulsion is put upon writers to become safe, polite, obedient, and
sterile. *Sinclair Lewis*

You become a good writer just as you become a good joiner: by planing
down your sentences. *Anatole France*

WRITING . . . See JOURNALISM

WRONG *Also see:* APATHY, CRUELTY, ERROR, EVIL, FOOL, FRAUD, SIN,
VICE, WICKEDNESS.

Two wrongs do not make a right. *English Proverb*

It is better to suffer wrong than to do it, and happier to be sometimes
cheated than not to trust. *Samuel Johnson*

The remedy for wrongs is to forget them. *Publilius Syrus*

Wrong is but falsehood put in practice. *Walter S. Landor*

There are few people who are more often in the wrong than those who
cannot endure to be so. *François de La Rochefoucauld*

The only right is what is after my constitution; the only wrong is what is
against it. *Ralph Waldo Emerson*

We ought never to do wrong when people are looking. *Mark Twain*

The man who says "I may be wrong, but—" does not believe there can be
any such possibility. *Kin Hubbard*

Y

YOUTH *Also see:* AGE, AMERICA, BOYS, CHILDREN, DEBT, DISAP-POINTMENT, GIRLS, MATURITY, SELF-IMPROVEMENT, SENSUALITY.

It is not possible for civilization to flow backwards while there is youth in the world.
Helen Keller

Youth is the first victim of war; the first fruit of peace. It takes 20 years or more of peace to make a man; it takes only 20 seconds of war to destroy him.
Baudouin I

Older men declare war. But it is the youth that must fight and die.
Herbert Hoover

When we are out of sympathy with the young, then I think our work in this world is over.
George Macdonald

I, for one, hope that youth will again revolt and again demoralize the dead weight of conformity that now lies upon us.
Howard Mumford Jones

Don't laugh at youth for his affectations; he is only trying on one face after another to find his own.
Logan P. Smith

Youth today must be strong, unafraid, and a better taxpayer than its father.
H. V. Wade

For God's sake, give me the young man who has brains enough to make a fool of himself.
Robert Louis Stevenson

It is better to be a young June-bug than an old bird of paradise.
Mark Twain

Youth is that period when a young boy knows everything but how to make a living.
Carey Williams

> All lovely things will have an ending,
> All lovely things will fade and die;
> And youth, that's now so bravely spending,
> Will beg a penny by and by.
Conrad Aiken

The Youth of a Nation are the trustees of posterity.
Benjamin Disraeli

Youth is a wonderful thing: what a crime to waste it on children.
George Bernard Shaw

In youth we run into difficulties, in old age difficulties run into us.
Josh Billings

If youth be a defect, it is one that we outgrow only too soon.
James Russell Lowell

Youth comes but once in a lifetime.
Henry Wadsworth Longfellow

Z

ZEAL *Also see:* AMBITION, ENTHUSIASM, FANATICISM, PURPOSE, SPIRIT, WILL.

Zeal without knowledge is like expedition to a man in the dark.
John Newton

Never let your zeal outrun your charity. The former is but human, the latter is divine.
Hosea Ballou

To be furious in religion is to be irreligiously religious.
William Penn

Zeal without humanity is like a ship without a rudder, liable to be stranded at any moment.
Owen Feltham

The greatest dangers to liberty lurk in insidious encroachment by men of zeal, well-meaning, but without understanding.
Louis D. Brandeis

Experience shows that success is due less to ability than to zeal. The winner is he who gives himself to his work, body and soul.
Charles Buxton

Zeal is very blind, or badly regulated, when it encroaches upon the rights of others.
Quesnel

There is no greater sign of a general decay of virtue in a nation, than a want of zeal in its inhabitants for the good of their country.
Joseph Addison

Zeal is fit only for wise men but is found mostly in fools.
Ancient Proverb

ZEST *Also see:* ENJOYMENT, ENTHUSIASM, PLEASURE.

Forbid a man to think for himself or to act for himself and you may add the joy of piracy and the zest of smuggling to his life.
Elbert Hubbard

Mirth is the sweet wine of human life. It should be offered sparkling with zestful life unto God.
Henry Ward Beecher

Zest is the secret of all beauty. There is no beauty that is attractive without zest.
Christian Dior

Author Index

A

Abbot, F. E., 14
Abbott, John, 70, 272
Acheson, Dean, 261
Acton, Lord, 62
Adams, Franklin P., 85, 96
Adams, George Matthew, 46
Adams, Henry Brooks, 97, 138, 152, 157, 168, 201, 215, 251
Adams, James Truslow, 280
Adams, John Quincy, 180, 269
Adams, Phelps, 41
Adams, Thomas, 131
Addams, Jane, 212
Addison, Joseph, 9, 28, 33, 44, 62, 63, 81, 96, 104, 112, 140, 149, 156, 182, 183, 194, 220, 231, 247, 256, 257, 283
Ade, George, 231
Adler, Alfred, 13, 43, 152, 172
Adler, Felix, 51, 198
Adler, Mortimer J., 220
Aeschylus, 11, 28
Aesop, 154
Agesilaus II, 163, 184
Aiken, Conrad, 282
Alcott, Amos Bronson, 35, 107
Aldrich, Thomas Bailey, 41, 194
Alfieri, Conte Vittorio, 67, 132
Alfonso X, 66
Alger, William Rounseville, 11, 21, 99, 114, 182, 244
Allen, Fred, 10
Allen, Hervey, 178
Allen, James, 79, 254
Ambrose, St., 105
Amiel, 53, 153, 186
Anderson, John, 191
Anderson, Joseph, 72
Anderson, Judith, 277
Anderson, Margaret, 221
Angell, Norman, 188
Anspacher, Louis K., 177
Antisthenes, 101, 117

Aristippus, 174
Aristophanes, 105
Aristotle, 21, 69, 82, 124, 151, 155, 168, 183, 191, 201, 224, 228, 248, 278
Armour, J. Ogden, 40
Armour, Richard, 95
Armstrong, Neil, 245
Arnold, Matthew, 85, 160, 169, 223, 236
Arnot, William, 91
Astor, Lady, 13, 190
Auden, W. H., 36
Auerbach, 58, 161
Aughey, John H., 237, 255
Augustine, St., 6, 58, 127, 133, 141, 199, 216, 256
Ausonius, 119, 153

B

Babson, Roger W., 80
Bacon, Francis, 5, 10, 11, 28, 35, 36, 44, 45, 64, 72, 80, 86, 105, 106, 129, 143, 149, 163, 182, 192, 195, 201, 206, 211, 213, 214, 218, 247, 264, 268, 275
Baer, Arthur "Bugs", 68, 190
Bagehot, Walter, 218
Bailey, Gamaliel, 120
Bailey, J. M., 24
Bailey, Philip James, 18
Bain, Alexander, 156
Bakunin, Mikhail A., 103
Baldwin, Stanley, 144
Balfour, Clara Lucas, 52
Balguy, John, 60
Ballou, Hosea, 38, 87, 102, 106, 133, 135, 155, 186, 193, 209, 265, 283
Balzac, Honoré de, 19, 70, 183, 196, 202
Bancroft, George, 29, 59, 88, 128, 133, 215

L

Laboulaye, Edouard R., 132
Lacordaire, Jean Baptiste, 12
La Fontaine, Jean de, 6, 76, 100, 197
La Guardia, Fiorello H., 142
Laharpe, Jean François de, 106
Lamartine, Alphonse de, 238
Lamb, Charles, 37, 60, 195
Landon, Letitia, 84, 151
Landon, Melville D., 37, 205
Landor, Walter S., 5, 21, 32, 141, 225, 281
Lardner, Ring, 112
La Rochefoucauld, François de, 5, 9, 11, 14, 22, 37, 44, 46, 53, 61, 68, 75, 76, 79, 89, 99, 104, 107, 111, 115, 117, 118, 123, 129, 131, 135, 136, 143, 147, 148, 153, 157, 159, 161, 162, 172, 176, 180, 181, 188, 196, 201, 206, 209, 211, 217, 246, 252, 264, 265, 267, 268, 276, 277, 279, 281
Lasker, Albert, 10
Lavater, Johann Kaspar, 14, 40, 79, 109, 113, 115, 131, 154, 191, 193, 196, 209, 218, 234, 242, 271
Laver, James, 113
Law, Andrew B., 272
Law, Vernon Sanders, 108
Lawes, Lewis E., 110
Lawrence, D. H., 182
Leacock, Stephen Butler, 10, 88, 139, 262
Lebret, R. P., 52
Lec, Stanislaw J., 136, 148, 173, 223, 247
Lee, Gerald S., 185
Lee, Robert E., 125, 272
Lehman, Herbert Henry, 129, 226
Leibnitz, Gottfried Wilhelm von, 172
Lenin, 68, 228
Leo XIII, 28, 152
Leonard, John, 252
Lerner, Max, 206

Levant, Oscar, 134, 150
Levenson, Sam, 155
Lewes, George Henry, 131
Lewis, Joseph, 249
Lewis, Sinclair, 156, 281
Lewis, William Mather, 212
Lichtenberg, G. C., 36, 46, 60, 88, 124, 127, 130, 192, 251, 253
Liddon, H. P., 85
Liebman, Joshua Loth, 87, 99, 161
Lily, William, 15
Lincoln, Abraham, 15, 40, 47, 51, 58, 78, 92, 117, 118, 129, 138, 143, 166, 185, 204, 213, 214, 228, 232, 238, 243, 249, 250, 261, 265, 269
Lincoln, John A., 54, 76
Lindbergh, Charles A., 220, 235
Lindsay, Ben, 43
Lindsay, Howard, 141
Lindsay, Vachel, 187
Ling, Nicholas, 146
Linn, Walter, 189
Lippmann, Walter, 158, 167, 216
Little, M. W., 248
Livy, 35, 132, 275
Lloyd, William, 159
Locke, John, 8, 61, 170, 216, 228, 260, 279
Lodge, Henry Cabot, 17, 261
London, Jack, 47
Long, Edward V., 210
Longfellow, Henry Wadsworth, 7, 12, 15, 26, 49, 64, 69, 100, 104, 117, 130, 131, 146, 152, 161, 172, 179, 186, 216, 224, 225, 226, 228, 236, 240, 244, 247, 254, 269, 275, 282
Lorimer, George H., 210
Lowell, Abbott L., 262
Lowell, Amy, 26
Lowell, James Russell, 14, 22, 28, 48, 55, 57, 78, 108, 113, 114, 119, 144, 145, 149, 156, 157, 169, 181, 192, 202, 219, 220, 221, 228, 232, 235, 238, 259, 268, 273, 282
Lucan, 20, 35, 73, 74, 105, 213
Lucas, F. L., 54

Subject Index

A

ABILITY, 5
Also see: ACTION, CHARAC-
TER, DISCRETION, FORCE,
GENIUS, PERSEVERANCE,
POWER, STRENGTH, SUCCESS

ABSENCE, 5
Also see: LONELINESS, MEM-
ORY, WANT

ABSTINENCE, 6
Also see: DRUNKENNESS, MOD-
ERATION, SACRIFICE

ABSURDITY, 6
Also see: RIDICULE, SARCASM

ABUSE, 6
Also see: CRUELTY, INJURY,
POLLUTION, SLANDER

ACCURACY, 7
Also see: FACTS, FIDELITY,
PUNCTUALITY, SCIENCE

ACHIEVEMENT, 7
Also see: ACTION, AIM, AM-
BITION, DECISION, LABOR,
PURPOSE, SUCCESS, WORK

ACTION, 8
Also see: ACHIEVEMENT, DE-
SIRE, LABOR, PROGRESS, WORK

ADAPTABILITY, 9
Also see: CONFORMITY

ADMIRATION, 9
Also see: FAME, FOOL, LOVE,
PRAISE, RESPECT

ADVENTURE, 9
Also see: DANGER, INVEN-
TION, SPACE, TRAVEL

ADVERSITY, 10
Also see: AFFLICTION, CALAM-
ITY, MISERY, PROSPERITY

ADVERTISING, 10
Also see: ART, BUSINESS, PUB-
LICITY

ADVICE, 11
Also see: CAUTION, EXPERI-
ENCE, HELP, WISDOM

AFFECTION, 12
Also see: ADMIRATION,
FRIENDSHIP, KISS, LOVE

AFFLICTION, 12
Also see: ADVERSITY, CALAM-
ITY, DISEASE, PAIN, SORROW,
SUFFERING

AGE, 13
Also see: AVARICE, YOUTH

AGGRESSION, 13
Also see: ANGER, ENEMY, WAR

AGITATION, 13
Also see: ARGUMENT, DISSENT

AGNOSTICISM, 14
Also see: ATHEISM, GOD,
SKEPTICISM

AGREEMENT, 14

AIM, 14
Also see: AMBITION, DESIRE,
END, IDEAL, PURPOSE, PUR-
SUIT

AMBIGUITY, 15
Also see: DOUBT

AMBITION, 15
Also see: AIM CONSCIENCE,
DESIRE, EFFORT, GLORY,
IDEAL, PURPOSE, WORTH,
ZEAL

AMERICA, 17
Also see: DEMOCRACY, NA-
TION, PARTY, PATRIOTISM,
PRESIDENT

AMIABILITY, 19
Also see: AGREEMENT, CHEER-
FULNESS, COURTESY, HAPPI-
NESS

AMUSEMENT, 19
Also see: ENJOYMENT, JOY,
PLEASURE, REVERIE

ANCESTRY, 20
Also see: ARISTOCRACY

ANGER, 21
Also see: AGGRESSION, QUAR-
REL, TEMPER

ANTICIPATION, 22
Also see: ANXIETY, DISAP-
POINTMENT, HOPE

ANXIETY, 22
Also see: ANTICIPATION, FEAR,
WORRY

How to Order
Extra Copies of This Book

This book is one of a series of books which make up the *Instant Reference Library*. Titles currently included in the series are as follows.

Instant Spelling Dictionary
Instant English Handbook
Instant Quotation Dictionary
Instant Synonyms and Antonyms
Instant Medical Spelling Dictionary
Instant Business Dictionary
Instant Medical Adviser
Instant Secretary's Handbook
Instant Sewing Handbook
Instant Home Repair Handbook

You may order any of the above books from your local bookstore, or send your order to Career Publishing, Dept. 267, 1500 Cardinal, Little Falls, NJ 07424. Individuals, send check or money order. Minimum order $10. No COD's. Business firms or other organizations must send cash with order if 5 or fewer books. For larger orders, use purchase order and we will bill you on open account. Each book $3.95 plus shipping, less the following quantity discounts.

Quantity	Discount
	None
1 to 5 books	15¢ per book
6 to 15 books	25¢ per book
16 to 49 books	35¢ per book
50 to 149 books	

Orders for different titles may be combined to take advantage of the above quantity prices. Postage and handling $1 for 1st book plus 25¢ for each additional book. New Jersey residents add Sales Tax. Prices subject to change.